Narrative Form

Suzanne Keen
Washington and Lee University

First published 2003 by
PALGRAVE MACMILLAN
Houndmills, Basingstoke, Hampshire RG21 6XS and
175 Fifth Avenue, New York, N.Y. 10010
Companies and representatives throughout the world

PALGRAVE MACMILLAN is the global academic imprint of the Palgrave Macmillan division of St. Martin's Press, LLC and of Palgrave Macmillan Ltd. Macmillan® is a registered trademark in the United States, United Kingdom and other countries. Palgrave is a registered trademark in the European Union and other countries.

ISBN -13: 978-0-333-96096-7 hardback
ISBN -10: 0-333-96096-3 hardback
ISBN -13: 978-0-333-96097-4 paperback
ISBN -10: 0-333-96097-1 paperback

This book is printed on paper suitable for recycling and made from fully managed and sustained forest sources.

A catalogue record for this book is available from the British Library

Library of Congress Cataloging-in-Publication Data
Keen, Suzanne.
    Narrative form / Suzanne Keen.
      p. cm.
    Includes bibliographical references and index.
      ISBN 0–333–96096–3 (hardback) — ISBN 0–333–96097–1 (pbk.)
        1. Narration (Rhetoric) 2. Fiction—Technique. I. Title.

PN3383.N35K44 2003
808.3'3—dc21

                                                         2003046946

10   9   8   7   6   5
12 11 10 09 08

Printed and bound in Great Britain by
Antony Rowe Ltd, Chippenham and Eastbourne

Narrative Form

Jane EYRE
Shapes of Narratives
Discourse vs Story 17

useful terms:
In medias Res
Kernal / Satellite Event

Narrative voice (who speaks?)
focalization (who sees?)
Narrative situation is a part of discourse
because it examines how the story is told.
narrative

Paratexts.

overt narrator — has a distinct personality
and opinions.
covert narrator — Hardly noticable.

kernel events
snares
fabula (story)   Sjuze (plot)

Distinguishing b/w
the story + the way
it is told.

For
Jake

Contents

Preface: Studying Narrative Form   x

1 Major Approaches to and Theorists of Narrative   1
   What is narrative fiction?   1
   Why study narrative form?   5
   Major theorists of and approaches to narrative: a selective
   sketch   7
   Studying narrative: selected resources   13
   Further reading   15

2 Shapes of Narrative: A Whole of Parts   16
   Analytical strategies   25
   Keywords   28
   Further reading   29

3 Narrative Situation: Who's Who and What's its Function   30
   Terms   32
   Narrators   36
   Perspective   44
   Second-person narration   45
   Analytical techniques   48
   Keywords   50
   Further reading   53

4 People on Paper: Character, Characterization, and Represented
      Minds   55
   Terms   57
   Representing consciousness   59
   Characterization and kinds of character   64
   Analytical techniques   69
   Keywords   71
   Further reading   72

5 Plot and Causation: Related Events   73
   Terms   75
   Analytical techniques   82
   Typological approaches to plot   83
   Feminist critiques of plot and closure   86

Generic approaches to plot 86
Keywords 87
Further reading 88

6   Timing: How Long and How Often? 90
Terms 92
Analytical techniques 95
Keywords 96
Further reading 98

7   Order and Disorder 99
Terms 100
Analytical strategies 104
Keywords 107
Further reading 107

8   Levels: Realms of Existence 108
Terms 108
Analytical strategies 112
Keywords 114
Further reading 114

9   Fictional Worlds and Fictionality 116
Terms 118
Analytical techniques 123
Keyword 124
Further reading 126

10   Disguises: Fiction in the Form of Nonfiction Texts 128
Terms 129
Analytical strategies 138
Keywords 139
Further reading 140

11   Genres and Conventions 141
Terms 141
Analytical strategies 147
Keywords 151
Further reading 152

Appendix A. Terms Listed by Chapter   154

Appendix B. Representative Texts: A List of Suggested Readings   163

Notes   167

Bibliography   179

Index   189

Preface
Studying Narrative Form

Advanced students of literature, creative writing graduate students, and teachers will find in this handbook a concise treatment of narrative form in fiction. A useful supplement to a course of study in the novel or narrative fiction, it also serves as a first introduction to the broad field of narrative theory. Throughout, I use the term 'narrative form' to encompass the strategies used in the making of narrative fiction and the traits, shapes, and conventions that a careful reader can observe in narratives such as novels and stories. The first full-length chapter, on major approaches to and theorists of narrative, begins with the problems entailed in defining narrative fiction and situates this text's focus on fictional narrative form within the most important schools of thought on the subject. Despite this emphasis, many of the techniques discussed are employed in nonfictional narratives as well, and the points of commonality are acknowledged. Towards the end of the text, chapters on fictional worlds and fictionality (Chapter 9) and disguises or fiction in the form of other texts (Chapter 10) raise some questions about the intrinsic formal distinction of fictional from nonfictional narrative. For the most part, readers of this book can expect a close focus on the techniques and formal qualities of narrative fiction.

Makers of narrative use identifiable tools and techniques to craft stories. Whether they work by inherited traditions, by habit, deliberately, unconsciously, according to formulas, in imitation of admired precursors, or with deliberate aims of experimentation and innovation, they take up tools of language and build fictional worlds in which narrators introduce readers to imaginary persons who move, think, feel, and act, in those patterned sequences of events that go by the everyday name of plot. Together the makers and receivers of narrative construct a matrix in which a story can be realized and interpreted. Readers or viewers, experts in narrative by virtue of being human, then enliven fictional worlds in their minds, completing them by responding to them imaginatively. There interpretation begins, with reading. This book aims to provide advanced students of narrative with a critical vocabulary and a variety of strategies for analyzing the formal qualities of fiction. It suggests ways to supplement thematic interpretations with accurate observations about form.

The specialized work of identifying, naming, and analyzing the formal devices of narrative has been accomplished, mainly in the twentieth century, by a diverse group of critics and theorists. In a few important cases these theorists are fiction writers themselves, but narrative theory for the last half-century has been separated, as a discipline, from creative writing. One of the many things that differentiates this book from others like it is its intention to write about narrative form for both critics and creators of narrative. Creative writers familiar with the many books on the craft of fiction will find that this book is less prescriptive and more descriptive than most guides to writing fiction. One of the precepts of narrative poetics, the descriptive theory of narrative, is to emphasize possibilities even when examples do not readily come to mind. Thus a creative writer may consider creating an external, authorial, third-person omniscient and *unreliable* narrator, even though unreliability more often appears in first-person narrators. (In fact, Ian McEwan just did it, in *Atonement* [2001].) Warnings against undertaking formal experiments, or against trying techniques that increase the degree of difficulty for the reader, I leave to handbooks written by literary agents. No tool or technique is disparaged here, for I take the view that, in the hands of a talented writer, any aspect of fictional form can be handled with persuasive or innovative results.

Knowing the names and possible applications of these tools and techniques enhances a reader's understanding and appreciation of the craft of fiction. For the advanced student, this book provides a way to acquire a more sophisticated theoretical vocabulary and a menu of critical strategies, both of which can augment the presentation of evidence in analytical essays. Creative writers may decide to try new techniques or experiment with the tools they are already using in their work. Teachers—I assume that graduate students are often also teachers or tutors—will find that the discussion of narrative form always includes suggestions about how noticing form might be used analytically—and by extension pedagogically—to open discussions or support assignments from a range of approaches to narrative literature.

A book on narrative form may safely be described as formalist in nature. 'Formalism' has often been used as a disparaging term, suggesting hopeless abstraction from the real world, blind obedience to unexamined standards of value, neglect of historical change, disinterest in what happens when people read texts, and, at worst, a sort of hermetic practice carried out for the benefit of a priestly caste of elite interpreters. I hope that it will become plain that this textbook attempts to avoid all these charges. *Narrative Form* does not argue that literary critics should return to some earlier, purer, more transparent, or natural, critical approach to literature, in which the study of form is self-evidently valuable. It expresses instead the modest view that narrative fiction is made using a diverse kit of tools and techniques, wrought into different shapes and sizes, and employed to a variety of ends. It suggests that an understanding of formal traits of narrative can be used to support and complicate arguments with extra-literary interests. In this, it will be obvious to professional readers, my perspective owes a great deal to the pluralism of several generations of Chicago critics. Their interest in genre and form and particularly in the changes that occur over time in the careers of genres or conventions has been accomplished in work that attends to ethics, readers, and real-world consequences of rhetorical choices.

Arising not in opposition to recent trends in literary and cultural studies, but in sympathy with them, this textbook rests on the assumption that critical conversations about content or theme gain from encounters with form. Though narrative theory may sometimes proffer an array of formal alternatives as if they were static, timeless, and universal, critics may undertake to show how those very formal possibilities are used, in historically specific contexts, with attention to the ideological implications of their use in particular circumstances. Thus, this text shows advanced students both how they can enrich thematic analysis and theoretical writing with observations about how the textual vessels embodying those themes are shaped, and also how they might see their topics differently by noticing the formal choices that may guide, limit, or enable certain representations. This handbook does not attempt to adjudicate the conflict between culturalist and structuralist approaches within cultural studies, or what an earlier generation understood as a dichotomy between extrinsic and intrinsic kinds of literary criticism, but it registers the fact that scholars experienced in varieties of New Critical close reading, structuralist analysis, and post-structuralist reading often assume (not always justifiably) a shared vocabulary for observations about form. In those circumstances, it makes sense to use the language of formal analysis accurately as well as innovatively. My own critical and pedagogical practices bring together form and content, structure and context, and history and theory. This handbook thus reflects the experience of a teacher and critic who is not a narratologist, but who has found it helpful to know and use the vocabulary for the technical analysis of narrative.

Thus, though some of the newer theoretical, interdisciplinary, or historicized approaches to literature and culture certainly arose in critical reaction to formalist methods of reading, I can see no reason why the most fruitful strategies of New Critical close reading, practical criticism, structuralist poetics, and post-classical narratology should not be grafted back onto our

already hybrid practices. I do not attempt to persuade those with philosophical objections to formalist analysis to change their views and practices; instead, I aim to assist those who would like to improve their
understanding of narrative form. The problematizing of formal analysis, or
of the very notion of literary form, this brief text does not undertake,
though it points the way for those who are interested in studying the controversies. For instance, Chapter 10, 'Disguises,' calls into question the
belief that distinguishing features mark a boundary between narrative
fiction and nonfiction, and concurs with the view that the location of such
boundaries depends on cultural contexts and paratextual apparatuses (such
as labels).

When studying narrative form to supplement or enrich their discussion
of narrative texts, advanced students will want to be sure that they can
communicate effectively with those for whom the technical vocabulary of
narrative form and technique is a second language. Employing the terms
and strategies described in this textbook will not make a critic into an
instant narratologist, though it will work as a starting point for students
developing interests in the structuralist or post-structuralist poetics of narrative. Instead, it allows a student of literature or cultural studies to benefit
from familiarity with some of the most useful practices and ideas of narrative theory and formalist criticism. I refer to a wide variety of theorists, but
the guiding spirits of the text are Gérard Genette (particularly on order,
duration, frequency, and narrative levels), Franz Stanzel (on narrative situation), and Dorrit Cohn (on fictionality and the representation of fictional
consciousness). Experts familiar with these theorists will know that Cohn
criticizes Stanzel, and that Genette and Cohn often disagree. It is not my
goal to recount these critical controversies, though they can be fascinating,
but to represent the most useful and enduring concepts and approaches for
the analysis of form. I am emboldened by the example of Monika
Fludernik, whose revisionist narratology has also had an influence on this
guidebook,[1] and by those who have argued for a contextualist narratology.[2]
However, I follow no single guide or school of thought in this selective
guide, and the concepts presented within, though comprehensive in cover-
age, contribute neither to an exhaustive system nor to a complete taxonomy. The suggested readings at the end of each chapter point the curious
reader to my sources and to more detailed discussions of each aspect of
form described briefly in these pages.

This book can be used in a variety of ways. It can be read straight through
or consulted as a reference book. It can accompany a course of readings in
narrative literature; it can even be used to help construct a syllabus

organized around narrative technique. The first chapter, 'Major Approaches to and Theorists of Narrative,' orients the advanced literature student within the field of narrative theory. Individual chapters can be read as freestanding essays on particular areas of narrative form. Any chapter may be skipped over by readers who seek information only on particular aspects of narrative form. Appendix A, 'Terms Listed by Chapter,' helps a reader unsure of terminology locate the relevant discussion by locating terms in their contexts. The suggested readings in Appendix B, 'Representative Texts,' illustrate the full range of techniques described in the book.

The chapters themselves offer definitions of technical terms used to describe the full range of formal techniques employed by writers of narrative fiction. Within the sections of terms, I integrate background discussions of the literary histories of techniques, mentioning the influential uses that have suggested a correlation between techniques and particular ideas, themes, politics, or literary movements. Throughout I follow the example of Susan Lanser's feminist narratology, which situates narrative practices in relation to historical contexts, including modes of literary production and dominant ideologies. The political and cultural significance of particular devices of narrative form I treat in brief accounts of background, and in the connections to critical 'Keywords,' discussed below. The chapters suggest a variety of 'Analytical strategies' and 'Analytical techniques' for the interpretation of narrative form. These strategies always possess formal components, but they are not limited to 'close reading' or 'practical criticism' methodologies, embracing as they do tactics that have been developed by more recent critics of a variety of theoretical persuasions. Brief bibliographies detailing 'Further reading' provide preliminary guidance for students seeking more information about particular aspects of narrative form. Finally, cross-referencing within the chapters sends selective readers to sections on related topics.

Each chapter discusses a few critical keywords which have become associated with particular narrative techniques through influential theories, relationships of theme or context, accidents of literary history, or the preoccupations of particular literary artists and their interpreters. The keywords can help the advanced student anticipate some of the associative leaps their professors and readers may make in response to specialized vocabulary for the analysis of narrative form. Sometimes a commonly used word, such as 'discourse,' signals an approach or a school of thought. While 'discourse' suggests an allegiance to Mikhail Bakhtin or Michel Foucault, it is also a technical term with a precise descriptive meaning within narrative theory. In those cases I suggest how the meanings differ, where they overlap, and where potential confusions might arise. Very often, identifying the theorist whose specialized use of a term has gained currency clarifies matters. For instance, a student of narrative might discuss a 'gap' in the plot without being aware of Wolfgang Iser's influential theory of the reader's response to gaps. This difference would be treated up front in the discussion of technical terms. But when a critic attributes to a narrative's 'gaps' the mechanism of Freudian repression, that usage becomes a connection worthy of separate comment under 'Keywords.' An advanced student would certainly want to know that the use of the term 'gap' might call up such an association in a professional reader's mind, and also that not every use of 'gap' is intended to signal an allegiance to psychoanalytic criticism, or to reception theory. Because the critical keywords section of each chapter can suggest only some of the connections between the vocabulary for narrative form and the language of theory, it should be regarded as a starting point for exploring the larger realm of theory, and as a preliminary checkpoint at which advanced students can verify whether they are identifying their interests accurately for their professional readers.

Jargon presents a serious challenge to the student of narrative form. Translated from French or Russian, borrowed from neighboring disciplines (anthropology, linguistics, psychoanalysis), or concocted in English to mimic scientific terminology, technical vocabulary for narrative form and technique repels readers as often as it informs them. Indisputably, the wielding of paragraphs heavily freighted with polysyllabic compounds ('extraheterodiegetic' instead of 'third-person omniscient' narrator) can signal the desire to belong to, or be taken seriously by, a small circle of likeminded theorists. Several excellent texts that can serve this need include Gerald Prince's *A Dictionary of Narratology* (1987) and Martin Mcquillan's *The Narrative Reader* (2000). Happily, Shlomith Rimmon-Kenan's accessible handbook *Narrative Fiction: Contemporary Poetics* (1983) has been re-released in a revised second edition by Routledge.

If it is clear that jargon has its professional uses, not least that of gatekeeping, it is equally obvious that a paper written in code can be read only by another possessing the key. Unless absolutely certain of their audience, then, advanced students take a risk if they adopt a vocabulary that may be perceived, even by other literature professionals, as arcane, elitist, or deliberately obscure. I would hesitate to recommend any method that risks repelling readers, or narrowing the already rather limited audience for criticism. Therefore, this text uses narratological terminology sparingly. When appropriate English labels for forms and technique exist, I use those terms. In some cases, the jargon terms simply must be employed, for lack of plain

English substitutes. I do not invent critical vocabulary in this textbook, but I do suggest in short plain paraphrases the 'translations' of technical terms that may freely be adopted. Anyone who has experience with a specialized activity—from gourmet cooking to car repair—knows how indispensable a specialized vocabulary becomes, though it may at first sound like obscuring jargon. A major purpose of this textbook is to explain the most useful terms so that students may communicate their insights about narrative form to the uninitiated without baffling them, and to experts without inadvertently suggesting a lack of sophistication.

Drawing on a wide array of approaches to narrative, in *Narrative Form* I assume that any critical encounter with novels or stories gains from attention to the way narrative fiction is made. Further, I assume that reading is itself a kind of making, a dynamic process in which the mind responds to cues in order to recognize and shape narrative forms. Thus, I emphasize the fictional worldmaking activities of readers as well as writers. If this work has an agenda other than the clear introduction of concepts related to the discussion of narrative form, it lies in the tacit case made for the importance of narrative form in shaping a reader's experience, and the equally important matching pressure brought to bear on narrative literature by the reader's formal knowledge and expectations of generic conventions. The textbook teaches critical vocabulary painlessly by suggesting its relevance to larger literary concerns; it eschews hyper-technical jargon, and translates it when necessary. It helps the advanced student understand the cultural influences, generic conventions, and material conditions that accompany certain formal traits. It aims to define the parts, and to demystify the analysis, of narrative form without aspiring to provide the last word on the subject. Each short chapter points the way forward with a brief bibliography of recommended reading.

Textbook writing is inspired by teaching and by daily interactions with students who love to read. I thank my students at Washington and Lee and Yale Universities for the questions they have asked and the clarity they have demanded of me. Librarians, departmental colleagues, and the list members on the Narrative list, where I lurk, have helped me in countless ways. David Perkins told me to take a course with Dorrit Cohn, years ago, and I thank them both. Brian Richardson and Gwyn Campbell helped me by answering queries and offering encouragement. I thank Jim Warren for arranging a fall term course release when I needed it most and for getting the carpenters to build another bookshelf. Josie Dixon, Eleanor Birne, and my anonymous readers for Palgrave all played important roles in steering my course. My father, William P. Keen, contributed significantly at the beginning and end of the process; he will recognize some of his useful phrases and examples. Sandy O'Connell assisted in a thousand ways without even noticing. In the end, of course, the flaws and errors are all mine. The author welcomes the comments and suggestions of her readers. These may be directed to her at skeen@wlu.edu, or by mail to the Department of English, Washington and Lee University, Lexington, VA 24450, USA.

1
Major Approaches to and Theorists of Narrative

What is narrative fiction?

One of the most striking commonalities of handbooks for writers of fiction and theoretical works for advanced students lies in the evasiveness of their opening gambits of definition. Narrative fiction ... what exactly is it? Neither sort of work typically comes right out and states a plain definition of narrative fiction; both assume that readers already recognize narrative and, more particularly, the fictional kinds of narrative. For definitions the advanced student turns to dictionaries and specialized texts, and here the consensus begins to break down. The *Oxford English Dictionary* (*OED*) refers the inquisitive to Scottish law, where narrative means 'that part of a deed or document which contains a statement of the relevant or essential facts.' (From this Scottish source, according to the *OED*, the words 'narrative' and 'narrate' enter common parlance, around the middle of the eighteenth century.) This definition gives primacy to the documentary nature of narrative and clearly leaves out fiction. For narrative as fiction, the *OED* offers 'An account or narration; a history, tale, story, recital (of facts, etc.),' which brings in oral narration and several examples of narratives real and fictitious. Finally, the *OED* offers 'narrative,' without an article, as 'the practice or act of narrating; something to narrate.' Here the emphasis falls on the implicit narrator: narrative is what the narrator does and what the narrator tells. Related definitions fill in more of the picture: in classical rhetoric, narration is the part of an oration in which the facts are stated; the etymology of the verb 'narrate' (to relate, recount) suggests derivation from a root meaning 'skilled' and 'knowing.' A glance at the definition for fiction brings us closer: 'The species of literature which is concerned with the narration of imaginary events and the portraiture of imaginary characters;

fictitious composition. Now usually, prose novels and stories collectively.'
However, to arrive at this definition, one must note its precedent meanings, which emphasize fashioning, arbitrary invention, feigning, counterfeiting, and deceiving. The senses of fashioning, from fiction, and skill,
from the root word for narration, both suggest craftsmanship, but they also
carry more negative meanings of deception. A relation of events may
proceed from 'mere invention,' and the receiver of such a tale may be
tricked or taken in. The continuing tensions between disciplinary understandings of the functions of narrativity (in literary theory and history, for
instance) may have a distant source in the vexatious relations of 'narrative'
and 'fiction.'

Gerald Prince, in his *Dictionary of Narratology*, scarcely deigns to notice
the word 'fiction.' He defines narrative as 'the recounting (as product and
process, object and act, structure and structuration) of one or more real or
fictitious EVENTS communicated by one, two, or several (more or less overt)
NARRATORS to one, two, or several (more or less overt) NARRATEES' (*Dictionary*,
58). Without the qualifying parentheses, this definition deflates the
recounting of events by narrators to narratees. From the *OED* definitions
we recognize the narrator, the act of recounting, and the real or fictitious
events (replacing the Scottish legal 'facts'). Prince, a major theorist of the
recipients of narration, emphasizes the narratee, an auditor, viewer, or
reader figure whose presence is implied by the activity of the narrator. This
contemporary view of narrative has a long pedigree, reaching back to Plato
and Aristotle, from whom we derive a traditional distinction between
'telling,' or relating (*diegesis*), and 'showing,' or enacting (*mimesis*). In the
narration of Plato's *diegesis*, the poet acts as a narrator in his own name,
telling about agents and events. (The imitation of *mimesis* involves a poet
who pretends to be the speaker responsible for the utterance.) Thus the
mediation of a narrator becomes a core characteristic of narrative.

For most people, narrative is defined by examples—the novels, short
stories, films, histories, music videos, epic poems, biographies, ballads, television series, and private conversations that tell stories true and made-up.
This incomplete list suggests how ubiquitous narrative is, and also how
hard it is to say what it is in a satisfactory short definition that would
encompass all the examples. Theorists propose definitions comprised of
bare minimums: narrative tells a story; so it has a teller, called a narrator
(but this doesn't work for film or narrative art); it relates events (at least
one, though some insist on two); it features characters or agents (though
not necessarily in human form). Contrasts have proven helpful: while
drama is enacted, lyric speaks, and narrative is told. Other contrasts hold

up less well: is it really the case that the first person of lyric is matched by the second person of drama and the third person of narrative fiction?[1] Both definition by exclusion and definition by minimal required ingredients often run into logical or practical problems.

Nearly every observation that we can make about narrative's core qualities can be confuted or extended to apply to other forms. Though not an exhaustive list, the following examples demonstrate some of the areas of contestation. Narrative fictions tell stories that are not necessarily true, though they should be distinguished from lies. However, deception through the production of fictions that masquerade as true stories continues to the present day. So sometimes fictions are still lies, or intend to deceive. Narrative fictions have plots; this differentiates them from chronicles of events, or mere lists, or other collections of events presented without causation. As one narratological version has it, 'a narrative is the semiotic representation of a series of events meaningfully connected in a temporal and causal way.'[2] The events in plots are causally linked, as E. M. Forster famously illustrates—'The king died, and the Queen died of grief.' However, some postmodernist narrative artists have made a point of breaking the causal connection between the events in their fictions: the actions are related in the sense of being narrated, but unrelated as far as causation is concerned.[3] From Aristotle narrative theory derives the observation that plots have beginnings, middles, and ends. So do dramas and all other art forms that transpire in time. Common qualities of narrative can be found in other forms, and the solution, to my mind, is not to extend the category of narrative to include everything that resembles it in some way.

Even Cleanth Brooks and Robert Penn Warren, whose *Understanding Fiction* (1943, rev. ed. 1959) remains one of the most influential works of Anglo-American criticism of narrative, evade the task of definition.[4] 'Fiction' they assume from the outset; their goal is to argue its artfulness and significance. When it comes to definitions, they suggest that fiction is a 'unity,' having a set of 'vital relationships' among its elements, relationships that are not necessarily harmonious, but which include conflict and tension. In Brooks and Warren's view, fiction comes down to the combination of elements. It has action, characters, psychology, moral content, social situations, ideas and attitudes, and literary style (*Understanding Fiction*, xii). Though Brooks and Warren resist the idea that fiction-writing lies in the deployment of the contents of a bag of tricks, their emphasis on relationships among elements makes the component parts the essential items in achieving 'a real unity—a unity in which every part bears an expressive relation to other parts' (*Understanding Fiction*, 645). Given that any other art form could be asserted to consist of the 'unity' much prized by followers of the New Criticism, the unity of its elements does not ultimately make a compelling definition of narrative fiction.

If the 'unity' of Brooks and Warren does not satisfy, the various divisions presented by structuralist theorists of narrative have also resulted in incomplete definitions. One common distinction sets *description* against *narration* as binary opposites. In description, story time stands still, while in narration, the chronology of events implies passing time (see treatment of temporality in narrative in Chapter 6). Description may have the objects, characters, and even the happenings of narrative, but it presents them without suggesting the succession of events that sets a plot in motion. This opposition makes the possession of plot a fundamental ingredient of narrative. In an even more basic and ubiquitous convention of structuralist narrative theory, the 'what' of the story is distinguished from the 'how' of the narration. In this binary arrangement, narrative consists of a *fabula* (story) and *sjuzet* (discourse), or the events as they actually happen, contrasted with the events as they are told by the narrator. This conception assumes that narrative consists of a sequence of events, told by a teller, and it posits an intrinsic tension between the events as they 'really' happened (though as fictions, they didn't happen) and the events as they are related in the text. Without events, without a teller, or without a sense of order in time, the basic materials of narrative would then be missing.

Where do *people* belong in a definition of narrative? Most lists of the fundamental ingredients of narrative acknowledge *characters*, the actors involved in plot events, though some critics use the term 'actants' to de-emphasize the human-like quality of characters in narrative. Fictional character poses some problems for the two-level understanding of narrative offered by structuralist narrative theory. Character and characterization bridge the ostensibly separate zones of *fabula* and *sjuzet*, for they belong equally to the realm of 'what really happens,' the story level, and the realm of 'how the narrator tells what happens,' the discourse level. The invitation that characters make to readers, that is to connect their fictional experiences with our real ones, makes character an especially important ingredient of narrative from the perspective of the reading experience.

By rephrasing the description of the discourse level to the realm of 'how readers come to know what happens as they read a text,' we can reinsert readers into structuralism's formal division. Much depends upon whether narrative is understood as a dynamic process involving a reader who does not yet know everything about a text's content, or whether it is conceived as a completed object, about which generalizations can be made and checked against other completed readings. Structuralist criticism usually assumes the latter. A parallel school of thought about narrative, speech act theory, emphasizes its function as a kind of speech act, a specialized form of utterance that has a teller and a recipient. This approach offers a dynamic view of narrative, and sees its object—a time-bound linear form—as the co-creation of recipients hearing, watching, or reading. The distinction between narrative as a kind of behavior (something humans do with words) and narrative as a kind of object, whose traits can be discovered through close scrutiny, results in very different emphases. This book draws insights from both approaches to narrative, because the influence of speech act theory has been felt in narrative theory. Structuralist models for the description of narrative objects have been challenged and modified by theorists informed by speech act theory (and the related areas of reader response criticism and reception theory) and by the work of Mikhail Bakhtin. These approaches have helped to make more central an idea of narrative as a thing that people do. Though a story is a specific thing and one of numberless instances of things of that type, narrative is also an activity. It is often conceived as a universal human trait, even, in the arguments of some cognitive scientists, a habit of the mind that precedes language.

Why study narrative form?

Scholarly interest in narrative has expanded rapidly in the past decade. Theorists and literary critics are more often engaged in interdisciplinary conversations with narrative experts from a diverse array of fields, including anthropology, art, architecture, artificial intelligence, cognitive science, ethics, film studies, history, legal studies, media studies, philosophy, narrative psychology and narrative therapy, sociolinguistics, and virtual reality theory. This exciting situation means that understandings of narrative that have been accepted for decades are being scrutinized from new angles and for different purposes. Years ago, structuralist theorists called for a comprehensive, interdisciplinary study of the poetics of narrative. Though recent developments in narrative studies do not point towards a new grand theory subsuming all examples and disciplinary approaches into one grammar or science, the scrutiny of narrative from so many different angles promises new understandings and new questions.

Advanced students of narrative are well positioned to contribute to this interdisciplinary conversation. In literary studies, they are likely to approach narrative through courses of reading in novels, short stories, and nonfiction prose. Indeed, courses on novels and narrative literature (as well as film) still vastly outnumber graduate level courses in narrative theory. This book cannot replace a full course of reading on narrative theory, but it provides a broad and comprehensive introduction to that field for advanced students. Because it is likely to be most useful as a supplement to a syllabus of narrative texts, it focuses on fiction. Questions about the formal distinctiveness of fictional narrative are addressed, and much of the terminology applies equally effectively to novels and stories, to nonfictional narratives, and to narratives in verse. A modest level of reference to films acknowledges narratives in other media. That said, *Narrative Form* is located squarely in the field of literary studies, where the study of narrative has been going on for nearly a century. Familiarity with the terms and techniques commonly used in literary studies should permit the venturesome to enter interdisciplinary conversations confident of their ability to identify and describe the aspects of narrative that interest them.

Even if an advanced student has no deep interest in narrative form, understanding the claims of narrative theory can still be useful. Narrative theory provides an extremely detailed vocabulary for the description of the component parts and various functions of narrative, but only a few advanced students will go on into the sub-field of narratology. Many will be drawn to narrative literature, but will find contextual, thematic, or other theoretical approaches more immediately compelling. The approach to narrative form that I take in this handbook emphasizes the craft of fiction, and honors the makers and feigners who shape words to build story worlds in the minds of readers. It is my hope that advanced students who are drawn to narrative simply because they love to read will find the description of the narrative artist's tool-kit of interest. In the process of reading this book, advanced students will acquire tools of their own for making critical distinctions and clarifying their observations about a writer's craft. It is true that many critics are skeptical of the underlying assumption of formalist analysis, and that others shrink from anything that sounds like theory at all. I believe that the evidence of contemporary writing suggests that formal choices still matter to the makers of fiction. Further, I believe a finely tuned sense of narrative form should matter to literary critics hoping to illuminate the way discourse moves through texts, through our lives, our self-understandings and misapprehensions, and into the story worlds where we float our theories about possibilities and problems. Describing narrative form cannot by itself answer all the questions that advanced students bring to the critical conversation, nor should it. However, precise observations about the handling of the formal qualities of narrative can easily be combined with many other modes of criticism.

Horrible jargon is the only significant obstacle. *Narratology* itself—a term coined by Tzvetan Todorov—has a pseudo-scientific sound, and many literary critics today disdain the structuralist emulation of science embodied by the word. It refers, in its classical sense, to the structuralist analysis of the nature and function of narrative, and it implies an interest in commonalities across all narrative instances. Like the structuralism and semiotics from which it is derived, it de-emphasizes historical and cultural contexts in favor of generalizations that hold true across a broad array of examples drawn from many periods (though in practice, narratology has been limited by the linguistic attainments of its practitioners). When the mere use of narratology's highly specific terminology, its jargon, provokes negative reactions in otherwise open-minded readers, critics of narrative form do well to demystify their language and to establish the broader-reaching relevance of their insights. Outside the small circle of dedicated practitioners of narratology, attention to narrative form is justified by its connection to larger interests—theoretical, thematic, cultural, cognitive, and historical. For those working in cutting-edge fields such as postcolonial or cultural studies, adeptness at technical analysis of narrative helps to win the respect of critics trained in formalist methodologies. These readers are sure to notice when the language of structuralist or post-structuralist analysis is handled awkwardly, or when critical terminology inadvertently clashes with the writer's declared theoretical principles. Perhaps more importantly, agreement on the definitions of key terms in narrative permits communication and collaboration across disciplines. For this reason it makes sense to try to understand the assumptions underlying frequently used terms for narrative form, and to use the terms accurately.

Major theorists of and approaches to narrative: a selective sketch

Influential ideas about fiction and narrative predate the development of narrative theory by centuries. Though the reintroduction of classical ideas by Romantic critics suggests a briefer career than the uninterrupted two millennia suggested by the dates, Plato and Aristotle of the fourth century BCE are often credited with introducing key concepts. These include mimesis (imitation), diegesis (telling), plot structures, unity, causation, and the proper place of the feigning fiction-maker in the world. In the English

Renaissance, the first poet-critic of a long tradition brought classical and continental views together in a treatise that articulates some of the central purposes of fictional worldmaking. Philip Sidney's *An Apology for Poetry*, alternatively titled *Defense of Poesy* (1595), adapts the Aristotelian view of mimesis to a world-making that promotes virtuous action in the real world. Sidney's focus on the effects of poesy on the judicious reader points towards some of the interests of reader response critics. The fact that Sidney's 'poesy' includes narrative fiction (he was himself the author of a long prose romance) is sometimes obscured by the modern tendency to read poesy and poetry as meaning verse, or lyric. Sidney's *Apology* is important for considerations of ethics and fiction, as well as for an understanding of theories of fictional worlds (treated at greater length in Chapter 9).

Every national literature has its writer-critics (Goethe, Umberto Eco, T. S. Eliot). Some have made lasting contributions to the understanding of narrative. In the Anglo-American tradition, Henry James deserves special mention. In his book reviews of his contemporaries, in his essays for periodicals, and in his prefaces to his own work, James outlines many principles of narrative form that can also be observed in his novels and short stories. James's insights transcend the belle-lettristic commentary typical of his time. Because Percy Lubbock made of James's work a central exemplar in his treatise *The Craft of Fiction* (1926), James's ideas about the proper handling of plot, character, and the 'center of consciousness' have had tremendous staying power. Another novelist, E. M. Forster, in his 1927 *Aspects of the Novel*, made comments about plot and 'flat' and 'round' characters that persist to this day. Undiscouraged by the development of professional literary studies, fiction writers have continued offering their thoughts about their craft, sometimes including quite well-informed rejoinders to contemporary theory. The most comprehensive reading of narrative theory would not neglect these remarks by practitioners, including John Barth, A. S. Byatt, John Gardner, Annie Dillard, Madison Smartt Bell, David Lodge, Christine Brooke-Rose, and many others.[5] The interviews with writers in the *Paris Review* are also a great source of experienced commentary on craft from a very wide variety of perspectives. In this book, the reader will find references to the theoretical work of Barth and Lodge, two novelists with cross-over roles as respected theorists.

At about the same time that Forster and Lubbock were publishing their contributions on the craft of fiction, a group of writers known collectively as the Russian Formalists were at work on the description of the traits of literariness. Like the French structuralists, they were influenced by linguistics, and Ferdinand Saussure's ideas about *langue* (system) and *parole* (individual utterance). Much of their work concerned prosody and qualities of poetic language, but in this context their contribution to the description of narrative form deserves mention. They attempted to employ objective methods for the analysis of literary form. In addition to pioneering the division between *fabula* and *sjuzet* (discussed above), individual Russian Formalists emphasized the function of literary language in defamiliarizing the world (Shklovsky, Tomashevsky). Vladimir Propp initiated the typological study of plot by analyzing a corpus of Russian folk tales and deriving the 31 functions by means of which these tales articulate their objectives, proceed in steps of a particular order, and reach successful conclusions. Boris Tomashevsky emphasized the peripety by means of which plots move from one situation to another and the role of 'free' and 'bound' motifs in plotting (resembling what Seymour Chatman would later call kernel and satellite plot events). Tomashevsky also described the 'laying bare of the device' and the defamiliarization that especially characterized the literariness of the language of fiction. From the perspective of later structuralist theory, the Russian Formalists could be seen as anticipating a great deal of what structuralists would re-label with a different set of terms. Through Bakhtin and the work of the Prague Linguistic Circle, both of which were influenced by and reacted to the Russian Formalists, their ideas reached the French structuralists who are ordinarily credited with the invention of modern narrative theory. The ideas of Mikhail Bakhtin, one of the most influential theorists of the novel and narrative form, receive separate treatment in this book. His 'chronotope,' 'heteroglossia,' and 'polyglossia,' and his conception of novelistic discourse all appear in the pages that follow.

At roughly the same time as the Russian Formalists, but wholly separate from them, the practical criticism and close reading of the loosely associated group of Anglo-American critics known as the New Critics also sought to find methods that would eschew emotional, biographical, or heavily psychological approaches to literary texts. Like the Russian Formalists, the New Critics believed that poetic language has special traits that rendered it intrinsically different from ordinary language. The New Criticism focused more on poetry than on narrative, though Kenneth Burke's work on symbolic form, F. R. Leavis's articulation of a 'great tradition' of the novel, and the widespread New Critical practice of producing 'close readings' of passages from longer narrative works have made a lasting mark on the study of narrative and the novel.[6] As I have argued above, the New Critical focus on the 'unity' of fiction and the elements of that unity most deserving of comment remain influential through the contemporary descendants of Cleanth Brooks and Robert Penn Warren's *Understanding Fiction*. The idea that, in the best works of literature, form and content work together to make meaning and to enhance artfulness comes out of the New Criticism as popularized by widely used and imitated anthologies such as *Understanding Fiction*.

In René Wellek and Austin Warren's *Theory of Literature* (1942., rev. ed. 1956), the insights of the Russian Formalists make a brief appearance in the short treatment of 'The Nature and Modes of Narrative' (*Theory of Literature*, 217–19). Yet the impress of the New Criticism still makes the deepest mark. Wellek and Warren display anxiety in their quarantining of 'narrative.' They treat the novel as if it were neither true literature nor quite appropriate to their 'intrinsic' mode of study of literature. To the extent that they admit the significance of narrative method, they reveal New Critical tendencies in their focus of the task of evaluation:

> We are content to call a novelist great when his world, though not patterned or scaled like our own, is comprehensive of all the elements which we find necessary to catholic scope or, though narrow in scope, selects for inclusion the deep and central, and when the scale or hierarchy of elements seems to use such as a mature man can entertain. (*Theory of Literature*, 214)

Easy as it is to scoff at these old cuties with their scales of value and their mature male readers doing all the adjudicating, Wellek and Warren were struggling to reinstate narrative among the 'great forms' of literature. They saw that the 'widespread association of the novel with entertainment, amusement, and escape rather than serious art—the confounding of the great novels, that is, with manufactures made with a narrow aim at the market' damaged the reputation of the form and its criticism. Their attempt to demonstrate the total coherence, the structure, and the aesthetic purpose of narrative led them to mention not only the *fabula* and *sjuzet* and motifs of the Russian Formalists, but also the early findings of French and German critics interested in narrative situation and the modes for representation of characters' consciousness. The total opposition of form and content that is supposed to be characteristic of New Criticism's formalism already shows signs, in Wellek and Warren, of acknowledging the dynamic relationships of structure, context, and the reader's role in fictional worldmaking.

Examining the role of the reader includes a variety of problems tackled by rhetorical critics of the Chicago School, speech act theorists, reception or phenomenological theorists, and reader response critics. The influence of these approaches permeates this book, especially where I refer to Wayne Booth, Peter Rabinowitz, John R. Searle, Mary Louise Pratt, Wolfgang Iser, and Robyn Warhol. This is not an exhaustive list. When I emphasize the function of ordinary or natural language (as opposed to a special, separate literary language) in narrative, and when I assume the reader's complicity in responding to cues in order to participate in fictional worldmaking, I rely on broadly accepted contributions to narrative studies from these fields, though they arose out of disagreements with structuralist narratology's core assumptions.

The transformation of the study of narrative form into narratology and narrative poetics resulted from the influence of structuralism on literary theory, particularly in France. Saussure's and Jakobson's linguistics and Claude Levi-Strauss's anthropology played important roles in inspiring the search for systematic ways of studying narrative that would not be limited by the individual work. Instead, grammars of narrative structure or investigations of the underlying logic of narrative, paradigms or codes of structural possibilities, and systems for the comparative classification of a wide variety of texts were proposed. Structuralism had the salutary effect of deposing the masterpiece from its position of representative greatness and replacing it with a broad view of many texts, including literary classics, but also including humble narratives such as advertisements, comic strips, and folk tales. The reliance of structuralism on binary oppositions (especially the two-tier description of narrative as story and discourse), its emphasis on systems over individual texts, and its disregard of change over time made it vulnerable to deconstruction and to other forms of post-structuralist critique. In this light, it is worth noting that many structuralists went on to be post-structuralists themselves. Tzvetan Todorov, Roland Barthes, and Gérard Genette all wrote influential works of structuralist literary theory, and each of these figures subsequently made striking contributions to post-structuralist thought as well.[7] In this book, readers will encounter the ideas of many structuralist and post-structuralist narratologists, particularly in my descriptions of Gérard Genette's work. Contextual narratology, feminist narrative theory, and much of narratology participate in the ongoing post-structuralist revision of structuralist narrative poetics. For an exemplary selection of the range of work being done under the name of narratology, see David Herman's collection *Narratologies* (1990).

Recent developments in the study of narrative include what is often termed 'the narrative turn' in disciplines outside literary study. For instance, fields of study such as narrative jurisprudence in law, narrative psychology in the area of therapy, life-story study in social science disciplines, and the use of narrative as an emancipatory method of giving voice to the silenced in political discourse bring ideologically freighted understandings of the purposes and capacities of narrative to light.[8] Rather than setting these other understandings of narrative aside, recent studies in narrative have taken markedly interdisciplinary turns. In addition to fields such as Law and Literature, in which narrative theorists have participated from the early days, contextual narratology brings ideological and historical concerns to bear on the analysis of narratives. For instance, as Gerald Prince writes, 'Susan Lanser has sketched the foundations for a socially sensitive, feminist narratology; [Marie-Laure] Ryan has argued that some configurations of events make better stories than others,' and Prince himself has proposed ways to consider 'narrative context as part narrative text' ('Narratology,' 527). Three examples of different varieties of contextual narratology suggest the range of options available to the advanced student: narrative ethics; feminist narratology; and cognitive approaches to literary study. These fields have in common the strong influence of reader response theory, whether or not they acknowledge it. The ways in which readers construct meaning in their minds are central assumptions of ethical criticism, feminist narratology, and cognitivism.

Influenced by reader response criticism, speech act theory, rhetorical criticism, as well as by philosophers such as Martha Nussbaum, lively discussions about the ethics of reading, the practice of ethical criticism, and narrative ethics have been launched.[9] Students seeking ways to avoid studying narrative texts in isolation, and hoping to observe how fiction works in the world through actual readers will find many provocative ideas in these related fields. Wayne Booth and Martha Nussbaum have produced many of the fundamental books and articles in this area, with the skeptical Richard Posner spurring them more persuasively to articulate their claims about the ethics of reading.

Feminist narratology, a post-structuralist variant of narrative theory, overlaps with ethical criticism in some areas and with contextual narratology, as it emphasizes historical context, including 'era, class, gender, sexual orientation, and racial and ethnic circumstances of producers [of narrative forms] and audiences' (Warhol, 'Guilty Cravings,' 340). Robyn Warhol summarizes: 'Feminist narratology borrows the feminist-epistemological critique of objectivity to question the "either/or" reasoning of classical narratology,' yet 'maintains structuralism's focus on identifying patterns among narrative forms of story and discourse' ('Guilty Cravings,' 340).[10] Feminist narratology, according to Warhol, scrutinizes women's texts in order to challenge the typologies and systems of classical narratology, examines gender differences in narratives, and seeks historical explanations for those differences. It employs the detailed reading strategies of narratology to observe the workings of gender in texts, and it asks how gender is produced through narrative ('Guilty Cravings,' 343).

Finally, the various approaches to narrative developing in the relatively new area of cognitive literary studies re-situate the study of narrative as a subset of cognitive science's scrutiny of the mind. An excellent new study making this case with a focus on how human minds construct and comprehend 'worlds' is David Herman's *Story Logic* (2002), the first book in the interdisciplinary 'Frontier of Narrative' series. Using Herman's bibliography and his forthcoming edited volume, *Narrative Theory and the Cognitive Sciences* (2003), an advanced student can get up to speed efficiently in this emerging field. Sabine Gross summarizes the state of the field as falling into three areas: cognitive research into reading; analysis of the relationship between narrative structure and discourse comprehension; and cognitive study of concepts and language ('Cognitive Readings,' 272). As this array of aims makes plain, the hybrid approaches of contemporary narrative theorists make room for questions and points of view that arise out of other theoretical stances and even other disciplines.

Studying narrative: selected resources

Journals

Consciousness, Literature, and the Arts. This journal publishes new work relating the arts and literature to the exploration of consciousness going on in philosophy, cognitive science, psychology, neuroscience, computer science, and physics. <http://www.aber.ac.uk/~drawww/journal/> (accessed 12 Dec. 2002).

Image [&] Narrative: An Online Magazine of the Visual Narrative. This site offers an academic e-journal on visual narratology. <http://millennium.arts.kuleuven.ac.be/narrative/index_main.cfm> (accessed 12 Dec. 2002).

JNT: Journal of Narrative Theory. <http://www.emich.edu/public/english/literature/JNT/JNT.html> (accessed 12 Dec. 2002).

Narrative. The official journal of the Narrative Society. Information about the journal and the society at <http://www.vanderbilt.edu/narrative/> (accessed 12 Dec. 2002).

Narrative Inquiry. This interdisciplinary journal offers studies of narrative as a way to give contour to experience and life, conceptualize and preserve memories, or hand down experience, tradition, and values to future generations. Particular emphasis is placed on theoretical approaches to narrative and the analysis of narratives in human interaction, including those practiced by researchers in psychology, linguistics, anthropology, sociology, and related disciplines. <http://www.clarku.edu/~narrinq/> (accessed 12 Dec. 2002).

New Literary History. Focuses on the reasons for literary change, the definitions of periods, and the evolution of styles, conventions, and genres.
<http://muse.jhu. edu/journals/new literary history/> (accessed 12 Dec. 2002).

Poetics: Journal of Empirical Research on Literature, the Media and the Arts. This journal publishes articles on theoretical and empirical research on culture, the media and the arts.
<http://www.elsevier.nl/inca/publications/store/5/0/5/5/9/2/> (accessed 12 Dec. 2002).

Poetics Today. Edited by Meir Sternberg. This influential journal comes out of the Tel Aviv School of Poetics. As well as the current issues, see vol. 11, nos. 2 and 4 (1990) for the overviews 'Narratology Revisited I and II.'
<http://muse.jhu.edu/journals/poet/> (accessed 12 Dec. 2002).

Websites

Literature, Cognition, and the Brain. Alan Richardson's comprehensive site dedicated to research at the intersection of literary studies, cognitive theory, and neuro-science. The reviews, abstracts, bibliographies, and 'Starter Kit' compiled by Richardson and Cynthia Freeland are all strongly recommended.
<http://www2.bc.edu/~richarad/lcb/ home.html> (accessed 17 Dec. 2002).

NarrNet. Narratology Network. A specialized site of the Narratology Research Group at the University of Hamburg, for students and researchers in narratology.
<http://www.narratology.net/index2.html> (accessed 12. Dec. 2002).

Narratology: A Guide to the Theory of Narrative. Manfred Jahn's extraordinary website, user-friendly, with a detailed table of contents and targeted links to definitions and examples.
<http://www.uni-koeln.de/~ame02/pppn.htm> (accessed 12 Dec. 2002).

Essential Reference Books

Groden, Michael and Martin Kreiswirth (ed.), *The Johns Hopkins Guide to Literary Theory and Criticism* (Johns Hopkins University Press, 1994). A comprehensive, international, and historical encyclopedia of essays about people, schools of thought, and ideas, written by major authorities. The first stop for orientation and basic bibliography on theory and criticism. Some definitions relevant to the study of narrative are available free online at
<http://www.press.jhu.edu/books/hopkins_guide_to_literary_theory/free/g-contents.html> (accessed 16 Dec. 2002).

Herman, David, Manfred Jahn, and Marie-Laure Ryan, *The Routledge Encyclopedia of Narrative Theory* (Routledge, forthcoming). Look for this encyclopedia in a university library in 2005; it promises to be the definitive resource for narrative studies.

Makaryk, Irene R. (ed.), *The Encyclopedia of Contemporary Literary Theory: Approaches, Scholars, Terms* (University of Toronto Press, 1993). The collaborative effort of over 170 scholars, this indispensable encyclopedia provides brief, clear, and sophisticated essays on a wide array of current theoretical approaches. Not only for students on narrative, but for all graduate students in literary studies.

Further reading

Abbott, H. Porter, *Cambridge Introduction to Narrative* (Cambridge University Press, 2001). An excellent introduction to narrative broadly construed, not only narrative fiction. Well worth reading for a solid introduction to a wide range of issues in narrative studies, with thorough integration of film and visual narrative.

Brooks, Peter and Paul Gewirtz (ed.), *Law's Stories: Narrative and Rhetoric in the Law* (Yale University Press, 1996). A selection of narrative studies in the field of law and literature.

Greimas, A. J., *Structural Semantics: An Attempt at a Method* (1966), trans. Danielle McDowell, Ronald Schleifer, and Alan Velie (University of Nebraska Press, 1983). A systematic account of structuralism.

Herman, David (ed.), *Narratologies: New Perspectives on Narrative Analysis* (Ohio State University Press, 1999). As the plural in the title suggests, this anthology collects essays and excerpts illustrating a range of post-classical approaches to narrative. An excellent resource that makes a compelling call for interdisciplinary collaborative research in narrative studies.

Lemon, Lee T. and Marion J. Reis (ed. and trans.), *Russian Formalist Criticism: Four Essays* (University of Nebraska Press, 1965). The most useful supplementary text of Russian Formalists for teaching purposes.

Martin, Wallace, *Recent Theories of Narrative* (Cornell University Press, 1986). A very useful survey of narrative theory from the 1960s through the early 1980s, with some attention to earlier twentieth-century approaches.

Matejka, Ladislav and Krystyna Pomorska (ed.), *Readings in Russian Poetics: Formalist and Structuralist Views* (Michigan Slavic Publications, 1978). A comprehensive selection of the Russian Formalists.

Mcquillan, Martin, *The Narrative Reader* (Routledge, 2000). A superb anthology for graduate students, but it makes no concessions to those who are new to narrative theory. Densely theoretical, comprehensive, and up-to-date.

Onega, Susana and José Ángel García Landa, *Narratology: An Introduction* (Longman, 1996). The title suggests a narrow focus on structuralist narratology, but this useful anthology excerpts works from a broader array of approaches to narrative.

Pratt, Mary Louise, *Towards a Speech Act Theory of Literature* (Indiana University Press, 1977). A good starting point for those interested in speech act theory.

Richter, David H. (ed.), *Narrative/Theory* (Longman, 1996). A useful anthology for students, but it has a flawed glossary. The definitions of prolepsis and analepsis are reversed.

2
Shapes of Narrative: A Whole of Parts

Narrative is a time-bound linear form that can be heard, watched, or read. Each of these circumstances for narrative's reception has its own effects on the length, shapes, and subdivisions of narrative, and each makes different demands on our time, attention, memory, patience, and physical endurance. Experience tells us that narrative takes a great variety of shapes, from the 30-second advertisement to the immense novel sequence. This chapter focuses on the most common shapes of prose fiction, only briefly noting oral, verse, and film forms. While 'narrative' conveys what all these storytelling shapes have in common, 'narrative literature' is comprised of a wide array of forms each with its own distinct literary history. The chapter defines these forms briefly and discusses narrative's most typical subdivisions, units such as chapters, sections, or volumes, which are so familiar as not to be noticed by a reader. The traits of genres and the expectations generated by conventions that play such an important role in the reader's experience of narrative are treated at the end of the book, in Chapter 11. Though this chapter suggests some relationships between genres and shapes of narrative, its central concern is the lengths, subdivisions, and labels that mark out the units of the reading experience.

Effective criticism of narrative fiction begins with accurate description and a willingness to start with its evidently simple traits, such as its length, the units that comprise it, and its overall shape. This approach has the advantage of conveying both the individual and the unique features of a work, while prompting recollection of reading experiences that may be rather distant. Few readers of George Eliot's *Middlemarch* (1871–72) need to be reminded that it is a very long novel, but many would be aided by the information that it comprises a prelude, eight 'books,' and a finale. The historically minded critic of narrative form will want to know that

16

Middlemarch came out in eight separately bound segments over a period of thirteen months, and that reviews of the parts appeared in journals before readers knew the outcome of the multiple plots of the novel. Feminists may be interested to know that Eliot was the only woman novelist to succeed with a method of publication—monthly numbers—that was associated with the most popular Victorian novelists (especially Charles Dickens).

The paragraph above indicates how swiftly a discussion of a work's shape may move into territory far afield from narrative form. Attention to the shapes of novels, short stories, and other narratives steps away from the core principles of structuralism. Much of structuralist poetics works to derive the *shared* features of narrative, treating folk tales, films, and novels as so many samples to be examined for similarities of strategy and technique. This approach has resulted in a rich descriptive vocabulary for the 'grammar' of narrative, and in useful taxonomies of form. Though it contains historical and generic commentary that structuralists would eschew, a great deal of this book is devoted to the explanation of the most useful terms coined by structuralists as they studied diverse narratives for their shared qualities.

For instance, we owe the distinction between story and discourse to the insights of structuralist theorists. Briefly, 'discourse' indicates the words of the narrative as they are actually presented, including—as they occur page by page—any digressions, repetitions, omissions, and disorderly telling. Discourse streams along in the linear path of language itself. In the 'discourse level,' the events of page 99 always come after those of page 75, and before those of page 250. Subdivisions of narrative literature are marked at the level of discourse with white space, page breaks, numbering, or the separation of individually bound volumes. In the more didactic or philosophical Spanish *novela*, chapters are sometimes labeled 'discursos,' which felicitously emphasizes how chapters and chapter breaks belong to the discourse level of the narrative.

In contrast to discourse, 'story' represents the whole narrative content as (re)constructed in a reader's understanding. Story has been defined by Gerald Prince as the 'what' a narrative tells (as opposed to discourse, the 'how' of the telling). Though some plots (in which events are linked causally) are presented in purely chronological order, flowing along in the order of the discourse from beginning to middle to end, many others involve the piecing-together of segments of narration that the writer deliberately disarrays. Authors from Homer to Toni Morrison have exploited the techniques of disordering at the level of discourse. It makes sense to consider how the form or sectioning of the discourse might play a role in shaping readers' experiences of the story, and in recording the traces of the narrative's making and publication, its individual literary history.

One matter of terminology that must be confronted directly is the difference between the structuralist sense of story explored in the preceding paragraph, and the commonsense usage of story to indicate a narrative fiction significantly shorter than a novel. None of the five definitions of 'story' in Gerald Prince's *Dictionary of Narratology* acknowledges the primary meaning for most readers and writers, the sense invoked in a phrase such as 'John Cheever's story "The Enormous Radio".' Since 'tale' is an inexact synonym for 'story,' invoking as it does a set of generic associations with folk or fairy tales, substitution of terms does not solve the problem. It may be helpful to know that in structuralist efforts to systematize the elements of narrative, the distinction between long narratives (novels) and short ones (stories and tales) is usually collapsed, in the interest of arriving at a universal grammar of narrative structure. This is one of the reasons (though not the only one) that structuralist or post-structuralist critics refer to their objects of study as 'texts.'[1] To the working fiction writer who creates both stories and novels, this conflation obscures a world of vital differences.

Although the minimalist short short story of barely a paragraph and the 900-page novel share many traits, their radically different lengths condition the way they are written, read, criticized, and theorized. Indeed, the historical, material, and cultural conditions surrounding the production of a narrative often have a profound effect on its presentation: the form in which it comes to a reader. This form in turn may have an impact on its immediate success in the marketplace, on its chances for surviving its immediate moment or short-term 'shelf-life,' and the statistically unlikely event that it will be studied, written about by critics other than book reviewers, or become canonical. Accurate description and identification of a narrative's provenance thus communicates a great deal to an informed reader. After naming the author, the title, and the date of first publication, conveying the shape and length of a narrative should be immediate priorities of a critic attentive to narrative form.

Ordinarily, critics handle the differences in the length of prose narratives by naming them novels—long narrative prose fictions[2]—or short stories— brief tales, or narratives that can be read in a single sitting, according to Edgar Allan Poe's influential definition. (Poe emphasizes the singleness of effect that can be achieved when a story can be read straight through and he prized the unity of a pre-established design, in which the end controls the beginning and the middle.) Though 'epic' is sometimes used as an adjective to indicate the exceptional length, ambition, or scope of a narrative in film or prose (as in 'epic novel,' 'epic history,' or 'Hollywood epic'), used as a noun it ordinarily means a long narrative poem that relates in an elevated style the adventures of a heroic figure through whom a nation's identity is defined, or fate decided.[3] (In the German tradition, 'episch' and 'Epik' can refer to any fictional narrative, long or short, in verse or prose.) Narrative poetry comes in short forms (ballads) too, but the narrative conventions of epic poetry have had the more influential impact on narrative form in prose. Though this book cannot address the aspects of form peculiar to poetry (many superb handbooks on poetic form exist already),[4] it does attend to qualities of narrative that verse and prose share.

Indeed, one of the most ubiquitous forms of narrative before the eighteenth century, the romance, appeared in verse as well as in prose. In Anglo-American literary criticism, the romance and the novel have most often been considered alternate types of long narrative prose fiction. I argue in the chapter on genres and conventions (Chapter 11) that novel and romance interpenetrate one another and that many of the subgenres of the novel are in fact variants of romance. In any case, it is helpful to know that in neighboring literary traditions, the prose narrative that we call in English a 'novel' goes by the older name 'romance,' or a cognate, as in the French *roman*. The opposite can also occur, as in the Spanish *novela*. In Spanish, a *novela* can be every bit as long as a novel in English; the *novela corta* is distinguished by its shorter length.

In English, however, the novella denotes a narrative fiction of intermediate length, such as Henry James's *The Turn of the Screw* (1898). Nevertheless, in the latter part of the twentieth century, many fictions of novella length are considered by their authors and readers to be novels. This shift in usage reminds us that market considerations, particularly publishers' ideas about how labeling affects sales, often govern the commonsense, real-world names given to narrative fictions. It is not unheard of for contemporary volumes of related short stories to be described and sold as 'novels,' to increase their distribution and enhance their eligibility for prizes. Thus Alice Munro, the brilliant Canadian author of short stories, found her volume *The Beggar Maid* (1978) short-listed for the Booker Prize, an award ostensibly reserved for novels.

The terms 'novel' and 'short story' disguise a multiplicity of formal arrangements—traditional, experimental, and often nearly invisible to a habitual reader. This chapter draws attention to some of the most prominent of these arrangements: in books, chapters, and regular and irregular sections. The nineteenth-century history of the three-volume novel and alternative serial forms of publication (in magazines, in monthly numbers, and in sequences of novels) can still be discerned in the forms of some recent fiction, including television series. The term most often used to indicate an installment on television (or, in earlier years, on the radio or at the movies), the 'episode,' has its roots in prose fiction, particularly in romances and picaresque fictions. In literary critical language, the episode is a unit of storytelling with its own plot and characters, combined with others of similar dimension and contents, or embedded contrastingly within a larger fictional world. Perhaps because in the Victorian period episodes were seen as marring the 'unity' of novels, the term is rarely used as a section-label.[5]

Books and chapters, in contrast, have pedigrees much more ancient and distinguished than the episode. Both terms antedate the novel. From classical epic early novelists adopted the notion of division into books, even mimicking epic associations by creating them in numbers that would remind readers of the division into 12 or 24 often used by epic poets. Thus Henry Fielding, who announces in his preface to *Joseph Andrews* (1742) his intention to write 'a comic epic in prose,' creates *Tom Jones* (1749) in 18 books, an epic-and-a-half by the numbers. Bible stories are conventionally divided into chapters and verses; writers of early prose fiction adopted chapters even as they dispensed with verse. Usually numbered and often titled, chapters and books give readers convenient places to take a break in reading. Their titles and number may contribute to the interpretation of the story. It is no accident, for instance, that Anthony Burgess's *A Clockwork Orange* (1962) was originally written in 21 chapters, though the American edition and the film Stanley Kubrick made of it truncated the story to end on a darker note. Burgess defends his intention by reference to the significance of 21, the 'symbol of human maturity.' He goes on to speak for novelists 'of his stamp,' with interests in 'arithmology, meaning that number has to mean something in human terms.' To these novelists, 'the number of chapters is never entirely arbitrary.'[6] For others it is a matter of little significance though real convenience. Chapter titles with or without numbers make their own contributions to the reading experience, as in Margaret Atwood's *The Handmaid's Tale* (1986), with its recurrent chapters called 'Night,' or in Seamus Deane's *Reading in the Dark* (1996), where the evocative titles of the very short chapters add to the effect of a novel comprised of units resembling prose poems and short short stories.

Though chapters predominate, they are not the only devices available for sectioning long narratives. Unnumbered sections employ white space and a fresh start at the top of the following page to create a break and a pausing place without the formal apparatus of a chapter number and title. Sections are more likely to vary dramatically in length than chapters, but they serve many of the same functions, and the curious are often rewarded for counting the sections of a novel. In the eighteenth century, Samuel Richardson capitalized on the vogue for letter-writing by creating novels comprised of letters and journals. (To complicate matters further, *Pamela* (1740–41) was issued in separate volumes.) The novel of letters (also known as epistolary fiction) employs the letter in lieu of the chapter. Though this strategy was in vogue in the eighteenth century (as in the bestsellers Pierre Choderlos de Laclos's *Liaisons Dangereuses* (1782) and Fanny Burney's *Evelina* (1778)), it has never disappeared entirely from the novel. A recent novel such as David Lodge's *Thinks ...* (2001) brings the epistolary fiction up to date by embedding email exchanges complete with their standard, machine-generated headers.[7]

Very few novels do without breaks altogether. Gabriel García Márquez's *The Autumn of the Patriarch* (1975) challenges the reader with a text that eschews even paragraph indentations. This sort of experiment reminds novel-readers of how much they rely on chapters, books, or sections to relieve the demands a novel makes on their attention. Playing with the conventions of sectioning, either by omitting the usual concessions to readers looking for breaks, or by calling attention to the usual way sections are ordered, for instance, can participate in a writer's project of 'laying bare' the devices of narration. Like the publisher's apparatus—such as ISBNs and back cover blurbs—authorial materials such as epigraphs, frontispiece maps, and the devices that typically announce chapter or section breaks, are known collectively as paratexts. They occupy a liminal position in relation to the fictional world, partly of it, partly of the realm that orients itself towards the reader's experience. Manipulation of reader's expectations about breaks and sectioning can draw attention to what is tacitly accepted as 'normal' in narrative fiction. Paratexts can play up the ambiguities or confusions about who has responsibility for various apparatuses that comprise the material text.

Interpreting sectioning and labels can be rewarding, especially because these paratexts sometimes reflect the material conditions of authorship and publication. Though most novel-readers today expect a novel to be a single book, a freestanding volume that starts and finishes within one set of covers, readers in the past consumed installments of various dimensions. In many cases they read a single novel spread out over the course of a year. The segments in which many nineteenth-century novels appeared for the first time can still be discerned when the whole story is assembled for republication in a single volume. The most common type of installment

publication was the magazine (or newspaper) serial. Many Victorian novelists, including Thomas Hardy, Elizabeth Gaskell, Anthony Trollope, Wilkie
Collins, and Charles Dickens, published some of their work in family magazines. The need to sustain readers' interest until the next issue (weekly,
biweekly, or monthly) required clever use of suspense (as in the 'cliff-
hanger' of early film serials, which adopted this form), or a carefully
deployed set of mini-climaxes, one per issue. It is a useful exercise to try to
discern where the installment breaks occur in a novel first published this
way, such as Thomas Hardy's *The Mayor of Casterbridge* (1886), for key turns
in the plot may be placed at the ends of the original installments. However,
the use of titled sections for a novel published in briefer magazine installments can conceal the formal traces of its first appearance, as in Thomas
Hardy's *Tess of the D'Urbervilles* (1891), apparently divided into seven
'phases,' and bearing few traces in book form of its weekly serialization in
The Graphic.

The advantage of serial publication for an author was a steady paycheck
to be received during the writing of the novel; the disadvantages lay in the
censorship some writers experienced at the hands of editors endeavoring to
protect their magazines' reputations for wholesomeness. Contrasting the
serial version of a novel published in a family magazine with the later issue
in volume form can reveal the restoration of racier material, though novels
in book form were not immune to censorship in the Victorian period.

A few of the most popular novelists avoided the constraints imposed by
working with a magazine editor by contracting with a publisher to produce
monthly numbers, paperback installments that could be sold independently over a period of months until the whole novel was out. Charles
Dickens, George Eliot, and William Thackeray all used this method of publication. Recently, Stephen King exploited this strategy, when he published
The Green Mile (1996) in six inexpensive paperback chapbooks, just like
Victorian monthly numbers. Later the parts were assembled for publication
in single-volume form. Especially for writers who produced enormously
long novels, the monthly number sustained contact with their readership
until the book could be brought out in hardcover form. It could be lucra-
tive, but a publisher might cut off a novel-in-process if the numbers sold
poorly. Thackeray's masterpiece *Vanity Fair* (1847–48) was almost cancelled
after the fourth number because it was not selling well. Like many of his
contemporaries, Thackeray wrote for the deadline; the cancellation of his
contract for monthly numbers might well have meant the end of the
novel. Luckily, the publisher took the risk and continued to put out the
parts of *Vanity Fair*. The most common clue that a Victorian novel was first

published in monthly numbers is its division into roughly eight to twelve titled books of approximately the same length, as in *Middlemarch*.

In the nineteenth century, most English novels were published in three volumes. This practice was encouraged by the private lending libraries that bought most of the print run of a new novel and virtually controlled its distribution. Hardcover books were too expensive for most readers to own. Most British middle-class readers borrowed their books from libraries such as the famous Mudie's, having paid their subscriptions. Triple-deckers, as three-volume novels were sometimes called, commanded three times the earnings for these libraries. Each subscriber paid a set fee to have the right to borrow a book; borrowing three required three subscriptions. Whether lending all three volumes of a new novel to a single subscriber rich enough to possess three subscriptions, or sending the three parts to three different readers, the libraries tripled their revenue for each book published in this fashion. As a result, publishers were loath to risk printing single-volume novels, as Charlotte Brontë found when she tried in 1846 to publish her first novel, *The Professor*, which was short (she got it into print in 1857, after her success with *Jane Eyre* (1847)). Until the domination of the circulating libraries was broken by more economical printing methods that enabled publishers to sell cheap books directly to readers, three-volume novels were the rule. Thus cultural influences, generic conventions, and material conditions influenced the division of a novel into three sections. For an 1850 British novel this is the sign of a practical response to the role of the circulating libraries. For a 1950 novel, division into three volumes is an aesthetic decision, perhaps parodying or wistfully invoking the vanished world of the Victorian triple-decker. There are other reasons for dividing a novel into three, however. For instance, Elizabeth Bowen's 1938 novel *The Death of the Heart* has three named parts, 'The World,' 'The Flesh,' and 'The Devil.' For Bowen's original readers these words comprise a phrase that would have been familiar from the Book of Common Prayer, in whose words Anglican worshippers prayed, 'From all the deceits of the world, the flesh, and the devil, Good Lord, deliver us.' Bowen makes an oblique and sometimes ironic use of the elements of this once familiar phrase, and perhaps also of the narrative expectations associated with formal division into three volumes.

As time passes, the associations readers make with particular modes of delivering narrative fiction change. The success of television, film, and mass market fiction series has given the narrative in series a reputation of lightness, popularity, or unseriousness. The use of this publishing format for juvenile readers, as in The Hardy Boys, The Babysitters Club, or

R. L. Stine's Goosebumps series, suggests the exploitation of generic formulas in highly repetitive narratives designed to be as similar to one another as possible. The low-brow appearance of the narrative in series, sequence, or cycle form is mitigated by an endpoint that suggests a conscious plan, a number dignified by association with prior literary works, or a title that justifies the grouping. Thus we have Lloyd Alexander's Prydain Cycle (1964–68) and Doris Lessing's Children of Violence series (1952–69), each comprising five separate novels. Numerous authors of trilogies, from J. R. R. Tolkien to Pat Barker, have insisted that the three volumes be read as one large novel. J. K. Rowling's immensely popular Harry Potter books (1997–) cleave to this pattern in a projected grouping of seven books, a number dignified by C. S. Lewis's The Chronicles of Narnia (1950–56). (Thanks to Anthony Trollope, 'chronicles' abound in the bibliography of novels in sequences, though historians, from whom the term is borrowed, would be reluctant to use it unironically.) Even more ambitious sequences, such as Anthony Powell's twelve-volume *A Dance to the Music of Time* (1951–75), extend the possibilities of the unified (though serially published) work's length. Perhaps no writer will exceed the ambition of French novelist Honoré de Balzac, who in 1841 named his entire, voluminous, body of work *La Comédie Humaine*, or the 'the human comedy.' (Though uncommon in Anglo-American criticism, the French term for these long narrative sequences, the *Roman-fleuve*, sometimes turns up.) Since the days of the Victorians and high modernists, novels in long or open-ended sequences have declined in status, or been relegated to zones of so-called genre fiction, a denigrating label for popular varieties of the novel such as westerns, fantasies, gothic romances, and so forth. Thus, it is of interest when contemporary writers with literary ambitions embark upon such projects. The most prominent example in contemporary literature is dramatic, not narrative—playwright August Wilson's as yet incomplete ten-play sequence chronicling the African-American experience in the twentieth century.

The variety of lengths, subdivisions, and sequences of novels demonstrate how the modes of publication or material conditions of authorship can have a shaping effect on narrative form. Within the area of short fiction, important formal differences also emerge through consideration of means of publication. Periodicals—newspapers, magazines, and literary journals—have provided an outlet for short fiction from the late nineteenth century to the present. Freestanding short stories, either previously published or original, may also be assembled into collections published in book form. From the early days of the modern short story, magazines published in installments linked story sequences such as Conan Doyle's

Sherlock Holmes stories (1891–93, 1901–5). Though these stories often appear later in collections, they differ from the stories deliberately grouped into a unifying volume form (such as Joyce's *Dubliners* (1914) or Sarah Orne Jewett's *Country of the Pointed Firs* (1896)). Though there is little consistency in critics' usage, a 'volume' of stories usually indicates the unified form, such as Tim O'Brien's *The Things They Carried* (1990) or Margaret Laurence's *A Bird in the House* (1970), whereas a 'collection' of stories more often refers to an assemblage of short fiction by a single author. This is by far the more common form of the two. Another arrangement, the short story cycle, may bridge the volume and the collection, as stories comprising cycles may not all appear in the same volume; they are usually linked by their subject, their speaker, or their setting. For instance, John O'Hara's stories of his fictional Gibbsville, Pennsylvania appeared over time in volumes of stories that also contained fiction set in other places, and were only later reassembled into cycle form, by an editor, in *Gibbsville, PA* (1992). Readers often encounter short stories in anthologies, a term reserved for collections of writings by multiple authors. The separation of a story from its context in a unified volume may matter to a critic. Arguably, it makes a difference to read Joyce's 'Araby' in the company of Ring Lardner and Eudora Welty, rather than as a part of the volume *Dubliners*.

Anthologies and inexpensive paperback teaching editions of novels may bear as much responsibility as the influence of structuralist theory for the tendency to gloss over the impact modes of publication make on the formal qualities of narrative fiction. The following section suggests several ways in which noticing the shapes of fiction can be brought to bear on the advanced student's critical practices.

Analytical strategies

As this chapter freely acknowledges from the start, discussion of the shapes and lengths of narrative fiction has not been a priority of the structuralist theorists who have devised most of the technical vocabulary discussed in the remaining chapters of this book. Today's advanced literature students are more likely to be interested in historicizing texts than structuralist vocabulary allows. One way to build a bridge between the useful aspects of structuralist formal analysis and contextualizing approaches is to attend to the way that the material conditions of authorship, including the modes of publication available to a writer, may be reflected in the form of the narrative. Attention to the cultural resonances of narrative shapes can also assist

advanced students in perceiving the writer's manipulation of those associations. Several suggestions regarding analytical strategies follow.

Close reading and reader response methods.   Most novels and many short
   stories are arranged in sections. Look at the narrative you are reading
   and describe its sectioning. Does it make use of chapters, volumes, or
   unnumbered sections? (Count the sections if they are unnumbered.)
   Are these sections named and labeled with titles? Does the numbering
   of the units contribute to the interpretation of the narrative? Do the
   sections fall into a pattern, and if so, does the author break or alter that
   pattern at any juncture that would reward close scrutiny? How do the
   chapter titles or names of the volumes condition the reading experience? A lengthy work with absolutely no concessions to readers' needs
   for breaks demands attention: what effect on the reading experience do
   you discern? Does the content or narrative situation mirror the narrative shape in an effective way? For instance, a deathbed discourse
   might appear awkward if divided up into chapters (see Hermann
   Broch's *Death of Virgil* (1945)). Narratives featuring multiple narrators,
   such as William Faulkner's *As I Lay Dying* (1930), or Andre Brink's
   A Chain of Voices (1982), may use sectioning to effect the shift between
   narrators. Can you justify the shape of the narrative by referring to its
   content? Can you find places in the narrative where the section breaks
   or section sizes emphasize aspects of the content?

Textual history method.   Find out when the work you are studying was first
   published (or, if it was published a very long time after its composition, as was E. M. Forster's *Maurice* (1971), when it was composed and
   also when it got into print). In what form was the work first published?
   Has it been revised or edited by the author or a scholarly editor? Was it
   published in a different form in another country, as in the cases of
   Lawrence Norfolk's *Lemprière's Dictionary* (1991, 1992) and Anthony
   Burgess's *A Clockwork Orange*? If you discover that there are likely to be
   significant differences between the edition you are reading and another
   edition, you can fruitfully compare the texts and speculate about the
   reasons for the differences or the effects on readers. An infrequently
   explored area of the novel lies in the condensed or expurgated children's versions of classic fiction. Charles Kingsley's *Water-Babies*
   (1863), for instance, is often published in modern children's editions
   with its offensively racist sections removed. Writers sometimes
   comment on the processes by which their works have appeared in different forms in published letters or interviews. For contemporary

writers, interviews are very easy to locate on Nexis's Academic Universe or other full-text databases of newspapers and journals. For earlier writers, the correspondence between author and editor has sometimes been published. Comparison of an author's text and the version produced in collaboration with an editor can be fruitful, as recent critics of Thomas Wolfe have demonstrated. In film, this sort of analysis is easier than ever to attempt in the classroom, because DVD versions of films now often feature director's cuts, and alternative versions in addition to the version released to movie theaters.

Formalist and contextual methods combined.   Determine whether the novel you are reading, most likely in a modern paperback edition, appeared in installments when it was first published. The introduction to the edition may provide this information. Even if you are far from an excellent research library, you can make use of this knowledge. Can you tell where the original episodes began and ended? Are the serial breaks marked by a climactic action? Does the book present a revised (franker, or longer) version of the story that first appeared in a family magazine, as the book form of Thomas Hardy's *Tess of the D'Urbervilles* does? See if you can get the work in its original, in a research library, through inter-library loan, on microfilm, or in an edition specially prepared to recapture the exact text of the original publication. Increasingly, original editions can be found online in pdf format, or for purchase through internet publishing ventures such as Elibron (www.elibron.com). If you can look at the original publication, for instance in one of many nineteenth-century periodicals, you can recapture a sense of the surrounding texts (advertisements, illustrations, articles) it is likely the earliest readers would have seen. How might the context of its first appearance have conditioned its composition or the reactions of the earliest reviewers? Alternatively, you could select a periodical in which narrative fiction appears (such as *Harper's*, *The Atlantic*, or *Cornhill*), and study the way fiction appears in the full run of the journal, or in the issues centered around a date of historical significance.

Even without access to a major research library, advanced students can get at much of the material needed to make contextual studies or to study rare or fragile materials. Microfilm or microfiche can sometimes be ordered through inter-library loan. In addition, increasing numbers of journals are now available on the World Wide Web in searchable etext forms. See, for instance, the Library of Congress's nineteenth-century periodical site at <http://memory.loc.gov /ammem/ndlpcoop/moahtml/snchome.html>. (The British Library is experimenting with digitizing its microfilm collections of early news- papers.) Many narrative texts in the public domain are already avail- able: start with the University of Virginia's Gutenberg Project at <http://www.gutenberg.net/>. Since the 1980s, textual recovery efforts such as the W. E. B. DuBois Institute's Black Periodical Literature Project have been in the process of making hitherto inaccessible narra- tive texts available for study on microfiche and in CD form.

Keywords

The 'Keywords' section of each chapter connects the terminology of the chapter with similar or related uses of critical or theoretical language. Keywords are presented alphabetically, with a brief explanation of the relationship between the terms discussed in this chapter and the other meanings.

Epic and novel.   Mikhail Bakhtin pairs epic and novel in order to advance his methodology for the study of the novel in 'Epic and Novel' (*The Dialogic Imagination*, 3–40). In this essay Bakhtin contrasts the novel, the only uncompleted genre, with the pre-existing form of the epic, a 'congealed and half-moribund' genre typified by its representation of a remote national heroic past, based on tradition, and located at an absolute distance from the teller and audience (13–14).

Loose baggy monsters.   This oft-quoted phrase is Henry James's damning description of long Victorian novels, from his 'Preface to The Tragic Muse,' in *The Art of the Novel*, edited by R. P. Blackmur (1934), 84. Repeating it implies a preference for short, tightly unified modern novels. For a good defense of long Victorian novels against James's charge, see Peter K. Garrett's Bakhtinian study, *The Victorian Multiplot Novel: Studies in Dialogical Form* (1980).

Textual editing.   Expressing an interest in the publication history of a narrative work, particularly one with a complicated history involving periodical installments later assembled into book form, may suggest an aptitude for textual criticism, the discipline that governs the produc- tion of scholarly editions of texts. A painstaking discipline that can involve bibliographic research, comparison of editions, correction of errors, and annotation, textual editing brings forth standard editions, paperback teaching texts, CD-ROM concordances, and searchable etexts like the ones available from the University of Virginia's Project Gutenberg.[8] See Jerome McGann's *A Critique of Modern Textual Criticism* (1983) for an introduction to the issues just prior to the electronic textual editing revolution.

Further reading

Doody, Margaret Anne, *The True History of the Novel* (Rutgers University Press, 1996). Doody takes on the critical commonplace that the novel 'rose' in the eighteenth century, arguing that long prose narratives have been around for 2,000 years.

Griest, Guinevere L., *Mudie's Circulating Library and the Victorian Novel* (Indiana University Press, 1970). A fascinating study of one of the major forces conditioning authorship and publication during a period celebrated for its novels.

Lohafer, Susan and Jo Ellyn Clarey (ed.), *Short Story Theory at a Crossroads*, (Louisiana State University Press, 1989). An excellent anthology of theoretical essays on short fiction, from its troubled definition to its formal traits.

McKeon, Michael (ed.), *Theory of the Novel: A Historical Approach* (Johns Hopkins University Press, 2000). A treasure trove of excerpts from major theorists from Henry James to Kwame Anthony Appiah. This textbook has a wonderful bibliography organized by topic.

Nagel, James, *The Contemporary American Short-Story Cycle* (Louisiana State University Press, 2001). A focused study of related short stories.

Price, Leah, *The Anthology and the Rise of the Novel: From Richardson to George Eliot* (Cambridge University Press, 2000). A subtle account of anthologizing, excerpting, and condensing of long prose narratives.

Sutherland, John, *Victorian Fiction: Writers, Publishers, Readers* (St. Martin's, 1995). A lively account of the material conditionals of authorship for Victorian novelists: practical matters have an impact on narrative form.

Watt, Ian, *The Rise of the Novel: Studies in Defoe, Richardson and Fielding* (University of California Press, 1957). The classic account of the impact of print culture, literacy, and middle-class ideology on the rise of the novel in the eighteenth century.

3
Narrative Situation: Who's Who and What's its Function

This chapter introduces the basic elements of narrative situation, the combination of narrator, perspective (point of view), and narrative level involved in first-person and third-person fictional narration.[1] A separate final section treats second-person narration and points readers to the growing bibliography on this unusual kind of narrative situation. This chapter deals exclusively with prose fiction, since the extent to which films have narrative situations, implied by the gaze of the camera, operates by rough analogies to the possibilities in prose fiction. Most films adopt the equivalent of third-person omniscience.[2]

Though characters and narrative levels are treated in depth in their own chapters (Chapters 4 and 8 respectively), they appear here first as ingredients of narrative situation. Briefly, characters, the active agents represented within narratives, may possess perspectives or points of view, or they may be depicted externally through reports of their speech and actions. Narrators, who are responsible for acts of telling, can be characters when they are positioned inside the story world, but often narrators are located outside the story world. A narrator positioned outside the story world can convey sufficient information to assume the status of a character, but unless the writer has a frame-breaking surprise up her sleeve, that kind of overt narrator still usually isn't a character within the story. These distinctions reflect the basic conception of narrative level, as comprised of (at least) a discourse level, a realm of narrated words-in-order, and the story level, a realm of imagined actions and agents.

Narrative situation describes where the narrator is located, how overtly or covertly the narrator makes his or her presence felt, and what relationship the narrator has to the characters, in one or more of whom perspective may be invested. In other words, narrative situation describes the nature of the mediation between author and reader, and it encompasses extremes: those narratives that seem to be the autobiographical outpourings of a narrator who closely resembles the author, as well as those that appear to record with perfect neutrality the actions of a set of figures moving on a remote stage, and those that have the feel of a first-person perspective while actually employing third-person reference—the 'center of consciousness' made famous by Henry James. Accurately using the language of narrative situation prevents two rudimentary errors: referring to a character in a third-person fiction whose perspective provides the central point of view as 'the narrator'; and calling an omniscient narrator by the name of the author. Understanding narrative situation offers far more than avoiding errors of terminology, however. The various combinations of narrators and reflectors (perspective-bearing characters; also called 'filters' or 'focalizers')[3] suggest different degrees of authority and reliability, and they profoundly affect the way readers interpret stories.

Virtually the first thing narrative theorists seek to ascertain about a text is its narrative situation. They ask themselves questions such as: Who tells the tale? (What kind of narrator does the writer create?); Does the telling imply speech, writing, or thought? (and a matching narratee—listener, reader, or self-auditor?); Who sees the actions? (Does a narrator provide the perspective from the outside, or do character(s) within the story view the events? Does the perspective of a single character or set of characters dominate the view of the fictional world?) Where do the functions of narration reside in relation to the story world? (Does the narrator perch outside or above the story world, or within it? Is the narrator also a character in the story?) Answering these and other questions about a text can be done handily with the vocabulary discussed in this chapter.

For some narratologists, the application of technical language in the accurate description of narrative situation may seem to be an end in itself. Taxonomy is indeed one of the aims of classical narratology; good taxonomy requires elaborate naming. The strength of narratology in this area, however, becomes its gravest weakness. Some of the most irritating jargon ever devised was invented for the purpose of discussing narrative situation, and accuracy does the literary critic no good if readers refuse to attend to insights produced by the use of difficult terminology. This chapter thus takes on a double task. First, it explains in relatively plain terms an aspect of narrative form most completely described by narratologists in hyper-technical language. Readers wishing to master the terminology can use the references in the notes and the bibliography to find their ways to the most technical narratological works (see especially

Genette and Prince). Second, this chapter makes a case for the immediate usefulness of narrative situation to the critic and teacher. In the classroom and in critical writing about narrative fiction, accurate observations about narrative situation lead to fruitful discussions of critical and interpretive problems. Form and content, structure and theme: these are not artificially bound together by critics seeking significance in co-incidental matters of narrative art. The manipulation of narrative situation is one of the most useful strategies possessed by fiction writers to elicit sympathy, to command respect, and to unleash the complicated effects that go by the name of irony. Furthermore, a reader attentive to narrative situation will be better able to interpret those occasions when a writer alters a narrative's perspective, or changes narrators, or even appears to 'break the rules' about what a narrator or reflector can do.

Terms

Narrative tells or shows a story. Whether it appears in the written verbal forms that are the central subject of this book, or in one of many visual or hybrid narrative forms (films, computer games, operas), narrative communicates. This communication works on different levels simultaneously, with several mediating figures performing different, albeit overlapping, functions. The *author* communicates with the *reader*; the *narrator* directs its discourse to a *narratee*; *characters* interact with one another. The actions, thoughts, and speech of characters occur inside the story world, or at the level of action. The narrator and narratee (recipient of the narrative) may also share the space of the story world with the characters, but they often occupy a distinct level separate from the story (often conceived spatially as existing 'above' the story). This realm, which is implied by the existence of the discourse, as the zone from which speech or writing emanates, may be elaborately or very lightly represented: it is the imaginary neutral zone from which a covert 'omniscient' narrator spins out language, or the cozy library in which an overt narrator props up his or her feet and 'speaks' to his or her guest. Outside the text itself, the author writes words to be read by other people; narrators may be represented as existing either inside or outside the story world, where they 'write,' 'speak,' or 'think,' but they can never escape their location in their own narrative discourse, which is the substance of their existence.

Conventionally, 'real' people such as authors and readers are firmly distinguished from the textual creations—narrator, narratee, and characters. Though many narratives endeavor to persuade readers of the roundness or psychological depth of their narrators and characters, these entities are use-fully differentiated from real people. E. M. Forster called characters 'word masses,' representatives of the species 'homo fictus.' Roland Barthes named them 'paper beings.' These estranging labels help us to avoid treating char-acters as if they possessed lives independent of the words which constitute them. Narrators whose views and attitudes appear to mirror those of their creator should also be distinguished from the real people who crafted their narration. This practice helps preserve terminological consistency when we are confronted with narrators whose opinions obviously differ from the recorded views of their makers.

real author → | | implied author → (narrator) → (narratee) → implied reader | | → real reader

Figure 1

Figure 1 reproduces Seymour Chatman's paradigm for narrative structure (*Story and Discourse*, 151). This model usefully identifies all the figural posi-tions located around, contained in, and implied by a narrative text. Chatman draws on work by both Wayne Booth (in *The Rhetoric of Fiction*) and Wolfgang Iser (in *The Implied Reader* and *The Act of Reading*) to create a model naming the participants in narrative transactions, when narrative is understood as an act of communication, with a sender and a receiver. Thus the diagram flows from left to right, from the real author to the real audi-ence or readers. In between those individuals, who necessarily exist outside the world of the text, Chatman places the entities projected by or implied by the text. Thus, drawing on both Booth and Iser, Chatman shows two additional extra-textual positions, the implied author and the implied reader. The following paragraphs briefly define these terms from Chatman's paradigm.

The author is the actual historical person who wrote the text. For instance, Charles Dickens is the author of *David Copperfield* (1849–50); Anonymous, an unknown woman or man of the Middle Ages, composed the ballad 'Sir Patrick Spens.' The *implied author* is the version of the author projected by the text itself and sometimes also conditioned by our knowl-edge about the actual author's life and career. Thus we can speak of the Dickens of *The Pickwick Papers* (1836–37), as contrasted with the Dickens of *Our Mutual Friend* (1864–65), or the Mark Twain of *Tom Sawyer* (1876) versus the Mark Twain of *Huckleberry Finn* (1885). This use of implied authors invokes contrasting characteristics, distinct temperaments, and narrative styles *implied* by the different books, without denying the histori-cal Charles Dickens or Samuel Clemens their roles as the *actual* or *real authors*. The use of pseudonyms in publishing distinguishes the actual author (Mary Ann Evans) from the implied author of her creation, projected by the text (George Eliot). Similarly, we can characterize the practices of the author of an anonymous narrative without knowing his or her historical identity. In these cases, the name given to the implied author ('the *Pearl* poet,' 'the *Gawain* poet,' 'the author of *Primary Colors* (1996)'), doubles as the name of the actual author until historical research or revelations in the news produce evidence of the real author's identity. The actions, intentions, aesthetic decisions, and motivations of the implied author, so often the subject of speculation in literary criticism, take present tense in formal writing. Thus the historical Dickens *lived*, *suffered* the indignity of the blacking factory, *wrote*, *made* loads of money, *left* his wife, *went* on reading tours, and *died* exhausted, whereas the implied author, 'the Dickens of *Bleak House* (1852–53),' perpetually *experiments* with a mixture of first and third person, *continues* to employ characters to do his bidding, and permanently *abides* in the realm of the present tense. It makes no difference whether an author is living or dead; the real author's actions belong to literary history, which takes the past tense, and the actions of the implied author belong with other projections or contents of the text, to which we conventionally refer in the present tense. Because literary critics and readers are free to attribute all sorts of motivations, qualifications, and aptitudes to the implied author of a text, it is axiomatic that implied authors are smarter and more capable than any ordinary flesh and blood human being who writes.[4]

In Chatman's scheme, the narrator, character(s), and narratee are textual creations. The narrator is the entity from whom the discourse comprising the story emanates. David Copperfield narrates the first-person novel of that name, while Dickens employs various unnamed narrators to do the telling in third-person novels. (Various kinds of narrator—first-person, third-person, internal, external, overt, covert, reliable, unreliable—are treated below.) The characters operate within the story world, where the narrator (and narratee) may also be located, especially when the story is self-narrated by a first-person narrator. See, for example, Edgar Allan Poe's 'A Tell-Tale Heart' (1843). However, the narrator and narratee often exist outside the story world. The communication of the narrator implies the existence of a narratee existing at the same narrative level. This is the entity to whom the narration is directed, overtly or covertly (implicitly). In some texts the narratee is given a name through direct address: 'O my Brothers' in Burgess's *A Clockwork Orange*; 'Reader' in Charlotte Brontë's *Jane Eyre* (1847); 'Sir' and 'Madam' in Laurence Sterne's *Tristram Shandy* (1759–67).[5]

Whether named or not, the narratee differs from the implied reader analogously to the way in which the narrator differs from the implied author. The implied reader is the name we give to the profile of readerly traits that seems to be assumed by the text. A novel may project an implied reader familiar with popular culture of the 1980s, as does Bobbie Ann Mason's *In Country* (1985), with its frequent quotations of contemporary music videos. It may demand a reader of a certain age or level of education. Like the implied author, the implied reader is a projection of the text, and differs in every instance from actual readers, many of whom will not exactly match the profile suggested by the text. Some novelists deliberately exploit the gap between narratee (seemingly in sympathy with the narrator) and implied reader (assumed to be skeptical and alert to signs of unreliability, for instance). Kazuo Ishiguro's *The Remains of the Day* (1989) makes good use of that ironic gap between narratee, apparently a fellow butler, and implied reader. Furthermore, all novelists whose work lasts beyond its initial publication will be read by actual readers differing markedly from the implied readers projected by their texts. Peter J. Rabinowitz augments this model with the notion of the authorial reader, an actual reader who actively attempts to enter the implied readership projected by the text and live up to the expectations projected by the text.[6]

Real readers are easy to define—the people who read narratives—and difficult to analyze. Literary theorists working in the fields of 'reception theory' (following Iser), reader response criticism (see Tompkins), and cognitive science (see Herman) have deepened our understanding of the practices of actual readers. In traditional literary criticism, we privilege those actual readers whose reactions to texts have been preserved in print (in book reviews or critical articles) or collected in archives of personal papers (in diaries or letters). This means that the readers who count often differ from the majority of readers in their social class or educational attainments. Some reader response criticism works to mitigate this phenomenon by setting up experimental situations in which the responses of ordinary readers are collected. Whatever its source, the published testimony about a text becomes part of its history, though this history may tell us more about the changing tastes of readers than about the text itself. Through sales figures, bestseller lists, bibliographic accounts of editions, citation indexes, college course syllabi, and through the comments of readers published on internet sites (as for instance in the reviews that Amazon.com collects), critics can trace the activities of real readers. But evidence from the marketplace should be treated carefully, for one can never know for sure if a person who purchases a text, for education or for pleasure, actually takes the step of becoming one of its real readers.

Narrators

The first distinction that the study of narrators demands is that of first-person from third-person narrators. New students who spot an 'I' here or there on the page may leap to the conclusion that the text must be a first-person narrative, but this isn't necessarily the case. As numerous commentators have pointed out, any overt narrator has the capacity to refer to himself or herself as 'I.' The use of the pronoun alone does not make a first-person narration. Instead, first-person narration, or self-narration, indicates those narratives in which the narrator is also a character, where the narrator and characters coexist in the story world, *and* the narrator refers to himself or herself as 'I.'

In one variety of first-person narrative, the experiencing self is also the protagonist, or the central character. Often called fictional autobiographies, these narratives do not differ formally from actual autobiographies of real people about their own lives, except in the fictitiousness and preconception of the events narrated. In both cases a narrating self presents the earlier life-events of an experiencing self. Examples range from Charlotte Brontë's *Jane Eyre* (1847) to Ernest Gaines's *The Autobiography of Miss Jane Pittman* (1971), a novel that fooled some of its early readers into thinking it was really the work of an elderly ex-slave woman. First-person fiction of this kind may be either consonant or dissonant, that is, it may present the experiences of the protagonist-self as reported by a narrating self positioned very close to the experiences (consonant narration), or it may emphasize the altered perceptions made possible by a gap in time between experiences and narration (dissonant narration). Dissonant narration lets the narrating self deliver judgments or make reflections that would be impossible or highly implausible for a narrator cleaving close to the experiences: see for example some of the adult language about a boy's experiences in James Joyce's 'Araby' (1914). This kind of first-person narration may then contain sharply differentiated voices of the 'same' figure, the experiencing self and the retrospective narrating self, structurally analogous to the reflecting character and the narrator in third-person fiction. At the start of Charles Dickens's *Great Expectations* (1861), Pip is presented in dissonant first-person narration. Throughout Don DeLillo's *White Noise* (1985), by way of contrast, Jack Gladney narrates his own experiences consonantly. In first-person versions of the novel of development, or *Bildungsroman*, the narrator may show a modulation from dissonant to consonant presentation of his or her experiences, which can suggest or underscore the character's growing maturity.[7] Alternatively, first-person fiction can be presented in sections with varying degrees of consonance or dissonance, depending on the fictional circumstances of the telling or composition, as in the separate depositions of Ned Kelly in Peter Carey's *The True History of the Kelly Gang* (2000).

As an alternative to first-person fiction in which the self is the central figure, some first-person narrators, while participating in the story, focus on the actions of others. The account this kind of narrator offers of the central characters is most often limited to what he or she could plausibly know, but there are exceptions, where a first-person narrator presents the thoughts and feelings of a character with whom he or she shares the story space. Though first-person narrators in general may reasonably be suspected of partiality if not of outright unreliability, many cases of unreliable narrators employ the narrative situation of a participating-self narrator who is not the central character. (Unreliable narrators are treated below.) Steven Millhauser's *Edwin Mullhouse: The Life and Death of an American Writer 1943–1954* (1972) presents a case in which the first-person narrator Jeffrey Cartwright acts as a highly unreliable Boswell to his childhood friend Edwin Mullhouse, the protagonist of Cartwright's fictional biography. Certainly not all first-person narrators who focus on other characters are suspect; Barry Unsworth's *Morality Play* (1995) employs reliable self-narration by one of a group of traveling players. Like self-narration in which the narrator is also the central character, this kind of first-person fiction can either be quite immediate in its reporting (consonant) or more retrospective (dissonant).

Plural first-person narration is uncommon but intriguing; William Faulkner's story 'A Rose for Emily' (1930) is considered a *tour de force* in its use of a communal, civic voice.[8] The better part of Joyce Carol Oates's novel *Broke Heart Blues* (1999) is narrated by communal voices variously comprised of the members of a high school class, sometimes speaking for the girls, sometimes for the boys, sometimes confined to an elite clique, and sometimes including the town's perspective. The use of the plural pronoun alone does not necessarily indicate a plural narrator, however. In Ayn Rand's novella *Anthem* (1938, 1946), the singular narrator Equality-7-2521 speaks of 'we,' but means 'I.' He has been indoctrinated to understand himself as a part of a group identity, and the novella reaches its climax when he discovers the forbidden concept of the individual and the sacred word 'Ego.' Perhaps because of cases like this, plural narrators can seem gimmicky; even more exceptional are the very rare cases of second-person narration, employing a singular or plural 'you.' I will return to these anomalous narrative situations after the next section, on the different varieties of third-person narration.

To say that a narrative employs third-person narration should immediately raise the questions 'What kind?' and 'How?' Further, a critical reader may inquire whether the narrator shares the space of the story world with the characters, or exists in a realm external to the events of the story. The capacities exercised by a narrator in either location ought also to be noticed: does the narrator provide an external view of events and characters, or does it give access to the thoughts and feelings of one or more characters? Does the narrator reveal himself or herself as an overt presence in the narrative, or does the narrator operate covertly, revealing no personality and avoiding direct address of the reader? The answers to these questions, when compiled, go a long way towards establishing the norms and potentialities of a work's narrative situation.

The most familiar distinction made by students of the novel or creative writing differentiates 'limited' from 'omniscient' third-person narrators. Third-person limited (or restricted) narration usually refers to situations where a single character's perspective governs the perceptions included in the telling of the story. The writer achieves this effect by limiting the representation of consciousness or perceptions to a single figure (not the narrator). This limitation of perspective does not prevent the writer from employing the narrator to perform mundane tasks, such as providing the tagging of spoken discourse ('he said') that exists outside the central character's perspective. Even in limited narration, in other words, the narrator and the reflecting or focalizing character remain distinct: Henry James's 1900 story 'The Tree of Knowledge' provides one of many examples of this technique in use. The center of consciousness (Henry James's term for what is now often called the reflector, the filter, or focalizer) provides the perspective, while the narrator employs the third person. Omniscient narration usually requires a narrator who exists outside the story world and freely informs the reader about any and all details about a host of characters; the standard accounts associate omniscient narration with nineteenth-century (English) novelists. The temptation with omniscient narrators is to equate them and their opinions with their creators, a move that is rarely justified and often misleading. (A better strategy is to establish the nature of the narrator and assert that the implied author projected by the text receives strong coloring from the personality of the narrator.) If omniscient narration is supposed to be a Victorian way of telling, twentieth-century novelists, according to the usual story, prefer limited narration. The fact that many counter-examples to both generalizations exist only emphasizes the fact that a narrow canon of works are often taken to be representative of whole centuries of literary production. Finally, the most cursory survey

of third-person narratives quickly reveals examples that fit neither description—'limited' and 'omniscient' are most useful in indicating two ends of a
spectrum of possibilities.

Franz Stanzel suggests the terms 'authorial' and 'figural' narration as
alternatives to omniscient and limited narration, respectively. Stanzel's
terms have the advantage of more neutral coloring: they suggest a narrator
who functions above and outside his creations, like an author, employing
an external perspective (authorial), or a narration focused on and reflecting
internally upon individual figures (figural). The traditional terms suggest a
narrator like a god (omniscient), and a narration stunted or blinded by its
'limits.'[9] In the *authorial narrative situation,* the narrator exists outside the
story world of the characters and possesses capacities consistent with an
external perspective—the narrator can offer panoramic descriptions and
observations about events occurring simultaneously in the story world. In
the *figural narrative situation,* the perspective of a reflecting character inside
the story world (Genette calls this function focalizing) overwrites the narrator, whose presence is downplayed. Stanzel summarizes his three categories
simply: 'What determines the nature of a particular narrative situation is,
above all, the first person as a character in the novel in the first-person narrative situation, external perspective in the authorial narrative situation,
and reflector-mode in the figural narrative situation' (*Theory*, 5). In Stanzel's
own examples George Eliot's *Middlemarch* (1871–72) employs an authorial
narrative situation, whereas James Joyce's *Portrait of an Artist as a Young
Man* exemplifies (until the very end), the figural narrative situation. The
fact that many readers regard Joyce's reflector, Stephen, as a thinly disguised version of Joyce's younger self, does not make the narrative situation 'authorial.' The internal perspective renders the technique 'figural.'

Authorial and figural narrative situations represent not absolute differences, but poles of a continuum (in Stanzel's original scheme the possibilities are represented as segments of a circle, shading into one another in
border regions). While a purely external narrator, like the narrator of Ivy
Compton Burnett's novels, who renders speeches and actions but keeps
thoughts and commentary to a minimum, may be easily identified as
authorial, an external narrator who takes the reader into just four perspectives, as Rohinton Mistry does in *A Fine Balance* (1995), can be seen as
authorial in some ways (the narrator provides an overarching external perspective conveying information outside the experience of the central
reflecting characters), or as figural within each section (the perspective of
Dina dominates some sections, Maneck other sections, Ishvar and Om still
other sections). Indeed, the central dilemma of the novel can be read in the

technique, as Mistry creates a fine balance between the perspectives of his characters as they break down the social barriers that would ordinarily prevent intimacy. Thus the decision to call a narrator authorial or figural can itself pose interpretive challenges.

Narratologists have developed an elaborate taxonomy of narrative situation to describe those cases that lie somewhere between 'figural' and 'authorial' narrative situations, but they have done so using vocabulary that confuses or puts off many readers of criticism (instead of 'authorial,' Genette uses the term 'extraheterodiegetic' narrator). If one is willing to describe a narrator using more terms rather than fewer, one can achieve much of the specificity afforded by narratology's taxonomies without sacrificing clarity. Having established the narration in terms of person (first- or third-person, figural or authorial, internal or external), the critic can then add several other observations to the description of narrative situation.

One of the most useful distinctions concerns the degree of personification of the narrator. Is the narrator overt or covert? An *overt narrator* announces his or her presence through self-reference; a *covert narrator* is the scarcely noticeable functionary who provides speech tags and indications of setting and temporal movements, identifies characters, and narrates actions, all untinged with personality. The first sort of narrator is extremely common in a figural narrative situation, where the personality of the reflecting character dominates the reader's impression of the narration. Covert narrators can be used in an authorial narrative situation, but even where few clues about the qualities of an external narrator exist, readers tend to fill in or assume they know features such as gender, age, and attitude. Overt narrators may or may not identify their age and gender, but they leave sufficient evidence of their existence in the text to create a sense of a distinct personality. Overt narrators can make summaries of time passing or provide bird's-eye views. They can identify characters with capsule descriptions of their traits, pasts, appearance, and what they think, as well as what they do not think or say. Overt narrators can offer commentary, including interpretation of the action, judgments about characters or events, generalizations, and even self-conscious remarks about the narration. A named narrator is by personification rendered overt.

Overt narrators are common in authorial narrative situations and automatic in first person. While few sophisticated readers would mistake a first-person narrator for the author (Molly Bloom is obviously not Joyce), overt authorial narrators (such as Trollope's narrators) are often mistaken for the author. (See the discussion above on implied and real authors for a set of terms that helps distinguish narrator, implied author, and real writer.) Finally, the overtness or covertness of a narrator can change during the course of a narrative, as an overt narrator fades from view or a covert one suddenly demands attention. Just because covertness seems to rule the opening 50 pages of a narrative does not guarantee that it will be sustained throughout the whole narrative. Henry James objected strenuously to the chatty breaking in upon his narration that exemplifies Trollope's overt narrator. Tastes change, however, and in recent fiction breaks with the apparent norms of a narrative situation, including a sudden burst of overtness from a previously covert narrator (as in the end of Iris Murdoch's *The Philosopher's Pupil* (1983)) have become more common, and not only in experimental or postmodern fiction. Noticing where and speculating why moments of overtness occur in an otherwise covert narration, or observing the retreat from overtness that can occur over the course of a novel, can provide opportunities for interpretation.

The degree of overtness of a narrator may have an impact on other aspects of narrative situation. Fully personified narrators may narrate either externally or internally. They may exist outside the story world or may coexist with the characters inside the story world. A personified, overt narrator who exists inside the story world with the characters about whom he or she narrates is perhaps the most logical bearer of the term 'limited,' since the circumstances of the narration would usually imply that such a narrator could not exercise omniscience, having good excuses for not knowing everything, or even for withholding information. However, a narrator who appears at first to be external and omniscient may be revealed at the end to be a singularly well-informed cohabitant with the characters. In *The Philosopher's Pupil*, the narrator at first appears to be covert and external (authorial), but is revealed at the end to be overt (though usually reticent) and involved in the action with the characters of the story world. Evidently, 'N' has interviewed all the participants in order to gain the copious evidence of their thoughts, feelings, and motivations that would usually be plausible only as funneled through an external authorial narrator. Murdoch's 'N' acts authorial despite existing inside the story world. As 'N' comments coyly, 'I also had the assistance of a certain lady,' presumably the author (*Philosopher's Pupil*, 558).

Narrative situation can be further complicated when more than one narrator is used. Both horizontal and vertical extensions of the narrative, function can be made, and each extension should be described independently in order to accumulate an accurate description of the narrative situation and perspective. The reader asks 'Does the text use more than one narrator?' and 'Does the narrator combine with a single reflector or with more than one reflector?' In cases with plural narrators, these tellers may exist parallel to one another (though they may not show awareness of one another's existence), or they may be presented within the story world (inside another's narration). There are two possibilities when a character narrates: the straightforward use of the first-person narrative situation, or the secondary or tertiary nested narration that occurs when a character in someone else's narration (delivered either in the first or third person) becomes a teller in his or her own right. By far the most famous example of this kind of nested narrative situation comes from Joseph Conrad's *Heart of Darkness* (1902). Properly described, Marlow is a secondary narrator inside a frame narrative that itself possesses a narrator who becomes one of the group of narratees on the ship to whom Marlow tells his tale. Nested narrations (frame tales and so forth) are treated in more detail in Chapter 8. When responding to a narrative that has more than one narrative level or more than one narrator located in a parallel level, the critic will not be wasting time by characterizing the narrative situation of each narrative level or section. As will be seen below, interpretations of the reliability of the narration often hinge on accurate descriptions of narrative situation.

Wayne Booth's description of the *unreliable narrator* in his magisterial *The Rhetoric of Fiction* (1961, 1983) has proven one of the most enduring contributions to the permanent vocabulary for the discussion of narrative, but it is nonetheless frequently misunderstood. A common mistake is to describe the fallibility of a reflector character in a figural narrative situation as an 'unreliable narrator.' As I have suggested above, the reflecting character (focalizer) does not actually narrate; the character can possess an incomplete or misguided perspective, but he or she cannot narrate unreliably if he or she does not do the telling, just the perceiving. Another failure of critical tact can occur when *all* narrators become objects of suspicion, including the most neutral, covert, external narrators. To say that a narrator is unreliable is not a value judgment, and it differs radically from an accusation of lying. It suggests instead that a writer deliberately exploits readers' awareness that the version of the story retailed by the narrator should be treated with skepticism (this awareness on readers' part often grows stronger as they read more). Seymour Chatman explains Wayne Booth's idea in an admirably clear formulation: 'what makes a narrator unreliable is that his values diverge strikingly from that of the implied author's; that is, the rest of the narrative—"the norm of the work"— conflicts with the narrator's presentation, and we become suspicious of his sincerity or competence to tell the "true version"' (*Story and Discourse*, 149).

Identifying an unreliable narrator is always to some extent interpretive (for one must also establish the 'norms' associated with the implied author), but there are some handy ground rules.

First, a covert external authorial narrator is unlikely to be unreliable. As a narrator becomes more overt (see discussion above), the possibility of unreliability grows. A first-person narrator's implicit values are quite likely to diverge from those of the implied author, though certainly many first-person narrators, and especially dissonant (or retrospective) ones, strike readers as highly reliable. Who would doubt the veracity of what Jane Eyre imparts to her Reader? A third-person narrator who operates inside the story world with the characters about whom he or she narrates is usually more fully personified, and the more personified the narrator, the more opportunities for unreliability arise. Plausible reasons for a narrator's unreliability include the following: psychological states, such as grief or denial; incapacities, such as a low IQ or incomplete grasp of the language, senility, or extreme youth; simple obtuseness or limited information; dishonesty or some other kind of motivation to spin a story in a misleading way. When an unreliable narrator is at work in a story, the effect can be irritating, amusing, shocking, or provocative of sympathy for seemingly antipathetic characters. The umbrella term under which rhetoricians would place most of the consequences of unreliability is irony, and the differences between the views of the narrator and the views that readers impute to the implied author must be significant enough to generate tension. If the identification of an unreliable narrator makes no difference to the interpretation of the story (what would it mean to find Eliot's narrator in *Middlemarch* unreliable?), then the term should not be used. Finally, like other aspects of narrative situation, the narrator may progress from a condition of unreliability to something closer to reliability, as Stevens the butler does in Kazuo Ishiguro's *The Remains of the Day*, or a narrator could devolve into unreliability through the onset of madness or decay of faculties.

Determining whether a narrator should be described as unreliable often comes down to questions of motivation: What effect would the author produce by rendering the narrator unreliable? What would change interpretively if the narrator were discovered to be withholding information, misrepresenting events, or slanting the story in a way to make it suspect? Would it matter what the reasons for unreliability appeared to be? Ring Lardner's masterful story 'Haircut' (1925) employs a first-person narrator, a small-town barber named Whitey, who speaks to the stranger in his chair. Whitey tells a story about the killing of a town character, Jim, who appears to the reader a monstrous fellow, not just the practical joker Whitey describes. Furthermore, the reader comes to realize that the accidental shooting of Jim is almost certainly a murder orchestrated by the town doctor in a revenge plot. Whitey appears not to comprehend the import of the anecdotes he tells. Yet everything that the reader needs to understand the underlying story is narrated by Whitey. If Whitey is judged unreliable, he could be so due to limited mental and moral capacities—a narrator incapable of comprehending the wrongdoing he has witnessed or heard about. He could simply be a disorganized teller—Lardner, who began as a journalist, excels at capturing the voices of ordinary people, including their meandering speech. Alternatively, Whitey could be a sly and knowing narrator, conveying a sinister warning to the stranger in the barber's chair: if he knows what he is telling, is he then still unreliable? (Dorrit Cohn suggests that the term 'discordant' narrator makes a useful supplement to the terms 'reliable' and 'unreliable' for those cases where the narrator imparts information about events accurately, but displays attitudes that jar the reader and seem to clash with the views attributed to the implied author.[10])That there is no way finally to decide questions about narrative reliability through formal tests is part of what makes it such a perennial discussion topic in the literature classroom. Readers are bound to disagree, and from those disagreements come the contesting interpretations so prized by teachers of literature.

Perspective

Thus far my discussion of narrative situation has de-emphasized the role of characters in favor of narrators (characters receive full treatment in Chapter 4). To review, narrative situation encompasses narrative levels, the narrator, and the relationship of the narrator to the characters. When a character self-narrates, then character and narrator overlap, though a gap between the experiencing self and narrating self may be emphasized (see consonance and dissonance, above). Any character within a story may also be used as a secondary narrator for an embedded narration (see Chapter 8). The most central function of a character in narrative situations, however, lies in a character's role as a 'reflector' (Genette's 'focalizer,' Chatman's 'filter').[11] This terminology has been mentioned earlier as it pertains to authorial and figural narrators. Discussion of a narrative fiction's perspective adds the dimension of character-centered perception that is implied by the popular term 'point of view.' In addition to the colloquial slippage between 'point of view' and 'opinion,' the term has other limitations. At least metaphorically, it makes a priority of the character's eyes and gaze that may not adequately capture the matrix of thoughts, sensations, memories, preoccupations, and interests that comprise a 'reflecting' character's 'perspective,' though perspective (and focalization) both also suggest lines of sight.[12] I like 'reflector' because it conveys both a visual direction and a cognitive component. Thus it works for external narration, featuring the slant of a character or the internal report of a character's interior: both can fit one piece of the metaphor of reflection. Reflector can also be smoothly integrated into description of narrative situations employing fixed, multiple, or variable perspectives, and it can work in combination with a narrator's externalized reports of objects, actions, and persons which the reader is also expected to visualize. Fixed perspective sticks with a set reflector (usually a single figure, though sometimes a fused unit such as a husband and wife). Multiple perspectives can be employed either in formal alternation (with different sections employing different centers of consciousness) or within the same scene, when more than one character's reflections on the action are offered. The former strategy is more consistent with figural narrative situation, and the latter more common in authorial narration, where the external perspective of the narrator makes the presentation of multiple characters' thoughts more plausible. Variable perspectives can be especially interesting, as when Doris Lessing almost imperceptibly withdraws the male perspective from what begins as a plural reflector, 'David and Harriet,' in her novella *The Fifth Child* (1988). This manipulation of narrative situation enhances the effect of David's alienation and Harriet's isolation, even before Ben, their fifth child, enters the tale. The modes of representation of fictional consciousness that contribute so significantly to a reflecting character's function are treated in detail in Chapter 4.

Second-person narration

It would be easy to dismiss second-person narration as rarely used, gimmicky, or even just irritating. (Certainly most creative writers' how-to guides advise against using it.)[13] That would be to ignore two phenomena: a marked increase in the use of second-person narration in recent fiction, and a flurry of theoretical articles grappling with the challenge second-person narration poses to the traditional formal analysis of narrative situation in fiction. Narrative theory has a weakness for atypical narrative strategies and borderline cases, and it can emphasize the unusual at the expense of accuracy about the ordinary. I proceed, therefore, with the

caution that second-person narrative fiction is uncommon, and that a critical consensus has not yet emerged on how to describe it, or rather, how to
delimit it so as to distinguish it from other narrative situations that include
the second person, such as the 'you' addressee of epistolary fiction, remarks
addressed to a narratee, or extended apostrophes.

Second-person narration refers to a protagonist as 'you.' This conflates the
protagonist called 'you' with the narratee, or even with the real reader,
though the more specific information about the thoughts, actions, and speech
of the protagonist accumulates, the less likely these features are to be confused
with the reader's. Most commentators on second-person narration emphasize
the blurring of boundaries between protagonist and reader invited by the use
of 'you.' I doubt that real readers are ever confused, though they may be
entertained or enjoined to sympathize, by the technique. Readers of fiction
tend to understand that they are not the characters in the narratives they
read; if their reading is aggressively characterized by the text, they still possess
the power to dissent or to cease reading. As both James Phelan and Robyn
Warhol observe, the more fully characterized a narratee becomes in a fiction,
the greater the sense of dissonance felt by the reader (whereas the less fleshed-
out the narratee, the more willingly a reader may comply with the imputed
identification). The 'you' narration tends in the direction of this narratee-
related dissonance, unless the reader simply converts the 'you' mentally into
the third person 'he' or 'she', as can be done nearly automatically when
reading an extended 'you' narration.

Like other narrative situations, second-person narrative can be external or
internal, authorial or figural. It can range from extended interior monologue
of a first-person character addressing himself or herself as 'you,' as in the
second-person passages of Carlos Fuentes' *The Death of Artemio Cruz* (1962,
trans. 1964), to an authorial narrator's telling of a story, where the degree of
omniscience apparently extends to include the reader's mind, as well. Second-
person narration can function as a device inviting identification with a main
character labeled and addressed as 'you,' as in Jay McInerney's *Bright Lights,
Big City* (1984): 'Already you feel a sense of nostalgia as you walk down the
narrow halls past all the closed doors. You remember how you felt when you
passed this way for your first interview, how the bland seediness of the
hallway only increased your apprehension of grandeur' (34). In that case the
second-person narration persists through the whole novel. It can also be used
intermittently, in combination with other narrative situations, in either the
first or third person, as a way of marking a particular character as especially
different. For instance, in Stella Gibbons's *Cold Comfort Farm* (1932), the dom-
ineering grandmother Aunt Ada Doom recalls:

When you were very small—so small that the lightest puff of breeze blew your little crinoline shift over your head—you had seen something nasty in the woodshed.

You'd never forgotten it.

...

That was why you stayed in this room. You had been here for twenty years, ever since Judith had married and her husband had come to live at the farm. (113)

This early extract remind us that second-person narration, though uncommon, is not simply the product of postmodern experimentation.[14] Secondly, it suggests that second person can be used with past tense narration, though it is certainly the case that it is often combined with present tense in imitation of what is sometimes called 'guidebook imperative': 'Put on some jazz. Take off your clothes. Carefully. It is a craft' (Lorrie Moore, 'How,' 56). You narration can also verge into a projected future or subjunctive narration,[15] as in the same story by Lorrie Moore: 'You will fantasize about a funeral. At that you could cry. It would be a study in post-romantic excess, something vaguely Wagnerian. You would be comforted by his lugubrious sisters and his dental hygienist mom' (61). In some uses of the imperative second person, as in Lorrie Moore's 'The Kid's Guide to Divorce,' the impression of an implicit first-person narrator speaking to herself becomes so strong that questions of the (self)-narrator's reliability arise. As David Herman points out, the location of the addressee can be horizontal, within the fictional world, or it can reach beyond the story worlds toward the reader.[16] Some readers find second-person narration annoying, but that may not be the desired effect. The novelist Helen Dunmore told me that she chose to use second-person narration in her book *With Your Crooked Heart* (1999) to enhance the intimacy of the reading experience. That novel is in fact a multi-personed narrative, with sections in first, third, and second person alternating somewhat erratically throughout the novel.

Acknowledging the many multi-personed narrative fictions makes a good place for this chapter to come to an end of its descriptive task. As soon as students of narrative form become comfortable in recognizing the different kinds of narrative situation, they will realize that many novels and stories combine narrative situations in patterns, in deliberate illogic, or in ambiguous ways. Indeed, the many-voiced quality of novelistic discourse, containing as it does the contesting voices, styles, speech, and thoughts of a variety of characters from different social realms, has sometimes been considered a defining feature of the novel. For Mikhail Bakhtin 'polyphony' emphasizes the variety of different positions available for the author within a text; the analysis of polyphonic effects can be accomplished handily with the vocabulary for narrative situation introduced in this chapter, especially if the critic grants multiple perspectives validity and resists the urge to ascribe an overarching point of view to 'the author.' The author's voice, according to Bakhtin, is mediated by the multiple alternative voices of characters within the text. These voices are themselves positioned in dialogic relation to one another, with a resultant emphasis on process, diversity of voices, and social types implied by these voices (*heteroglossia*). The description of the novel as a dialogic form means not only that narrative fiction embeds dialogues among characters, but also that it is constituted out of diverse voices, languages, and social speech types. For Bakhtin, the representation of interaction among voices and the personalities or social beings implied by them is a core feature of novelistic discourse, though he traces its prehistory in earlier, non-novelistic genres. Bakhtin especially admires Dostoevsky's achievements in this form of the novel, but other critics following Bakhtin have observed polyphony or dialogic form at work in modernist fiction, in the mainstream realist tradition, in Victorian multi-plot novels, and in postmodernist and feminist texts.

No matter how firmly creative writing handbooks enjoin aspiring writers to stick to the contract they establish with their readers, and avoid shifts in narrative situation, in published writing, narrative situation is as often as not manipulated and altered during the course of the story's unfolding. As Brian Richardson remarks, 'contemporary fiction is replete with a polyphony of competing narrative voices; even where the narrator's speaking situation seems fixed, the proliferation of alternative voices threatens to destabilize that situation.'[17] These circumstances make the description of narrative in its component parts all the more rewarding, for when changes in technique can be detected and identified, then rich interpretations can be generated.

Analytical techniques

If the habitual use of early twentieth-century formalism is to demonstrate how particular literary works are unified, narratology, by way of contrast, aims to identify and name the components of narrative, suggest grammars of narrative function, or explain the nature of narrativity in narrative texts taken as a group (see Chapter 1 for a fuller account). Only a minority of advanced students will wish to pursue the calling of post-classical narratology. For the many more who would like to employ the analysis of narrative situation in their interpretations of narrative fiction, following a simple set of precepts may lead the way to the integration of narrative form and the thematic, contextual, or theoretically driven insights of compatible approaches, such as gender studies, cultural studies, or post-colonial theory and criticism.

The precepts are as follows:

- Establish and name the techniques employed (ask 'Who's who and what's its function?').
- Ask 'Why?' or 'To what end?' of each narrative situation.
- Discover any marked changes in technique within the text.
- Ask 'Why?' or 'To what end?' of each change in narrative situation.

Among the many different elements of narrative situation discussed in the preceding pages, several have proven of perennial interest to literary critics. Many contemporary narratives combine sections with contrasting narrative situations, as in Ali Smith's *Hotel World*, where the sections employ different persons and tenses. Counterfactual questions can be particularly useful: Ask, 'What difference would it make if the text were consistent with the technique of its first section?' Ask, 'Does the change from one set of norms to a different one undermine or support prior understandings of the text?'

When texts employing figural narrative shift the reflecting function from one character to another, or when authorial texts provide information about the minds of one set of characters while systematically excluding others, these choices and any alterations to the apparent norms of narrative situation can be interpreted by the student alert to formal cues.

Many first-person narrators and some overt narrators in third-person narration provoke discussion of reliability. (This should be strictly distinguished from the potentially partial views and opinions of the reflector in a third-person figural narrative.) If a narrator seems to be unreliable, and a gap between the values of the implied author and the narrator emerges, not only the evidence of reliability but also the ostensible underlying causes or motives can be interpreted. Differentiating discordance in values or perspectives from out-and-out unreliability in narrating what happens in a text can also be a useful exercise. Sensitivity to the historical context of the work's first appearance (perhaps the text was published in a time when very different ideas or feelings prevailed) and attention to the motives that attend our own reading can lend nuance to discussions of narrative reliability. Care should be taken not to overuse imputations of unreliability. No one wants to return to the days when any view clashing with the reader's own values could be explained away as 'irony' on the part of the author.

Though reader response criticism and reception theory are now over three decades old, lots of fruitful work remains to be done with narrators, narratees, implied readers, and real readers. In addition to the research that could be conducted into the reactions and behavior of real readers, implied readers can be characterized and historicized. Feminism and gender studies approaches to narrative can be usefully combined with an interest in implied and real readers, narrators, narratees, and narrative situation generally. Examining actual readers' assumptions about the gendering of narrators or implied readers or narratees can produce fresh interpretations, and opens the way for the richer reading of texts such as Jeanette Winterson's *Written on the Body* (1992) which features a conspicuously ungendered narrator. Attention to implied readers also opens up rewarding avenues for the discussion of narratives in its various genres.

Keywords

Author: author-function, death of the author, authority.   Narrative theory distinguishes the real author from an implied author, but this isn't the end of the possibilities. Wayne Booth's second edition of *The Rhetoric of Fiction* contains an afterword in which he develops with considerable nuance not just two but five potential meanings of the word 'author' with each type's qualities and functions, as well as consequences for the reader (428–31). Discussing authors, implied or real, can suggest an uncritical acceptance of intentions and meaning. Structuralist and some post-structuralist criticism de-emphasizes or even rejects the perspective of the author in favor of the text, textual relations, and what Julia Kristeva named intertextuality. According to these theoretical perspectives, the author should serve as neither a source nor a measure of a text's meaning. Authority can appear tyrannical at worst, limiting at best. If words have unstable meanings and texts are best understood as parts of larger intertextual networks, avoidance of authors and authority can help a reader subversively resist the imposition of constraining meanings and final answers. The central assumptions in cultural studies about the author derive from these ideas, as elaborated by Roland Barthes and Michel Foucault, among others. (Barthes's career encompassed structuralist and post-structuralist phases, and while Foucault is usually read as a post-structuralist thinker today, his early work was influenced by structuralism. From that early phase comes his work on the author-function. Two key texts for the questioning of authors and authority are Foucault's essay 'What is an Author?' and Barthes's essay 'The Death of the Author.'[18])

In narrative theory, authority usually designates the degree of knowledge or the extent of the powers of a narrator in an authorial narrative situation. While feminist criticism has often pointed out the ways in which authority is constituted in sanctioned rhetorical arrangements that support the dominant patriarchal social order, it has also shown how authority and author-functions can be appropriated to empower women or other marginalized groups.

Discourse. Two influential post-structuralist uses of the term 'discourse,' by Mikhail Bakhtin and Michel Foucault, differ significantly from its sense in narrative theory, where it means the words of the narrative as they actually appear rather than the content of the story. Paul A. Bové points out in his essay for Lentricchia and McLaughlin's *Critical Terms for Literary Study* that the New Critics used 'discourse' to mark generic differences and to establish a hierarchy in uses of language, with 'poetic discourse' elevated over the 'discourse of the novel,'[19] but few confusions are likely to arise from this quarter.

The use to which the Russian critic Mikhail Bakhtin puts 'discourse' (a translation of the Russian word *slovo*) links words, speech, and the way that languages as social or generic indicators interact in the novel. For Bakhtin, novelistic discourse refers to a diverse system of languages that 'mutually and ideologically interanimate each other' ('Prehistory,' 47). Both the medium and object of representation, 'double-voiced' novelistic discourse includes indirect discourse, in the sense that narrative theorists name it. Bakhtin's use of discourse is more inclusive than the indirectly represented thoughts and speech of characters, however, emphasizing as it does the dialogue amongst competing languages, including literary language and extra-literary languages, that he places so centrally in his account of the novel.[20]

Michel Foucault in *The Archaeology of Knowledge* (1972) recasts discourse to mean the bodies of statements, not only collections of text, that comprise the disciplines (such as medicine, political economy, heredity). Foucault recommends both a critical approach to discourses, emphasizing their validating functions, ordering principles, and exclusionary practices, and a genealogical approach, examining and affirming the power of discourses to constitute domains of objects. In both cases the emphasis is on the political function of language; the analysis of discourse aims, in the words of Bové, 'to describe the surface linkages' among 'power, knowledge, institutions, intellectuals, the control of populations, and the modern state as these intersect in the functions of systems of thought' ('Discourse,' 54–5). Using the word 'discourse' in the Foucaultian sense implies (to some degree) the writer's assent to a number of other post-structuralist skeptical doxa concerning human identity, subjectivity, sexuality, truth, authority, origins, history, and causation.

For full discussions of discourse in the narrative theoretical sense, refer to Chapters 7 and 8.

Voice.   Gérard Genette's influential use of the term 'voice' to designate the combination of effects that contribute to narrative situation can be the source of confusion to other literary critics, poets, theorists of the romantic lyric, and feminist and multicultural critics, for whom 'voice' is a contested term. The idea that the voice of a text or an author might authentically represent experience receives full elaboration in the works of Romantic poets and in many contemporary writers, especially poets, who strive to 'find their voices' in confident expression and effective performance. However, both structuralist and post-structuralist critiques of authority insist that language cannot neutrally express anything; instead language constitutes the subject. Bakhtin's multiple competing discourses (as in polyphony or heteroglossia) are sometimes translated as the different 'voices' of a narrative text, in the sense that voice embodies ideologies and expresses responses to particular historical conditions. Many feminist and multicultural critics place a priority on recovering and hearing the voices of those who may have been silenced or ignored in the past. Another kind of feminist reading emphasizes hearing the double-voiced qualities of narration that simultaneously tells and implies different messages to different narratees (see Lanser, 'Toward a Feminist Narratology'). The advanced student of narrative form may want to avoid association with any of these positions when describing a narrative text's participants and the relations among them. The simplest way would be to employ the terms 'narrative situation,' adding if necessary a parenthetical reference to 'what Genette calls "voice".'

Further reading

Bakhtin, Mikhail, 'Discourse in the Novel,' *The Dialogic Imagination*, ed. and trans. Caryl Emerson and Michael Holquist (University of Texas Press, 1981), 259–422. See this essay for dialogic form and heteroglossia.
— *Problems of Doestoevsky's Poetics*, trans. Caryl Emerson (University of Minnesota Press, 1984). See this book for polyphony and dialogism.
Benjamin, Walter, 'The Storyteller,' in *Illuminations: Essays and Reflections* (1955, trans. 1968), ed. Hannah Arendt, trans. Harry Zohn (Schocken Books, 1969), 83–109.
Booth, Wayne C., *The Rhetoric of Fiction*, 2nd ed. (University of Chicago Press, 1983). See Booth for discussions of implied author and reliable/unreliable narrators.
Chatman, Seymour, *Story and Discourse: Narrative Structure in Fiction and Film* (Cornell University Press, 1978). A comprehensive and readable handbook on narrative theory. Caution: many theorists find Chatman's idea of a 'nonnarrated' prose narrative unconvincing, and prefer the alternative he proffers, of 'minimally narrated' texts.
Cohn, Dorrit, 'Discordant Narration,' *Style* 34:2 (2000), 307–16.
— 'The Encirclement of Narrative: On Franz Stanzel's *Theorie des Erzählens*,' *Poetics Today* 2:2 (1981), 157–82.
— *Transparent Minds: Narrative Modes for Presenting Consciousness in Fiction* (Princeton University Press, 1978). On consonance and dissonance in first-person narration, see especially 145–72.
Genette, Gérard, *Narrative Discourse: An Essay in Method*, trans. Jane E. Lewin (Cornell University Press, 1980), 212–62. Genette's chapter on 'Voice' is the classic narratological treatment of narrative situation. Genette makes the case that his precise terminology of extra- or intra-, heterodiegetic or homodiegetic narration should replace the looser terms 'first' and 'third person.' He views all narration as at least potentially in first person, since any narrator could refer to himself or herself as 'I,' though many do not.
Herman, David, *Story Logic: Problems and Possibilities of Narrative* (University of Nebraska Press, 2002). An exemplary reconsideration of central precepts of narrative theory in light of cognitive science.
Iser, Wolfgang, *The Act of Reading: A Theory of Aesthetic Response* (Johns Hopkins University Press, 1978).
— *The Implied Reader: Patterns of Communication in Prose Fiction from Bunyan to Beckett* (Johns Hopkins University Press, 1974).
Lanser, Susan Snaider, *The Narrative Act: Point of View in Prose Fiction* (Princeton University Press, 1981). Lanser argues that in addition to authorial and 'personal' narration, a 'communal' narrative situation representing collective voices should be recognized. Her treatment of the philosophy of point of view is also very useful.
— 'Toward a Feminist Narratology' (1986), in Robyn R. Warhol and Diane Price Herndl (ed.), *Feminisms*, rev. ed. (Rutgers University Press, 1997), 674–93. Here Lanser demonstrates the need for a comprehensive theory of voice, including tone and rhetorical contexts as determinants of meaning.
Prince, Gerald, 'Introduction to the Study of the Narratee,' in Jane Tompkins (ed.), *Reader-Response Criticism* (Johns Hopkins University Press, 1980), 7–25.

Rabinowitz, Peter J., *Before Reading: Narrative Conventions and the Politics of Interpretation* (Cornell University Press, 1987). Rabinowitz's work advances a nuanced view of the different kinds of narrative audiences, beyond the implied reader of Booth and Chatman.

Stanzel, F. K., *A Theory of Narrative* (1979), trans. Charlotte Goedsche (Cambridge University Press, 1984). My source for authorial and figural narrative situation.

Tompkins, Jane, *Reader-Response Criticism* (Johns Hopkins University Press, 1980). A now classic collection of essays.

4
People on Paper: Character, Characterization, and Represented Minds

'What is character but the determination of incident? What is incident but the illustration of character?' asked Henry James in his 1884 essay 'The Art of Fiction.' More than a century later, we can still ask the same questions when we begin thinking about the nature of fictional character in narratives. Separating plot from the characters who experience events, cause them through their actions, meditate on them, or react in one way or another, wrenches apart the two elements of fictional narrative that are most securely bound to one another. How indeed can we think about characters without discussing their actions? (We can't!) How can we judge a set of actions in a plot without referring to the agents we come to know through those actions? (We shouldn't!) This discussion thus begins with an acknowledgement that it artificially separates characters from the plot that couldn't function without them. The benefit of temporarily isolating characters from their story-matrix lies in the observations that can be made about how writers build out of descriptive, illustrative, and demonstrative passages their invitations to imagine the people who populate story worlds.

Some narratives emphasize character and some emphasize plot. No narrative can do without either element, though writers and critics have disagreed over which element should be given the higher priority. Furthermore, character and plot resemble one another functionally in that the reader's knowledge of both shifts and changes during the reading experience. During a first reading, details of both plot and characters are received through the narration; these details can provoke the questions that drive the desire to continue reading. After a first reading of a narrative has been completed, a reader can then reflect critically on the 'full story' and the 'fully revealed characters.' Both a concluded plot and a character about whom no more words exist paradoxically persist in the imagination in a way which allows rethinking, questioning, and speculation. The notorious question 'How many children had Lady Macbeth?'[1] represents for several generation of critics an extreme case of the kind of question that should not be asked of a fictional character—an entity made out of a finite number of words. Yet readers who have surrendered themselves to a fictional world will almost certainly lend extra characteristics (from their experience of people or of other fictional characters) to the characters they have read. Further, many narratives demand that the reader work to figure out what has happened to a character during a gap, a skip in the discourse in which plot events are implied, though not narrated.

Acknowledging that readers of narrative routinely add and fill in as they reconstruct people on paper into inhabitants of fictional worlds raises challenging questions for formal analysis. How much of character can (or should be) attributed to formal devices? How broad a range of responses to character can be addressed within a formal analysis? Can counterfactual speculations about what characters might have done or said in extra-textual situations *ever* contribute to a formal discussion of character? Generations of New Critical, structuralist, and some post-structuralist critics would have answered 'no,' but reader response critics, genre critics, some feminists, and many practitioners of cultural studies have good reasons to move beyond the strict conception of character as purely textual. Making room for reading against the grain, historically contextualized reading, and reading that acknowledges the openendedness of interpretation requires a more flexible interpretation of character, including characters as entities which readers understand as related to people, or what Baruch Hochman calls 'substantial hypothetical beings' (*Character in Literature*, 26).

This approach to an imaginatively fleshed out fictional world and its inhabitants leads to a different kind of insight than the equally useful attention to the small textual building blocks that are put in place, in a fixed order, by the writer who creates both character and plot out of words. The questions that students of narrative ask about character thus range widely. They may address the fictive personality of the character: Why is Mr Woodhouse, Emma's father, so stingy? They may react to generic expectations: Does Thomas Hardy succeed in making Henchard a tragic hero? They may focus on external details: How does Dorothea Brooke's clothing reveal her attitudes and ideals? They may draw attention to representations of characters' embodiment: How do these details shape the characters' thoughts and actions and plot trajectories? They may emphasize conflicting responses: Why do contemporary readers find Little Nell sappy and implausible when Victorians found her believable and moving? They may focus on matters of narrative technique: Why (in *July's People* (1981)) does Nadine Gordimer allow the reader to have access to the adult characters' minds, but not to the children's minds? They may establish criteria for success or failure on the part of a writer: Does the author invoke sympathy for the characters or do they 'fail to come to life' for the reader? Indeed, the response to character is so profound a part of the reading and viewing experience that some students will be content to organize most of their critical observations about a narrative around questions about its creation and use of characters.

Terms

Characters, those anthropomorphic entities who carry out the plot actions of narratives, strongly resemble real people (or plausible people in fantastic situations). Certainly many narratives, from children's stories to beast fables to novels like Richard Adams's *Watership Down* (1972), employ animals as characters. All of these animals open up to interpretation as human-like as soon as thoughts, feelings, or motivations are attributed to them. Some of the stories in Italo Calvino's *Cosmicomics* (1968) stretch the point by giving an element an unpronounceable name and putting it in situations that no human being could experience. This strategy points up the fact that science has its narratives, too, whose actors and agents are then forces, elements, or entities that can be named only by formulae. As soon as one of those entities has a feeling, such as longing, or a thought that implies consciousness, it becomes human-like. As theologians can attest, the avoidance of anthropomorphizing language is a demanding task. Fiction writers ordinarily accept characters' quality of seeming like human beings, even though they know as well as anybody that characters are inventions constructed out of words.

Normally, readers create fictional characters in their minds by assembling the textual details relayed by the narrator into patterns that seem like people. Thus, fictional characters (and not only those in realistic texts) invite comparison with the real people of a reader's experience. When a reader judges a character 'believable,' he or she tacitly calls up his or her knowledge of real people (or, to complicate matters, of other fictional characters in similar fictions). The following discussion of character follows a line of thought in narrative theory that urges critical readers to recognize and respect the profound difference between real people and fictional characters, even when the narratives that contain them work hard to make the reader erase that difference. Nonetheless, I acknowledge the truth of the observation that as embodied readers, we bring a level of expectation that characters and stories will correlate in some degree to our embodied experience. Indeed, readers may create versions of embodied characters out of very few cues, as we project fictional worlds around characters out of sometimes quite minimal data.

Artists themselves complicate the reader's understanding of characters as different from people. The standard legal statement that often appears with the publisher's information claims that any resemblance to persons living or dead is entirely coincidental. Not coincidentally, this assertion often appears in the front matter of novels filled with characters 'drawn from life.' For instance, Emma McLaughlin and Nicola Kraus's *The Nanny Diaries* (2002) asserts that though the authors have worked as nannies for over 30 New York City families, 'none of these families is portrayed in this book. Names and characters are the product of the authors' imagination. Any resemblance to actual events or persons, living or dead, is purely coincidental' ('A Note to Readers'). Yet at the same time the novel suggests that it is dishing the dirt on a very real scene, providing an inside view of an otherwise closed world. In a delicate balancing act, novels and films marked with legal denials of responsibility for semblance can manage to convey elliptically that apparently fictional characters are 'based on' real people.[2]

A common alternative to direct portraiture of the living can be achieved through the combination of traits from a variety of sources. A writer who acknowledges taking a way of speaking from one living person, combining it with a manner of dressing from another, or with a profession entirely made up, has employed tools of the craft to make a plausible and believable character, not a real person. The goal of such a technique may be to create a character that seems like a real person, but it may also be to use the fresh combination of traits to create the sorts of implicit problems out of which interesting plot lines develop. Character building can be one of the 'what if' strategies used by writers to create narratives. Many writers report that in the process of creation, characters seem to take on lives of their own, and some writers speak of their characters as if they were friends or relations (Iris Murdoch indulged in this sort of imagining). Most often, writers show that they understand very well the difference between the figures of their imagination and real people. Novelist Jill Paton Walsh's response to the question 'Do you put real people in your books?' is typical. She says, 'I hope the people in my books are real to you. They are real to me. Sometimes I seem to be able to hear them talking in my head. I don't make up what they say; I just listen and write it down. But they aren't portraits of people that I know in real life. You can't put actual people into books, because you don't know enough about them.'³

What seems at first glance like a paradoxical claim, 'you don't know enough' about real people to put them in books, addresses a fundamental difference between fictional characters, the creatures E. M. Forster named '*Homo Fictus*,' and actual living beings. Unlike *Homo Sapiens*, *Homo Fictus* possesses a mind and feelings that can be rendered accessible to readers of narrative fiction. While your friend can tell you what he is thinking, or you may guess what your mother feels from her expression, or you may read in a diary entry another's private thoughts, no living being experiences the sort of access to consciousness—including thoughts, emotions, memories, motives, and sub-verbal states—that modern and contemporary fictional narrators routinely render up to the reader about fictional characters. The explanation of the techniques that allow narrators to generalize about, report on, quote, or narrate characters' mind-stuff make a central part of this chapter. The representation of consciousness is one of the technical accomplishments that distinguishes modern narratives, especially novels, from ancient precursors such as the epic and the saga. That this technical development arises in tandem with modern notions of the individual as a discrete self who possesses rich interiority, an unconscious mind, memories, and partially recognized motivations does not mean that earlier fictional characters completely lack interiority. Certainly, the external actions and narrator's epithets for Odysseus suggest a complicated mixture of feeling, understanding, and planning, along with blindspots and failures to think ahead. It suggests instead that the novel provides an especially flexible means of representing an aspect of experience (living inside a mind in the company of others who themselves possess minds) that modernity foregrounds.

This chapter works from the inside out. Following the discussion of modes of representation of fictional consciousness, which applies to written narratives, the reader will find a discussion of other elements of characterization, most applying equally to film fiction and written texts. This in turn is followed by a treatment of some of the important ways that fictional characters have been categorized by critics: for example, as flat and round, by function, and as types.

Representing consciousness

In her book *Transparent Minds*, Dorrit Cohn names the three modes of representing consciousness in fictional characters. The discussion here summarizes her discussion of these modes in third-person narrative situations (both authorial and figural; see Chapter 3 for a full explanation of narrative situation). Cohn's book also describes with parallel terminology the versions of these techniques as employed in first-person narratives, but in the interest of brevity, I shall not discuss them in detail here.[4] The three modes of representation of consciousness—psycho-narration, narrated monologue (also called free indirect discourse), and quoted monologue (also called interior monologue)—often coexist in a single work or even in a single passage. Though the heavy reliance on one mode may be associated with a particular period or style of narrative (modernist fiction with quoted monologue, for instance), combinations are common. Before discovering the modulations often found in representations of characters' mind-stuff, the student must first confidently identify the three modes.

Psycho-narration consists of the narrator's discourse about a character's consciousness. Often employed in an authorial narrative situation, psycho-narration allows the narrator to generalize about what a character has thought about for a long time, as well as reporting in the narrator's language on the gist of characters' thoughts and feelings. ('Mary, a working mother, hated Neal because he had tried to shut down the day-care center.') Psycho-narration can be used effectively to convey what a character has *not* thought or felt ('She forgot to call the allergist for the third day in a row.'). Psycho-narration preserves the tense and person of the narration, smoothly following the narrator's reports on external features, quoted speech, and characters' actions without any shift in the norms of the narration. All of the features of psycho-narration thus described can be observed in narratives with overt external narrators, and eighteenth- and nineteenth-century English novelists use psycho-narration generously. Psycho-narration can be spread around, when the narrator explains what a host of characters think or feel, but it can also be useful in figural narrative situations, for it can be used to report on sub-verbal states and dreams of a central consciousness (reflector). Thus, despite its association with the god-like omniscient narrator of the mainstream realist tradition, psycho-narration is by no means absent from modernist, postmodernist, and other contemporary narratives. Though she is well known for her use of quoted monologue, for instance, Virginia Woolf also employs psycho-narration for conveying her central characters' states of mind through analogies, metaphors, and images.

Narrated monologue, also known as free indirect discourse when it omits tagging (with words such as 'she thought'),[5] is considered one of the most significant innovations in technique in the nineteenth-century novel, though some critics have spotted it in earlier texts.[6] Narrated monologue presents the character's mental discourse in the guise of the narrator's discourse. Most theorists thus consider it a double-voiced kind of discourse.[7] In other words, reading narrated monologue gives the impression of the words and modes of expression of the character, while retaining the tense and person of the narrator's language. While a narrator employing psycho-narration might report of a character, 'She thought about calling the allergist,' in narrated monologue the same character's thought patterns might appear: 'She really ought to call the allergist to see about a better sun screen for Jake. His rash was bad, worse than yesterday, and it wasn't the chlorine, because they'd been at the lake.' As this invented example shows, the thoughts of the character are told in language that retains the third-person reference and the basic tense of the narration (in this case, as in by far the bulk of narrative fiction, the past tense). Yet the feel of the character's inner speech to herself comes through. Because narrated monologue retains the tense (usually past) and person (third) of the narration, it can be smoothly combined with psycho-narration, sometimes even in the same sentence about a character's thoughts. The sentence of psycho-narration, 'Dread of the child's illness filled her like a dark sludge,' could be combined with narrated monologue without alteration of tense or person: 'She really ought to call the allergist to see about a better sun screen for Jake. His rash was bad, worse than yesterday, and it wasn't the chlorine, because they'd been at the lake. Dread of the child's illness filled her like a dark sludge.' Neither psycho-narration nor thoughts rendered in narrated monologue could plausibly be spoken aloud by the character without significant revisions into present tense and first-person discourse (the standard modes for speech and dialogue). In that significant subset of contemporary narrative that employs present tense throughout, narrated monologue can still be spotted by its preservation of the third-person reference to characters.

Quoted monologue, by way of contrast to the other two modes, presents the character's mental discourse (with or without quotation marks and tagging) by shifting from the past tense of narration to present tense and from the third person of narration to the first person of thoughts. (In the case of present tense narrations, it still shifts, from third- to first- person narration.) These thoughts, though unspoken, are written in such a way that they could plausibly be spoken aloud without violating the reader's sense of grammatical speech. Thus, the narrated monologue presented above could be converted into quoted monologue: 'I've got to call the allergist to see about a better sunscreen for Jake. His rash is bad, worse than yesterday, and it isn't the chlorine. We were at the lake.' Note that the past tense that remains is the kind of past tense that can be used in speech about something that has happened in the *characters'* past. The entire thought could be plausibly spoken aloud without alteration. By Cohn's nomenclature, this sort of thought is 'quoted,' not told, as in 'narrated monologue.'

Extended passages of quoted monologue are sometimes called interior monologue or stream of consciousness (see the discussion of 'stream of consciousness' in 'Keywords,' below). Strongly associated with modernist fictional techniques under the name of interior monologue, quoted monologue, with and without tags, appears in early prose fiction (such as the narratives of Aphra Behn). In addition, quoted monologue very often appears not in the long flowing passages associated with 'interior monologue,' but in short bursts of thought-stuff that dispenses with formal syntax entirely. Perhaps more mimetically, the quoted monologue for the concerned mother might be rendered 'Allergist. Rash worse. Not water ... sunscreen?' Admittedly, this passage of thoughts would sound very strange spoken aloud, and it is so fragmentary as to elide most signs of tense and person, but it comes closer to quoted monologue than to either of the other modes for representation of consciousness. In some passages of rendered thoughts, the writer leaves too little syntactical or grammatical evidence for the reader confidently to decide whether the character's thoughts are quoted or mediated through a narrator. In those cases a sense of the norms of the text (what modes of representing consciousness are most often used?) can inform a reader's interpretive decision.

The combinations and modulation of modes of representation of consciousness within passages containing characters' thought reward close attention. Because of the congruity of tense and person, psycho-narration and narrated monologue are often combined. For instance, Joyce uses narrated monologue in the concluding passage of his story 'The Dead' (1914): 'The time had come for him to set out on his journey westward. Yes, the newspapers were right: snow was general all over Ireland.' These are clearly Gabriel Conroy's thoughts, though they appear in the tense and person of the narration. Combined with the narrated monologue, however, Joyce describes Gabriel's inner state using psycho-narration: 'His soul swooned slowly as he heard the snow falling faintly through the universe ...'

Quoted monologue, though more formally distinctive, also appears in combination with the other two modes. While writing handbooks often advise the aspiring fiction writer to avoid combinations and to choose consistency (and often, to avoid psycho-narration altogether as too much narratorial 'telling'), twentieth-century fiction in a variety of genres demonstrates that combinations are common. For instance, the following passage from Virginia Woolf's story 'Mrs. Dalloway in Bond Street' (1923) contains all three modes, first quoted monologue, then alternating phrases of psycho-narration and narrated monologue, with a return to quoted monologue at the end:

> Poor little wretches, she sighed, and pressed forward. Oh, right under the horses' noses you little demon! and there she was left on the kerb stretching her hand out, while Jimmy Dawes grinned on the further side. ...
>
> Big Ben struck the tenth; struck the eleventh stroke. The leaden circles dissolved in the air. Pride held her erect, inheriting, handing on, acquainted with discipline and with suffering. How people suffered, how they suffered, she thought, thinking of Mrs. Foxcroft at the Embassy last night decked with jewels, eating her heart out, because that nice boy was dead, and now the old Manor House (Durtnell's van passed) must go to a cousin.

Few of the rules that fiction handbooks offer are consistently observed in the wide range of published narratives.

For instance, the use of a figural narrative situation with a single reflecting character would imply that the consciousness of that character alone would be represented. However, serial reflectors (yielding to one another the central perspective), or even briefly interrupting passages of thought attributed to a previously externalized character, are common in contemporary fiction. As the previous chapter suggests, writers sometimes construct novels with multiple narrative situations (alternating first- and third-person sections, for instance); similarly, multiple modes of representation of consciousness can be employed to dramatic effect. For those writers (by far the majority) who allow access into at least some of their characters' minds some of the time, the representation of consciousness is a powerful tool in creating believable 'substantial hypothetical beings.'

It should be stressed that there is nothing especially natural or inevitable about the privileging of consciousness as an aspect of characters. The treatment of character as possessing interiority is an historical phenomenon, and some commentators see the focus on represented consciousness in modern literature as a symptom of a crisis of privacy. For instance, Michael Goldman writes, 'it is no accident that the terrible puzzle over self and language, persons and texts, that constitutes the post-structuralist or postmodernist moment is coeval with what appear to be the final stages of this crisis of privacy. Our radical doubts about selfhood and identity seem the inevitable product of a long history of increasingly excruciating scrutiny of inward, private spaces' (*On Drama*, 74). Analysis of represented minds may thus seem to participate in a bankrupt project of shoring up the boundaries of a self that is a delusion or a projection of wish fulfillment. It may be used to deconstruct the very notion of separable consciousnesses and selves. It may demonstrate, through the polyphony it traces within the verbal representation of a single mind, how thoroughly permeated by external discourses human character appears. A private inner sense of person may be shown to be the constructed projection of a number of external networks of significance. Or, as is most often the case in narrative fiction, it may assert with technical ease the human-like qualities of consciousness that mark characters as 'real' and 'sympathetic' to the readers who could never, in real life, gain access to another's mind. In any case, the preoccupation of modern narrative with the representation of interiority demonstrably results in an array of techniques for capturing what and how characters think.

Characterization and kinds of character

Characterization can be achieved directly, through the statements of the narrator (or another character) about the character, or indirectly, as when the reader deduces from actions, speech, or context key traits of the character. Seymour Chatman writes well about the way in which readers recognize and label character traits out of a widely available popular psychological vocabulary. The language of protagonist and antagonist calls upon commonly held views of those personal roles in human relationships. Chatman suggests that the repetition of particular actions constitute the 'habits' belonging to characters, about which readers make the assumptions that can then be called traits (*Story and Discourse*, 122–38). A trait may be part of a label given to a character (as in the Homeric epithet), but more often it is an adjective applied to a character in response to 'habits.' Thus the villainous MoJo JoJo of cartoon *The Powerpuff Girls* is not called 'verbose,' but earns the label of that trait through repeated wordy speeches. Some critics would resist the assent to popular psychology that Chatman's ideas imply. 'Attributes' could be substituted for 'traits' in order to dehumanize the process of character building a bit. Roland Barthes goes further, writing of his code of connotation (SEM) that 'when identical semes traverse the same proper name several times and appear to settle upon it, a character is created' (*S/Z*, 67). While Chatman acknowledges the tendency of readers to draw on popular psychology in creating characters, Barthes emphasizes the coding of the discourse as it unfolds in a narrative. Both theorists suggest that it doesn't take much characterization of a figure to set character creation in motion. Thus close attention to the words about characters, or the words inviting characterization, can reveal how a writer goes about creating characters of different dimensions.

The choice to represent a character only inwardly, including thoughts, feelings, memories, but excluding external details, can contribute to a powerful use of the figural narrative situation or first-person narration. Though the most extreme externality may also be observed (rendering no thoughts or feelings), most fictional characters are rendered by a blend of information about their appearance, gender, age, social circumstances, and their states of mind. These external details of characterization can have a significant impact on the reader's person imagining. Perhaps the most significant feature marking most fictional characters is a name. Avoidance of naming can itself be a powerful effect, as in Daphne DuMaurier's hands. The narrator, the 'second Mrs. DeWinter,' never reveals her first name in the novel about her discoveries regarding the first Mrs DeWinter (*Rebecca* [1947]). This contributes to the reader's sense of the narrator's lack of self-esteem. Normally, the writer provides a name. Such a label possesses considerable meaning all by itself. Without knowing anything else about them, for instance, the reader intuits strong differences between two characters of Trollope, Eleanor Bold and Mr Slope. Names can be allegorical—'Faithful' in Bunyan's *Pilgrim's Progress* (1678), or ordinary—Elizabeth Bennett. Slightly allegorical or symbolic names survive outside allegorical narratives, as Brontë's Lucy Snowe and Joyce's Stephen Dedalus illustrate. Often names combine realistic and symbolic effects through generic resonances: Pamela Andrews of Samuel Richardson's epistolary novel *Pamela* (1740–41) has a solid ordinary English last name, but a first name straight out of the prose romance tradition, via Philip Sidney's *Arcadia* (1580). In realistic fiction with a sociological edge, names can reflect ethnicity or other aspects of identity (Jimmy Gatz/Jay Gatsby). Henry James uses near-miss names with a slant-rhymed relation to a character trait, and William Faulkner's Homer Barron falls ambiguously between his homonyms, Baron and barren. Naming itself may be the cue that stimulates the activity of imaginative character building in a reader's mind.

Beyond a name, some characters appear with a passage of detailed personal description, including gender, race, appearance, age, dress, social position, and past experiences (as in a reference to a character's recent divorce). This strategy of *block characterization* can be avoided by employing instead indirect or scattered brief references to a character's physical qualities and social identity. The most revealing things about characters, of course, are their actions, speeches and thoughts (if these are represented). These elements of characterization add up in the reader's mind, where the character as 'existent,' in Seymour Chatman's phrase, is created along with the other elements of a fictional world. Recently, Genie Babb has called for theories of character that respect the representation of embodiment, not only through description, but through reference to the lived experience of embodiment shared by readers. Attending to what Babb calls embodied subjectivity (or psychical corporeality) means tracking a character's sense impressions (of both external and internal stimuli), their movement through space, their awareness of visceral processes (such as digestion or blood circulation or breathing, their automatic, habitual practices, and the ways that all of these traits contribute to the trajectory of their actions and the content of their thoughts.[8]

Knowledge of *types* aids readers in the understanding of fictional characters. Having read or watched a villain at work in a thriller, for instance, a reader may test his perceptions of a wrongdoing character against that model. The process of recognizing and revising one's first assessment of a character's possible type can be a dynamic process, and different readers may bring different perspectives about how a character is typical. Conflicting traits can call up an alternative model: Raskolnikov invites more sympathy than the typical bad guy in a thriller, so perhaps he is a different type, the social outcast, or the fugitive from justice. Each character type can itself imply a host of other generic associations, including likely story lines. For instance, a buffoon who often stumbles in pratfalls is likely to experience humiliation (as the butt of others' jokes), but he is unlikely to be a murder victim. Readers and viewers of narrative possess a huge amount of passive knowledge of character types, drawn from experience and from fiction. This stock of knowledge has its earliest sources in tales told to children and in jokes. Writers and filmmakers rely upon readers' knowledge of character types for reasons of economy as well as to establish generic boundaries. Though a type may veer too close to an offensive stereotype for a reader's comfort, there is nothing intrinsically wrong with the invocation of a character type. Minor characters are often sketched in as types, and even quite complex major characters may begin as conventional types.

The common distinction between *flat* and *round* characters comes from E. M. Forster's *Aspects of the Novel*. Both kinds of characters may start as types, but the flat character usually does not transcend the typical. Flat characters do not change; they possess a fixed set of traits, often a catch phrase, and they are comfortingly predictable in their functions. While it can be a damning criticism to judge a central character in a narrative 'flat,' in fact flatness is a desirable trait in a minor (foil) character. Forster did not mean for his paradigm to be applied pejoratively; if all characters were 'round,' narratives with large casts of characters would be unmanageably long. Flat characters, says Forster, are easily recognizable, easily remembered, and likely to be enduring for both of those reasons. A novel composed only of flat characters, Forster admits, might get boring. Round characters, according to Forster, are capable of surprising the reader in a convincing way (*Aspects of the Novel*, 78). This suggests the complexity and appearance of psychological depth of central or major characters. One way that a writer can achieve this surprising complexity is to begin with one type (the beautiful young love interest) and to fuse it with another type and its possibilities (the action-adventure hero). The function of being wooed by the protagonist might then be followed by the function of rescuing him from mortal danger. Hitchcock's film *Rear Window* plays with just such a surprising combination of character types in Grace Kelly's role (from caretaker girlfriend to intrepid sleuthing sidekick). Another strategy begins with a type, such as the innocent American girl, and shows how secondary characters react differently to her, thus creating the ambiguity and mystery from which a sense of roundness may come. Henry James's *Daisy Miller* (1878) does this. Both strategies achieve the surprises of roundness by combination. All characters in texts that feature more than a solo figure are in part created by the interactions with other characters dramatized, recalled, or otherwise reported by the narrator. Flat characters can thus play a major role in provoking a sense of roundness on the part of a central rounded character.

An influential structuralist way of looking at fictional character emphasizes their functions in the plot over their potential wholeness as fictive persons. This kind of analysis ultimately privileges story over character, but it can be a useful tool in deciphering why a character behaves in a particular way, carrying out its narrative function(s) in a predictable trajectory. The Russian theorist Vladimir Propp listed 31 plot functions (acts that play roles in a plot trajectory), a selection of which always occurs in a fixed order within Russian fairy tales. (Propp's functional analysis initiates this line of thought for structuralism. It is treated in Chapter 5.) An important revision of Propp's model by A. J. Greimas revises Propp's long list into six deep structural roles, which can be enacted by one or more characters. Greimas named these roles *actants:* the subject, object, sender, helper, receiver, and opponent. For instance, in *Great Expectations*, Pip is the subject. His object (or goal) is to become a gentleman. His helper is Magwitch, though he mistakenly believes it to be Miss Havisham, who is actually a sender, teasing Pip into making Estella an additional object. She is also an opponent, sharing that role with the prickly Mrs Joe. Dickens's rich cast of characters provides many other alternatives to fill out the paradigm: in their own ways, Joe and Herbert Pocket are also helpers. The entire paradigm can be revised, and the richness of Dickens's investment of roles in his characters emphasized, by altering the object. Perhaps the real goal of this *Bildungsroman* plot is self-knowledge. In that case, senders, helpers, receivers, and opponents can be fruitfully rearranged. Even a cursory application of Greimas's actantial model can suggest how ideas, things, setting, or social forces can play roles as significant as characters in narratives. For instance, in Thomas Hardy's fiction, a chance event can function as either a helper or an opponent. Greimas's model thus allows a more complex account of roles and functions in narrative than that afforded by the old-fashioned 'man versus man,' 'man versus nature,' or 'man versus himself' rubric.

Somewhere between the analysis of character as performing a function in the plot and character as the accumulation of textual details that suggests traits, types, and relative flatness or roundness lies much of the criticism of fictional characters. James Phelan advances a rhetorical view of narrative, and recommends three categories for the understanding of character: the *synthetic*, for artificial characters whose constructedness shows; the *mimetic*, for those who are most person-like; and the *thematic*, for those characters which exist to fulfill social roles or to represent ideas. Clearly some fictional characters could be placed in all three of Phelan's categories: Leopold Bloom surely is synthetic, mimetic, and thematic all at once.

Baruch Hochman suggests a set of pairings that may assist a student in discussing fictional characters sensitively. Each pairing represents the far ends of a spectrum of possibilities: stylization and naturalism; coherence and incoherence; wholeness and fragmentariness; literalness and symbolism; complexity and simplicity; transparency and opacity; dynamism and staticism (perhaps the traditional terms dynamic and static character could be substituted here); and closure and openness (*Character in Literature*, 89–140). Though he calls his approach a taxonomy, which suggests a static set of mutually exclusive categories, Hochman in fact recognizes that some characters may present aspects of both poles at different points in a narrative or a reading experience. His emphasis on describing characters' combinations of traits comes as close as anyone has to providing a formal method for analyzing fictional characters in their wide variety.

Analytical techniques

I begin with a caution. Whether you believe that fictional characters are nonhuman word masses, or if you think they can legitimately be treated as quite like people, your work will at some point or other be read by a critic who adheres to the principle that fictional characters should not be referred to as if they were human. Despite recent calls for a revival of ethical criticism, the strictures of New Criticism (which in this case are echoed by some structuralist and post-structuralist criticism of character) still have adherents. Moral judgments about characters, speculations about their lives beyond texts, and assumptions about their 'psychology' may provoke such a critic. For instance, Richard Posner recently wrote that stories can pose, but not resolve, moral dilemmas:

> a critical difference between fictional characters and real people is that the evaluation of a fictional character is made within a framework created by the work of literature, and the framework is an artificial world rather than our real social world. Who is a hero, who a villain, is relative to the values that furnish the character's fictional world rather than to our values. This defeats any project of comparing the characters (or their implied authors) in different works of literature along an ethical dimension. We cannot say, without seeming ridiculous, that Pip is a better man than Achilles, or Leopold Bloom than Odysseus, because to make such comparisons requires ripping the characters out of their context and so destroying the aesthetic structure of which they are components.[9]

The knowledge that influential commentators hold these views should not of course impede you from making a case for an ethical or edifying view of fictional character (Wayne Booth and Martha Nussbaum could be marshaled to your cause). It may, however, stimulate you to articulate the principles that underlie your treatment of character; often, acknowledging awareness of an alternative practice is sufficient.

Another method entails adding a layer to your statements. If you feel comfortable invoking 'the author' as an active agent with discernible intentions, you can surround observations about character with state-ments about the maker. The dubious 'Emma shouldn't respect her father because he is a manipulative skinflint' can then become a more nuanced statement about Austen's craft: 'Jane Austen invites the reader to dislike Mr. Woodhouse's controlling behavior even as she demonstrates Emma's desire to please her father in spite of his faults.' The statement about Emma alone may come too close to the kind of judgment we might make about a real person, a neighbor, or a relative.

The section above should provide starting points for students looking for methods of analyzing characters by function (applying Greimas's models) or by traits (using Chatman or Hochman). A combination of traits and function may also be useful in treating character from the perspective of genre. Some knowledge of character types and of the conventions of various genres is needed to get started in this sort of analysis. If your initial research into a genre suggests that the narrative under scrutiny belongs to a larger group or class of texts that can be named, then suppositions about the conventions of that genre, subgenre, or kind can be used to analyze character. Few literary critics working today would judge a narrative's success or failure based on its fulfillment of a recipe for a particular kind, though agents and publishers often look for just that: 'formula fiction' is a denigrating label, but successful writers often depend on formulas—recognizable generic conventions. The analysis of conventions about char-acters can be particularly useful when dealing with texts that employ mix-tures of genres—in novel combinations, or in contesting relations with one another.

Finally, to return to a central subject of this chapter's treatment of char-acter, you might try analyzing the representation of fictional conscious-ness. Asking what modes dominate (Mostly narrated monologue? Mostly quoted monologue? Attributed to a single character? Or to more than one character?) can help to explain the techniques that a writer uses to guide readers' responses to characters (always acknowledging that readers may have responses that work against a writer's apparent intentions: see the dis-cussion of real readers and implied readers in Chapter 3). Are we more or less likely to sympathize with a character whose mind is never shown, like Ben, the fifth child in Doris Lessing's novel of that title? Or does this effect only work when others' minds are represented in modes that give the impression of access to their real thoughts and feelings? Some writers so rigorously avoid internal representations (Ivy Compton Burnett, for example) that a break into even the shortest passage of psycho-narration or narrated monologue can provide a bracing shock for the reader.

Because fictional characters appear to possess agency within their fictional worlds, discussions of who does what in a narrative ought to be handled delicately (and accurately: see Chapter 3). Careful handling of the distinction between the reflector (who in third-person fiction may be represented as possessing a fictional consciousness) and the narrator helps to avoid confusion. (The narrator in first-person and in some third-person fiction may, of course, be a character as well.) While many statements about the actions or the implications of actions of characters and narrators are perfectly logical, some will strike most readers as out of bounds. There are some actions pertaining to a narrative that can be carried out only by an author! If textual evidence can be provided for an insight about a character, it is much less likely to be challenged. Since impressions of characters to a great extent depend on extrapolations from accumulated textual evidence, the steps in the analytical sequence can be shared to increase the likelihood of assent to your views.

Keywords

Aristotelian character. When discussing character by type, Aristotle's thinking from the *Poetics* may come up. Though Aristotle writes about drama and emphasizes actions (and by extension plot), his ideas about intrinsic qualities of those actions spills into the analysis of dominant character traits (such as goodness and badness). Aristotle's 'agent' ('pratton') possesses two qualities, thought and character ('ethos'). Character shows though the agent's actions and decisions; these actions and responses to conflict not only reveal but create character. Thus character in an Aristotelian sense inheres in action, is unfolded in plots over time, and reveals the intrinsic traits of the agent.

Stream of consciousness. This term is often used to indicate long passages of quoted monologue, and particularly to those passages in a subgenre of 'stream of consciousness' novels, where attempts to represent pre-verbal or pre-speech thought are made. According to the critics of this subgenre, stream of consciousness, in combination with free-association techniques, may also suggest psychic depth or the 'unconscious' of characters. Though he did not originate the concept, William James's discussion of stream of consciousness in his *Principles of Psychology* lent the word to literary criticism. Dorrit Cohn points out that James's conception of stream of consciousness includes nonverbal, or imagistic elements. She also argues that interior monologues cannot present a character's mind at multiple levels simultaneously, due to the linear consecutiveness of the language of fiction (Cohn, 87).

Further reading

Burroway, Janet, *Writing Fiction: A Guide to Narrative Craft*, 5th ed. (Longman, 2000).

Chatman, Seymour, *Story and Discourse: Narrative Structure in Fiction and Film* (Cornell University Press, 1978). On 'existents,' see pp. 96–138.

Cixous, Hélène, 'The Character of 'Character,'' *New Literary History* 5 (1974), 383–402. Cixous argues that the very idea of character is repressive.

Cohn, Dorrit, *Transparent Minds: Narrative Modes for Presenting Consciousness in Fiction* (Princeton University Press, 1978).

Fludernik, Monika, *The Fictions of Language and the Languages of Fiction: The Linguistic Representation of Speech and Consciousness* (Routledge, 1993). The definitive treatment of modes of representation of consciousness and speech, for specialist readers.

Forster, E. M., *Aspects of the Novel* (Harcourt, 1927). See the two chapters on 'People,' 43–82; 67–78, for the influential idea of 'flat' and 'round' characters.

Harvey, W. J., *Character and the Novel* (Cornell University Press, 1965). A defense of and exploration of a mimetic theory of character.

Hochman, Baruch, *Character in Literature* (Cornell University Press, 1985). Highly recommended nuanced recuperation of fictional character from New Critical, structuralist, and post–structuralist denigration.

Lodge, David, *Consciousness and the Novel: Connected Essays* (Harvard University Press, 2002). A novelist and theorist meditates on the representation of consciousness in fiction, including his own recent novel *Thinks ...* (2000).

Phelan, James, *Reading People, Reading Plots: Character, Progression, and the Interpretation of Narrative* (University of Chicago Press, 1989).

Price, Martin, *Forms of Life: Character and Moral Imagination in the Novel* (Yale University Press, 1983).

Scholes, Robert and Robert Kellogg, *The Nature of Narrative* (Oxford University Press, 1966), 160–206.

5
Plot and Causation: Related Events

The problems begin with the definitions. Plot is a sequence of narrated events. Or, plot is a set of events related by causation. Plot is the story in the way the narrator tells it (in the text's discourse). Or, plot is what the reader understands as the real story, having deciphered the narrator's telling and gotten at the underlying events. Discussions of plot can emphasize narrative's complicated relations with time (chronology), order (and disorder), and generic conventions. (Each of these elements is treated in its own chapter, following this one.) Plot's deep structures have been studied by structuralist theorists interested in the 'grammar' of narrative. Aspects of plot, including episodes, digressions, multiple plots, and closure, have in themselves attracted a great deal of critical attention. An influential school of thought in feminist criticism sees some women writers as working against plot or traditional plot devices. Along with a narrator (one who tells) and characters (those existents or figures who embody actions and thoughts), plot is a core feature of narrative fiction. Not everyone has been happy about this fact.

As E. M. Forster famously lamented, 'Yes—oh dear, yes—the novel tells a story' (*Aspects of the Novel*, 26). According to Forster, the way it tells that story, with events linked by causal relations, is the plot. It will be discerned that Forster uses story and plot to mean somewhat different things. The story, for Forster, is the sequence of events 'as they happen'; the plot is those same events as they are told, with an emphasis on their causal relations. Forster's example from *Aspects of the Novel* illustrates the difference well. He writes: 'We have defined a story as a narrative of events arranged in their time-sequence. A plot is also a narrative of events, the emphasis falling on causality. "The king died and then the queen died" is a story. "The king died, and then the queen died of grief" is a plot. The time-sequence is preserved, but the sense of causality overshadows it' (*Aspects of the Novel*, 86). Forster adds that the question readers ask of story is 'and then?' while the question readers ask of a plot is 'why?' For narratives in which the order of the telling and the order of events match one another, these distinctions may seem minor. However, so many narratives employ some kind of delay, disorder, or omission in the telling that the story (the events) and the plot (the events with their causal connections revealed) do differ profoundly. One need only think of the experience of reading a detective novel: the full plot, the events in causal relation to one another, is not fully revealed and reconstituted until the telling is over, despite the fact that an abundance of story (events following one another in chronological order) carries the reader through the text. For instance, each of the narrators in Wilkie Collins's *The Moonstone* (1868) tells a story, but the plot of the novel can be assembled in full only after each deposition has been read and combined in the mind of the reader.

Since Forster's time, the elements of narrative have been named and renamed so many times that few theorists would agree to stick with these terms as Forster uses them, though most creative writing handbooks employ Forster's distinctions and examples, even when admitting that plot and story are often used interchangeably in real world discussions of fiction. For would-be critics of narrative, the situation is more complicated. Indeed, as Jeremy Hawthorn points out, in different theorists' usage, plot and story rarely convey stable meanings.[1] As has been suggested earlier (in Chapter 2), 'story' conveys a generic meaning about length that is nearly never addressed by narrative theorists. Many alternative terms for the events as they occur in chronology, for the events with causal connections, for the events in the order they are narrated, and for the text on the page have been suggested. These include 'story' and 'discourse' (Chatman); '*histoire*' and '*recit*' (Genette); '*fabula*' and 'story and focalization' and 'narration' (Bal); 'story,' 'text' and 'narration' (Rimmon Kenan); 'narrated' and 'narrating' (Prince), and '*fabula*' and '*sjuzet*' (assorted Russian Formalists). Forster's emphasis on the presence or absence of causal information as the key distinction is not shared by all theorists. The Russian Formalists, for instance, emphasize instead the distinction between the events as they occur (in a restored chronology)—*fabula*—as opposed to the events as they are told (by a narrator who may not tell in the order of the happening)—*sjuzet*. As Boris Tomashevsky puts it, the story (*fabula*) is 'the action itself,' the plot (*sjuzet*) 'how the reader learns of the action' ('Thematics,' 67n.). Manfred Jahn writes that 'Ideally, one should distinguish three action-related aspects: (i) the sequence of events as ordered in the discourse;

(ii) the action as it happened in its actual chronological sequence (= story); and (iii) the story's causal structure (= plot).'[2]

In the face of this terminological confusion, Jeremy Hawthorn's caution bears repeating here. He suggests that 'when reading these terms always proceed with care and try to confirm what convention of usage the writer is following. When writing, explain your own convention of usage by making reference to what seems to be the one reliably unambiguous term, the paired *fabula* and *sjuzet*. Do not use terms such as *story* or *plot* on their own without making it very clear how you are defining them' (*Glossary*, 337–8). In the discussion that follows, I attempt to follow Hawthorn's sensible advice, except when I present the ideas of those who employ markedly different vocabulary. For despite the lack of consistent terminology, critics do agree that related events, connected either by logic or chronology, enacted by characters, provide the substance of a narrator's telling.

In this chapter I survey some of the major ways of thinking about plot that may be useful to the advanced student of narrative. These range from approaches that emphasize the component parts of plots (beginnings, middles, and ends) and plot's minimal units (events) to theories that look at plots in an overarching fashion, by types, genres, or shared structures. In the previous chapter, I suggested that the separation of characters (existents) from the actions they contribute to plots is artificial, a convenience employed for the sake of definition and discussion. That same artificial separation occurs in this chapter as well, where I de-emphasize the agents in narratives and focus on the events that comprise plots. To be sure, in narrative literature, plot may be downplayed in favor of the representation of a character's interiority, for instance, but whenever events are presented in an order that implies relatedness, a minimal plot exists.[3]

Terms

In the discussion that follows, *story* means the events of the narrative as 'they happened' in the imaginative chronological ordering of fictive time. The *story world* and the *story level* are imaginative zones, projections of the text, which a reader constructs out of the information presented in the discourse. The *discourse* is the words of the narrative in the order in which they appear in the text. The *discourse level* is thus a textual level. The creation of a story world and a story level require first that the words of the discourse be read or heard. The events of which plots are constructed reach the reader through the discourse, but they are then assembled in the reader's mind into a chronology of before and after, or 'and then and then and then.' (It should be obvious that even a bare summary of story of this kind also requires the naming of character, the agents in the action.) The fully reconstituted set of narrated events, complete with causal relations and consequences (and a clear sense of what does *not* happen), makes up the *plot*. In this sense a plot can be fully apprehended or discussed only after the reading experience is finished. Nonetheless, many discussions of plot emphasize the reading experience that transpires in time over the completed, causally linked events. Seymour Chatman puts it well: 'Narrative turns on the fundamental human need to know what is going to happen next. That need is manipulated by narrative *plot*' (*Reading Narrative Fiction*, 20).

As Aristotle commented in the *Poetics*, a plot has a beginning, a middle, and an end. A reader can have a hunch about where a plot is headed, but not until the whole set of events is known can the plot be fully characterized. The most general accounts of plots suggest that they move from stasis, to disruption, to a restored (though altered) stasis. Tzvetan Todorov describes plot as the movement from equilibrium, through disruption, back to a new and restored equilibrium, and he emphasizes the transformations implied by that movement. In the past, critics have drawn diagrams of what such plots look like, graphically rendering, for instance, tragic plot's rising action, complication, climax, catastrophe and denouement.[4] Creative writing handbooks are full of terms for plot lines that call up graphic analogies (pyramids, checkmarks, spirals, snakes, etc). Whatever their imagined shape, plots rely on related events, while reading narrative fiction provokes a desire to continue turning pages. These two features may support one another closely, or they may be manipulated through techniques of disordering and digression, as I discuss below. Recalling that the reading experience (which transpires as an effect of the discourse level) may or may not mirror the development of the plot (whose causal links are finally filled in after a completed reading) helps avoid confusion.

Plots require conflicts, while reading stories depends on the desire to know both 'what's next' and the answers to enigmas large and small. The events or actions that produce conflict may or may not be the same events that pose narrative enigmas and stimulate a reader to continue reading. The reading process thus has its own beginning, middle, and end, which may not map exactly onto the plot's beginning, middle, and end. However, much of the middle of reading the discourse will make up, in some version or another, the middle of the plot.

If disruption and its ensuing complications and conflicts are the business of the middle and the body of narrative plotting, the beginning alludes to a state of affairs that is about to change. The middle develops from the beginning and heads toward the end. The end may or may not create strong closure (in which a satisfying set of answers and conclusions appear).[5] Virtually everything about Aristotle's definition can be questioned, including the notion that plots inevitably have endings. He was writing about drama, particularly Greek tragedies, and of course he was right that these texts had endings: the performances did not go on forever, and the stories they told tended to have strong closure. But this is not true of all narrative. Porter Abbott points out that

> Soap operas, by contrast, can go on forever. Some sagas, myth cycles, comic strips, TV series seem also to have no proper end. And the phenomenon of the 'prequel' (the opposite of the sequel) suggests that even beginnings are not sacred, but can be pushed back endlessly into the past. Much as we, like Aristotle, want shape in our narratives we seem also frequently content with postponing the end—and therefore some final perception of narrative shape—indefinitely.[6]

The desire for a never-ending story may only be finally refused by writers' and readers' mortality.

Despite these compounded problems of definition, plots in their unruly variety remain to be discussed. As a practical matter, when summarizing a *plot line*, a critic indicates where the plot starts and stops, as well as where it goes in between. Some critics insist that the chronologically earliest fully dramatized scene marks the starting point of a plot, its true beginning, even when earlier events (such as the birth of a character to parents of a particular economic status) appear in the discourse. Thus a sorting out of which events count as essential, and which ones can be de-emphasized in a *plot summary*, complicates the relationship of event to plot. The beginning of the plot line need not exactly match the beginning of the discourse, although the two beginnings can coincide. Even in ancient times, many narratives began *in medias res*, or in the middle of the action.

Homeric epic observes this convention and provides a good example of how tricky it can be to establish the beginning of a plot line. The text of Homer's *Odyssey* begins with Telemachus and Penelope's suffering at the hands of the suitors, but in fact those scenes fall chronologically quite close to the climactic return of Odysseus. Odysseus' own story—the attempted return—begins in the weeks after the end of the Trojan war, and takes up ten years of adventures, most of which the reader learns about in a long embedded *flashback* or *analepsis*. Indeed, many of the most famous

adventures of the *Odyssey* occur in the time before the imminent home-
coming. Some might argue that the true beginning of the story of the
Odyssey lies in the initial separation of Penelope, Odysseus, and their infant
son. Indeed, one can understand neither the recognition of long-separated
husband and wife, nor the violent conclusion of the plot without knowing
something about the early days of the marriage. Particular pieces of that
knowledge (the marriage bed's construction) become consequential details
in the plot of testing that precedes the reunion. So where is the beginning
of the *Odyssey*? Does it have more than one plot, and do their beginnings
start at different points chronologically? For instance, Telemachus' coming-
of-age plot does begin contiguously with the beginning of the discourse.
However, few readers would place Telemachus' plot line at the center of the
Odyssey. Value judgments about the relative importance or unimportance
of particular characters and themes often color discussions of beginnings,
since starting points set up the disruptions and conflicts that generate
plots. Identifying the beginning of the narrative in *your* interpretation can
in itself be a strong interpretive act.

The situation becomes ever more complicated in narratives with multiple
plots. Aristotle believed that plots should be single and unified, though few
creators of narrative or even playwrights have agreed with him.
Shakespeare's plays often employ *subplots*, those secondary plot lines that
appear in subordinate roles to a main plot. Many narratives, from the prose
romances of the late Middle Ages to the Victorian multi-plot novel, boast
multiple plot lines.[7] As numerous critics have pointed out, Aristotle was
describing a particular form, not writing a recipe for all narrative. One of
the most vital first steps in the analysis of plot, then, is the enumeration of
plot lines in a particular text. Does a single plot emerge from reading, or do
double or multiple plot lines require separate consideration? This is what
Dickens, a great artist of the multi-plot novel, as well as serial publication,
says about the form:

> It is the custom on the stage, in all good murderous melodramas, to
> present the tragic and comic scenes, as in regular alternation, as the
> layers of red and white in a side of streaky bacon ... Such changes appear
> absurd; but they are not so unnatural as they would seem at first sight.
> The transitions in real life from well-spread boards to death-beds, and
> from mourning weeds to holiday garments, are not a whit less startling;
> only there, we are busy actors, instead of passive lookers-on, which
> makes a vast difference ... As sudden shiftings of the scene, and rapid
> changes of time and place, are not only sanctioned in books by long

usage, but are by many considered as the great art of authorship: an author's skill in his craft being, by such critics, chiefly estimated with relation to the dilemmas in which he leaves his characters at the end of the chapter. (*Oliver Twist*, ch. 17)

Dickens's analogy with a dramatic form makes the contrast with Aristotle's view all the more striking. Peter K. Garrett has written well about how the multi-plot novel exhibits the qualities of what Bakhtin calls the novel's dialogic form (see Keywords, below), and certainly a plenitude of plot lines characterizes certain very long narrative fictions. Interpreting the relationships among plot lines, and noticing how the narrator shifts from plot to plot in the discourse, can be fruitful lines of inquiry for the formal analysis of plot.

This topic moves us along towards the consideration of *events*, the component parts of plot lines. Events, or actions, are the things that happen in a narrative. A narrator tells about these events as they transpire, or as the characters enact them. A number of theorists have proposed terms for the description of significant events in relation to those events that appear to be subsidiary to the plot. Seymour Chatman's terms 'kernel' and 'satellite,' though oddly mixing agricultural and astronomical metaphors, convey vividly how the two kinds of plot events relate to one another. Kernel events make up the points on the connect-the-dots trajectory of a plot line. Each kernel event acts with gravitational force to collect around it the satellite events that are subsidiary actions in a plot summary. Plots are made up of sequences of events, but not all events presented in sequence suggest a plot, nor do all events contribute to the plot. A student may usefully discover, using Seymour Chatman's terms, which events are essential to the plot (kernels) and which ones are subsidiary (satellites). Satellite plot events can be omitted from a plot synopsis without resulting in serious inaccuracy: we can do without a report that Jane Eyre suspects Grace Poole of strange behavior. The omission of a kernel event from a plot synopsis would result in an incorrect summary and could lead to misinterpretation: an account of *Jane Eyre* leaving out Rochester's bigamous proposal or Bertha's death would be incomplete (Chatman, *Story and Discourse*, 53–4).

Plot events that at first appear to be kernel events, but which on a completed reading are revealed to have been misleading satellites are called 'snares.'[8] The filling out of an extended plot with a long sequence of events that may in retrospect appear to be satellites rather than kernel events could lead to the description of a plot as episodic, though an episode in and of itself is a minimal unit of plot, consisting of its own kernel and satellite events (see Chapter 2 for more on episodes as sub-units of narrative). Episodic fiction, long associated with picaresque and romance, has been criticized as insufficiently unified at the level of plot. However, as the earlier quotation from Porter Abbott reminds us, episodic fiction is a staple of our narrative diet in film and television, as well as in childhood reading. Some writers have been criticized by their contemporaries or later readers for writing dispensable episodes. This criticism suggests that an entire sub-unit of narrative could be rendered as a satellite set, and demoted from the kernel position in a plot summary. No one would miss it; the episode is present only to fill out the length of the fiction. Such a narrative might also be criticized as overly digressive. A digression, a term borrowed from rhetoric, is an interpolated story or anecdote, which appears to have been inserted into a narrative in order to lead away from the main plot, albeit temporarily. Laurence Sterne's *Tristram Shandy* (1759–67) makes an art out of the digression, at the expense of plot. Some writers, especially Victorian novelists, employ what I call narrative annexes in order to admit unexpected characters, impermissible subjects, and plot-altering events into fictional worlds whose norms would ordinarily exclude them. Marked by a boundary crossing carried out by the reflecting or narrating character, a narrative annex is a briefly realized zone in which both setting and genre differ from the surrounding fictional world. Narrative annexes contain kernel plot events in a modified story world.[9]

The common term 'plot turn' indicates the unpredictability that some theorists of plot have preferred, following Aristotle, who described *peripety*, or a sudden change of direction or reversal of circumstances, as one of the key qualities of a tragic plot. A plot with too many turns for a reader's taste or patience may be disparaged as hard to follow or implausible. Other qualities of narrative that can render a plot challenging or more intricate include repetitions, disorder in the telling, and disruption of the usual assumptions about causation.

Some experimental fictions set out to suggest that the causal relation between plot events is itself a product of the reader's wish that such a relationship exists. The experience of reading a text like Julio Cortazar's *Hopscotch* (1966) or B. S. Johnson's *The Unfortunates* (1969) emphasizes this arbitrariness by laying bare the device of sequential plot events through game-like techniques of scrambling. Johnson's novel presents 27 fascicle-like pamphlets in a box. They are presented this way to invite their reading in any order the reader chooses. Cortazar's novel has a fixed order in bound pages, but subverts it by instructing readers to 'hopscotch' through the book according to a numerical plan. Within each of the subsections, however, the normal habits of reading for a sequential plot take over. Causation is disrupted, but not entirely dismissed: the habit of making sense of chains of events is very strong in most readers, viewers, and listeners. Even in conventional realistic fiction, however, just because plot events follow one another guarantees no causal relationship.

The assumption that sequential events are causally related goes by the name of the *'post hoc ergo propter hoc* fallacy.' As the name suggests, this fallacy describes the habit of assuming a 'because' relationship of two events that happen to follow one another. Detective fiction and psychological thrillers both exploit the effect of the *post hoc ergo propter hoc* fallacy in the form of 'red herrings'; these genres count on the reader making assumptions about causal relations which later revelations prove to be arbitrary connections. Some works of metafiction or fabulation can take a resistance to plot so far as to break the sequence of the causal chain, making it virtually impossible to suggest a relationship between events without recourse to nonsense. Lyn Hejinian's lyrical prose work *My Life* (1980) provides a good example of this sort of challenging manipulation of narrative conventions.[10]

A more common manipulation of the need to know what happened next (and why) occurs when writers present events out of their chronological order. This strategy puts a greater demand on the reader to reassemble events into their chronological order than plots that match clock time or calendar time in their narrative order. William Faulkner uses this technique to powerful effect in his story 'A Rose for Emily' (1930), where profoundly disorded telling nonetheless conveys a set of related events that can be reconstituted into their order of happening. As mentioned earlier, some genres such as classical epic often employ the disordering technique of beginning in the middle of the action, and using flashback to fill in the prior events. In subsequent chapters I treat the various kinds of relationship between the order in the plot and the narration, including frequency, pace, and timing (as Genette describes them).

All of these techniques of narration have an impact on the way a reader encounters the events that will be reconstituted as a plot. While reading an unfolding or developing plot, one may encounter disorderly narration, repetitions of the same event from different perspectives or with different details or satellite events emphasized, and other manipulations of the desire to know, such as the use of a gap, in which the reader infers a plot event without its direct narration. Throughout this chapter, I have argued that it is useful to separate the fashion in which plot events are narrated from the discussion of plot per se. The organization of the next few chapters as separate sections endorses a view common in narrative theory that events in the story (*fabula*) and events in the order of the discourse (*sjuzet*) should be distinguished. Yet common sense tells us that a reader or viewer develops a sense of plot *during* the consumption of a narrative, while still absorbed in the discourse. The requirement of completeness that the observation of the *fabula/sjuzet* distinction demands by positing a realm of story in which the events of a finished plot are rearranged in the order of their happening makes no sense to a person who is in the middle of reading. That person would, if interrupted in the middle of the reading or viewing, capably convey the plot 'so far,' with the caveat that further 'plot twists' or 'surprises' were as yet unknown. This commonsense challenge to the conventional separation of story events and the order of their telling is elaborated with great sophistication by Peter Brooks, with significant support from Paul Ricoeur, the most important theorist of time in narrative.[11]

Peter Brooks has written well about the activity of 'reading for the plot' in an influential book of that title. Brooks focuses on the temporal dynamics of plot, 'the play of desire in time that makes us turn pages and strive towards narrative ends,' using Freud's dynamic model of psychic processes as an analogy (*Reading for the Plot*, p. xiii). In Brooks's use of Freud, the text itself possesses 'energies, tensions, compulsions, resistances, and desires' (p. xiv). According to Brooks, narrative is a mode of understanding whose instrumental logic is plot (10). As he uses it, plot means 'an embracing concept for the design and intention of narrative, a structure for those meanings that are developed through temporal succession, or perhaps better; a structuring operation elicited by, and made necessary by, those meanings that develop through succession and time' (12). Brooks suggests that the reader possesses an 'anticipation of retrospection' that helps make sense of the assumption that what is yet to come in a story will make sense of what has already been read (23). His central interest lies in the compulsion readers feel to continue to read, and thus he emphasizes the narrative desire that initiates narrative, motivates and drives reading, and 'animates the combinatory play of sense-making' (48). Whether or not one shares Brooks's conviction that Freud's Eros operates in people and in our narrative texts, his description of reading is one of the most persuasive in modern literary theory.

Analytical techniques

Avoiding the pitfall of plot summary can appear to be at odds with analyzing plot. As fundamental as plot is to narrative, its extensive discussion can get a student into trouble. Devoting too much space to plot summary or synopsis can seem a weakness, and many guides to writing about literature recommend that students avoid plot summary altogether. While recounting the plot of a narrative may seem like a necessary step before moving on to interpretation, the synopsis or summary (especially of complex plots) can take over and result in a piece of writing that seems uncritical to its professional readers. Comprehending the plot is of course an important phase of deliberation. One undertakes this step, if it does not occur automatically, prior to advancing an argument about a narrative. Because some disorderly or complex narratives have plots that are harder to grasp on a first reading, the effort that a reader puts into understanding the causal links between events may be significant. That does not mean that retelling the story in a plot synopsis is always an appropriate form of critical writing. When is plot summary acceptable?

- In a book review for general readers, though care should be taken not to reveal the whole plot or to reveal the ending (these slips are called 'spoilers').
- In a critical essay about a text that is not well known. Recounting the plot of *Jane Eyre* is not recommended, but briefly summarizing the events of *The Death of Felicity Taverner*, by the less well-known writer Mary Butts, would be considered helpful (unless the audience were exclusively made up of Butts scholars).
- Very briefly, and in excerpt form, to locate a reader in a complex text before analyzing it in detail: 'At this point in the novel, Pip does not suspect that Magwitch is his true benefactor, though he has reason to doubt Miss Havisham's intentions ...'
- When the plot itself is the subject of analysis. In this case, you should declare the methodology of the analysis to be undertaken (for instance, examining the role of satellite plot events in a complex novel, or arguing that a narrative takes on and alters the expectations generated by a particular genre and its conventional plot lines). This guards against the criticism that you are indulging in unnecessary plot summary.

Typological approaches to plot

Many narrative theorists have suggested typologies of plot, which abstract patterns from many texts and arrange them into charts of options, or attempt to boil all plots down into a very few plot patterns. For even an advanced student or a classroom teacher, the disadvantages of these methods lie in the up-front demands that they make: one must undertake bulk reading in many narrative subgenres in order to test the typologies. An extraordinarily influential book of this type is Northrop Frye's *Anatomy of Criticism* (1957), a founding text of archetypal criticism. Though *Anatomy of Criticism* does not even contain the word 'plot' in its index, Frye's theory of 'Modes' in fact depends upon the differentiation of plots by type. The book is rarely used in the classroom today except in classes on the history of theory and criticism, but its influence is still palpable.

Structuralists' interest in plot functions provide two methods that can be used in the classroom or in essays to explore the components and shapes of plot, the expectations they generate, and the way in which they deviate from norms. The two approaches I suggest here belong to a Russian Formalist, Vladimir Propp, and a French structuralist, A. J. Greimas.

Vladimir Propp's analysis of Russian fairy tales produced an ordered list of 31 plot functions, to be carried out by the seven dramatis personae (the Villain, the Donor, the Helper, the Princess and her father, the Dispatcher, the Hero, and the False Hero).[12] The functions are reproduced in Gerald Prince's *A Dictionary of Narratology* (36–7). In addition to the functions themselves (a set of actions that comprise the structure of Russian fairy tales), Propp also proposed four theses, arguing that (1) the functions are stable, constant elements no matter which actor carries them out; (2) the number of possible functions is limited to 31; (3) the sequence of functions is always identical, though no tale contains all the functions; and (4) all fairy tales are of one structural type. This last claim can be tested by applying Propp's model to fairy tales from other cultures or to literary texts modeled on fairy tales. Scrutinizing Propp's list of functions soon reveals that his study of a fixed corpus produced idiosyncratic results which cannot be applied to all narratives, but the exercise of describing narratives other than Russian fairy tales by their plot functions is a useful way to begin thinking about what groups of texts may have in common with one another. Reductive explanations, if coherent, are useful as scaffolding to stand upon while looking into the real (and possibly endless) complexity of the structure.

A. J. Greimas redacts Propp's 31 functions and seven dramatis personae to a much smaller and more flexible actantial model. A narrative has a subject, an object, a sender, helper, receiver, and opposer. These actantial positions can be filled by characters, but concepts, settings, or objects can also occupy the roles. Furthermore, a single character may fill more than

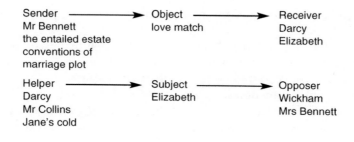

Sender ⟶ Object ⟶ Receiver
Mr Bennett   love match   Darcy
the entailed estate   Elizabeth
conventions of
marriage plot

Helper ⟶ Subject ⟶ Opposer
Darcy   Elizabeth   Wickham
Mr Collins   Mrs Bennett
Jane's cold

Figure 2

one actantial role. For instance, *Pride and Prejudice* might be diagrammed accordingly (Figure 2).

Depending on how the central pair (subject and object) are defined, the diagram of actants can turn out differently, and the placement of each actant can itself generate arguments about the interpretation of the novel. Attempting to fill out an actantial diagram can be a useful step in the interpretation of a complex narrative, as it challenges the interpreter to specify the central goals and oppositions of the story's conflicts. In this sense Greimas's actantial approach, which may at first appear to emphasize character, helps to get at the core conflicts or stresses around which a plot is constructed.

In the following chapters of the book, on 'Timing' (Chapter 6), 'Order and Disorder' (Chapter 7), and 'Levels' (Chapter 8), you will find additional vocabulary that will help you analyze the construction of some complex plots. Try to find out if these narratological approaches would be helpful by asking the following questions about the plot you are studying:

- Does the story tell everything that happens, or does something important get left out (a gap, or an ellipsis)? (See Chapter 6.)
- Does the plot emphasize some events over others by repeating them, dwelling on them at length, or otherwise stretching out the number of pages and story time spent on them? These are matters of frequency and pace. (See Chapter 6.)
- Does the story get narrated in the order that it happens, or does the writer employ anachrony (disordering)? (See Chapter 7.)
- What is the effect of the order of telling on the subsequent understanding of the plot? (See Chapter 7.)
- Does the plot contain a secondary or tertiary plot within it? (Note: this differs from the multiple plots described above, in that a nesting structure is employed.) (If so, see Chapter 8.)

Feminist critiques of plot and closure

In the early 1990s, Margaret Homans noticed what had by then become a stream of feminist treatments of narrative that emphasized women's fiction's resistance to traditional plot lines and closure.[13] These critics have been divided on the degree to which any fiction writer can resist what is sometimes depicted as the tyranny of plot, especially plots associated with a patriarchal tradition. Indeed, some theorists (and not only feminists) see plots as inherently ideological. Nancy K. Miller, Susan Stanford Friedman, Rachel Blau DuPlessis, and other feminists have described women writers' evasion, disruption, or subversion of closure, authority, conventional plots, and even narrative itself. As Friedman points out, Virginia Woolf was one of the most eloquent theorists as well as practitioners of the break with sequence. Friedman advocates the creation of theories of narrative that would honor Woolf's example, breaking with hegemonic stories about authoritarian narratives in favor of 'supple and multishaped' theories of 'polyvocal and polymorphous' narratives ('Lyric Subversions,' 180). A student interested in this kind of feminist criticism should begin with Nancy K. Miller's influential 1981 essay, 'Emphasis Added: Plots and Plausibilities in Women's Fiction.'

Generic approaches to plot

Generic approaches collect a number of narratives that resemble one another in their use of conventions into a common pool. Noticing the similarities and differences among these texts (as well as learning the literary history of the genre or subgenre) can open up interpretive avenues. Perhaps your work will focus on the way a plot conforms to generic expectations, or perhaps you will find a plot that alters or challenges a tradition. Possibly the narrative you are studying combines conventions from more than one genre. Perhaps you will have discovered a whole new way of naming and clustering related narratives that have not been brought together by critics before. The plot lines or types of plots employed in a group of text can be revealing elements confirming the usefulness of such an approach. One begins by asking these sorts of questions:

- What kind of story does the narrator tell (murder mystery, love story, etc)?
- What sorts of expectation does the story generate as it is narrated? Do you find these expectations fulfilled in the completed plot?

- If not, what happens to change the direction of the plot? Can it be explained by a generic shift or combination?

Keywords

Dialogic form.   Mikhail Bakhtin contributes this concept to the study of the novel, and it does not necessarily refer to the represented dialogue of characters, though dialogue certainly makes a substantive contribution to the array of voices present in novels. Bakhtin holds that novels, among literary forms, are uniquely 'dialogic,' employing as they do multiple competing voices, not ultimately subordinated to the voice of the narrator (see my treatment of Bakhtin's 'discourse' in Keywords, Chapter 3). These multiple voices interact in a polyphonic way, generating harmonies and tensions as well as out-and-out contradictions that may not be resolved by the text.[14] Though it would seem at first that each voice or discourse might be tethered to a fictional character (and that may be the case in some fictions employing representative types), plot lines may embody the competing discourses, particularly as they are associated with institutions and their assumptions. Dickens's Circumlocution Office and the plot associated with 'trying to get something accomplished by a bureaucracy' provides a good example of a 'voice' (in the Bakhtinian sense) which is not wholly bound to character, consisting as it does of place and (in)action, as well. (See also the discussion of Bakhtin's chronotope in Chapters 6 and 8.) Peter K. Garrett has argued that Victorian multi-plot novels especially exhibit the fruitful creative tensions of dialogic form. Garrett writes: 'Here structures can be related to the manifest concerns of Victorian fiction: the large loose baggy monsters mean many things and in many different ways, but one thing they repeatedly mean to do is to transcend the limitations of the individual point of view and envision the life of the whole community. Yet in every case we can observe, not the realization of a secure and comprehensive vision but a continual, shifting, unstable, and unpredictable confrontation between single and plural, individual and social, particular and general perspectives' (*Victorian Multiplot Novel*, 22).

Grammar of narrative, or story grammars.   An approach to plot (and narrative) that specifies (and sometimes predicts) the relationship among component units of plot, or episodes, moving towards an endpoint or goal. The linguistic or structuralist versions of these models, which are developed in a specialized field of their own, employ rules for both the large structures of plot and the possible behavior of its component units. They are based on an analogy between language and narrative; references to narrative syntax, to deep and surface structures, and to transformational rules announce an allegiance to theories of narrative grammar. Influential theorists include Tzvetan Todorov, Thomas Pavel, A. J. Greimas, Teun A. van Dijk, Marie-Laure Ryan, and Gerald Prince. This approach has currency in a very specialized area of narratology.

Masterplots.   A term that means two radically different things, either (1) a volume of plot synopses of major works of fiction, or (2) one of the major 'metanarratives' or governing fictions by which Western civilization understands itself. Examples of metanarratives include the redemptive Christian story, the liberal or Whig version of history emphasizing progress towards parliamentary democracy, and the Marxist description of the fate of global capitalism. See the discussion of metanarratives in Chapter 9. Hayden White is one of their most influential theorists, in his *Metahistory*, a work bearing significant traces of White's encounter with the ideas of Northrop Frye in *An Anatomy of Criticism.*

Further reading

Bal, Mieke, *Narratology: Introduction to the Theory of Narrative* (1980), trans. Christine van Boheemen (University of Toronto Press, 1985). Bal uses 'story' and 'fabula' differently than this chapter (her 'story' means my 'plot'), but her book provides a useful introduction to the structural elements of plot.

Brooks, Peter, *Reading for the Plot: Design and Intention in Narrative* (Knopf, 1984). Brooks resists the division implied by *fabula* and *sjuzet*, suggesting that a proper consideration of plot must consider both story's component parts and their ordering in the narrative.

Chatman, Seymour, *Story and Discourse: Narrative Structure in Fiction and Film.* (Cornell University Press, 1978). Kernels and satellites.

Forster, E. M., *Aspects of the Novel* (Harcourt, 1927). 'Story' and 'Plot.'

Friedman, Susan Stanford, 'Lyric Subversion of Narrative in Women's Writing: Virginia Woolf and the Tyranny of Plot,' in *Reading Narrative: Form, Ethics, Ideology*, ed. James Phelan (Ohio State University Press, 1989), 162–85.

Genette, Gérard, *Narrative Discourse: An Essay in Method*, trans. Jane E. Lewin (Cornell University Press, 1980).

Richardson, Brian, *Unlikely Stories: Causality and the Nature of Modern Narrative* (University of Delaware Press, 1997). Richardson argues that causal connections are a defining feature of narrative; he also treats chance, cause, and fate in postmodern and post-colonial texts.

Rimmon-Kenan, Shlomith, *Narrative Fiction: Contemporary Poetics* (Methuen, 1983). See especially her chapters 'Story: Events' (6–28) and 'Text: Time' (43–58).

Todorov, Tzvetan, *Introduction to Poetics,* trans. Richard Howard (University of Minnesota Press, 1981).

— *The Poetics of Prose*, trans. Richard Howard, foreword by Jonathan Culler (Cornell University Press, 1977).

Tomashevsky, Boris, 'Thematics,' in *Russian Formalist Criticism: Four Essays*, trans. Lee T. Lemon and Marion J. Reis (University of Nebraska Press, 1965), 61–95. Useful for story and plot (*fabula* and *sjuzet*), bound and free motifs (cf. Chatman's kernels and satellites).

6
Timing: How Long and How Often?

Story Time, when the narrative is written

Reader is effected by what time period

Time plays a fundamental part in narrative fiction. The sequential related events of plot imply the passing of imaginary time (what theorists call story time). Narratives take time to tell and receive. Writers create narratives in time, and if the stories of their lives and authorship are recorded, they become part of the non-fiction narrative of literary history. Alternatively, much of what we believe we know of a remote time may be derived from a narrative dated from that period. Genres as well as writers have their times, and very often criticism's narratives about the rise of a genre or the disappearance of another intersects with history. Readers, too, are rooted in their own cultural times and locations, which in turn affect what fictions they read and, to some extent, the way they read them. Finally, many narratives are set in a particular time, which becomes an intrinsic part of the fiction's setting.[1] Despite these commonsense connections of time and narrative, the 'time' discussed by narrative theory has little to do with the 'time' of history. When they refer to 'time' in narrative, most theorists mean some combination of the temporal unfolding of narrative in the act of reading, the duration of time depicted in the plot, the pace at which the narration relates the events of the plot, and the order or disorder of the events of story time. Narrative theory relies on the conceptual division of story time (the time that transpires in the imaginary story world of the plot) and discourse time (the amount of narration expended on the relation of the story events—really a quantity of pages, though it would have a correlate in reading time). To reintroduce the time of history, or philosophical meditations on conceptions of time in different eras, to the discussion of narrative form significantly changes the subject.

For instance, Raymond Williams, one of the founding thinkers of contemporary cultural studies, brings historical time into contact with the literary history of forms. Williams argues that one can discern in a particular time period the dominant, residual, and emergent forms of expression. The old, the new, and the everyday forms of a particular time overlap with one another, though Williams emphasizes the scrutiny of the 'social present.' There we find the emergent forms in which new 'structures of feeling' are embodied. Williams argues that in any given historical moment in a culture, old, new, and everyday forms coexist, overlapping with one another: 'The effective formations of most actual art relate to already manifest social formations, dominant or residual, and it is primarily to emergent formations (though often in the form of modification or disturbance in older forms) that the structure of feeling, as solution, relates.'[2] Williams's terms place scrutiny of form into a social and temporal matrix that many structuralist narrative theorists would set aside. (Contextual narratology is more welcoming to cultural studies approaches.)

In order to convey the most influential methods for examining time in narrative fiction, without suggesting that I can take on historical, philosophical, or scientific understandings of time, I use the narrowing term 'timing.' Timing is a matter of the fiction writer's craft, like the timing of a stand-up comedian. Repeating details, dwelling on some events to the exclusion or reduction of others, employing story-stopping descriptions or leaping over events with gaps, modulating the pace of narration with scenes and summary: these are the techniques of timing as employed by storytellers, filmmakers, and novelists. For a storyteller or a novelist or a kindergartener, mastering the use of timing in narration helps to avoid boring or irrelevant storytelling.

We criticize a boring narrative by saying that it drags or that it is slow, both terms referring to our expectations of good timing. These terms do not just report the experience of untrained readers reacting to unfamiliar texts. Since we don't in fact have all the time in the world to give to the imaginary related time of narrative, we need the compression, speeding up, and skipping that makes a coherent story about centuries, generations, or lives other than our own manageable. We also need narratives to slow down to linger on significant scenes or thoughts, to repeat in order to explain, enhance clarity, or heighten drama, and to be ample enough to afford a temporary escape from our own time. Of course, in order to enter fictional worlds imaginatively, we give time to the reading experience. A reader's sense that a fiction is 'slow' or 'fast' may have more to do with how many pages are turned during a session of reading than with the narrative's timing. Indeed, the conventional uses of timing in narrative may be virtually unnoticeable to many readers, who may react only when a narrative fails to offer the conventional blends of scene and summary. Understanding the concepts introduced by French narratologist Gérard Genette helps the advanced student accurately describe the handling of timing in narrative texts, whether typical or experimental. This chapter combines with Chapter 8 (on levels of narration in fictional worlds) to introduce some of the most useful contributions of Genette to the description of narrative form. It ends with some suggestions about how the formal analysis of timing might be enriched by combination with other elements, such as place and time as in Mikhail Bakhtin's concept of the chronotope (see Keywords, below).

Terms

[handwritten annotation: Story Time vs. Discourse time.]

The analysis of time in narrative depends upon a conventional distinction between story time and discourse time. Both kinds of 'time' are unreal compared to the real time in which we live and read. *Story time* is the time that transpires within the imaginary world projected by the text. It can be a single day, as in *Mrs. Dalloway* (1925) or *Ulysses* (1922); it can cover generations, in sagas such as Colleen McCullough's *The Thornbirds* (1977); or it can move through millennia, as in the fiction of James Michener and his imitators. Expectations about story time may be governed by generic conventions, as in the *Bildungsroman*, which usually tells one life story, but not two. A good example of this can be found in V. S. Naipaul's *A House for Mr. Biswas* (1961), which stops just as the author's father's story ends. *Discourse time* refers to the time implied by the quantity of discourse, in its linear arrangement of elements in the text (it is therefore sometimes called *text time*). Discourse time actually describes the amount of space, in lines or pages, given to the representation of narrative contents. It only becomes meaningful in relation to the story time, for the allotment of a smaller or larger amount of discourse to the narration creates the sense of the different speeds described under Genette's term of 'duration.'

Duration indicates the relationship between story time elapsed and amount of discourse time expended. Genette himself emends this term usefully to 'speeds' in his *Narrative Discourse Revisited* (34). Conventionally, pure dialogue (*scene*) is considered the meeting point of story time and discourse time. This convention comes from the drama, where scenes of dialogue are enacted in real time. Most readers in fact consume a page of print dialogue much faster than it would take to deliver the lines as dramatic dialogue, so it must be stressed that the equivalence of story time and discourse time in scene is a useful fiction. By contrast, *summary* covers 'more'

Name	Story time		Discourse time	'Speed'
Gap	ST	/	0 DT	fastest
Summary	ST	>	DT	fast
Scene	ST	=	DT	'real time'
Expansion	ST	<	DT	slow
Pause	0 ST	/	DT	slowest

Figure 3

story time than it takes to convey in discourse. (Scene and summary have long been associated with the contrasted methods of showing (mimesis) and telling (diegesis) in traditional accounts of narrative.) Genette's terminology accounts for three other options in the relative speeds of the narration. The greatest amount of story for the least discourse occurs in *ellipses*, or *gaps*. These have no discourse, but they implicitly consume story time, by leaping over time between events. At the far extreme from gaps are *pauses*, in which a great deal of discourse appears, but progression of the story stops. Description or authorial excurses can make up the substance of the discourse in a pause. Between pause and scene the reader may find passages of narration that expand upon or dilate a scene. This speed has been called *expansion*, *dilation*, or *stretching*. The whole paradigm of possibilities can be represented in a diagram (Figure 3).

The relations among the various speeds of duration go by the name of *pace*. Constancy of pace is very unusual, and ordinarily takes the form of fiction in pure scene (representing dialogue and nothing much more): the canonical examples are the novels of Ivy Compton Burnett and 'The Killers,' by Ernest Hemingway (1927). In film a constant pace is also very rare, though there are interesting examples, such as Iranian director Jafar Panahi's film *White Balloon* (*Badkonak*) (1995) which employs a constant pace matching real time throughout. Theoretically, among the other speeds of duration, summary and expansion could be employed in a constant fashion, though it is impossible to imagine a narrative that it is either all pause, or all gap. Typically, speeds are modulated in narrative, even within single passages of narration. The critic attuned to variations in narrative tempo notices acceleration and deceleration, as well as the more obvious pauses and gaps.

Until Genette drew attention to issues of frequency in *Narrative Discourse*, repetition was far more often noticed as a technique of verse than of narrative fiction. For students of narrative, repetition means something different from than the clock-ticking patterns that allow us to count and thus discern time passing. Like duration, or speeds, frequency describes a relationship between instances in story time and instances in the discourse or narration. Using Genette's terms, repetition in the discourse can be described by how many times an event occurs in relation to the number of times it is narrated. *Frequency* indicates the number of times an event occurs and number of times it is told. It can be a *'normative' frequency* of 1 to 1. This frequency indicates telling once what happened once (a pattern that often holds for all the events of the plot). *Repetitive frequency* tells multiple times what happened once. It may employ different narrators or reflectors' perspectives, as in Errol Morris's 1988 documentary film *The Thin Blue Line*, or Akira Kurosawa's *Rashomon* (1951). Alternatively, a single narrator may repeat himself, as in Kazuo Ishiguro's novel *The Remains of the Day* (1989), where several key events are visited more than once by the narrator. Finally, a form of frequency that is strongly associated with the speed of 'summary': *iterative frequency* tells once what happened many times. A brilliant experiment with repetition was made by Harold Ramis in his 1993 film *Groundhog Day*, starring Bill Murray as a weatherman who is doomed to repeat a single day of his life until he gets it right.

The emphasis here and in many repetitive narratives falls on plot events, but the same terms can be employed to describe the modulations of frequency in represented thoughts. For instance, consider the following passage from Virginia Woolf's *Mrs. Dalloway*:

> Elizabeth turned her head. The waitress came. One had to pay at the desk, Elizabeth said, and went off, drawing out, so Miss Kilman felt, the very entrails in her body, stretching them as she crossed the room, and then, with a final twist, bowing her head very politely, she went.
>
> She had gone. Miss Kilman sat at the marble table among the éclairs, stricken once, twice, thrice by shocks of suffering. She had gone. Mrs. Dalloway had triumphed. Elizabeth was gone. Beauty had gone, youth had gone. (*Mrs. Dalloway*, 201)

Not only does Woolf relate the departure of Elizabeth using expansion, stretching out her act of leaving by emphasizing Miss Kilman's thoughts (in a vivid image conveyed in psycho-narration), but she also employs repetitive frequency in her relation of Miss Kilman's thoughts. Woolf relates the 'shocks of suffering,' counting out the three strokes of pain using normative frequency (one mention for each event). However, Woolf then turns to relate Miss Kilman's thoughts inwardly, narrating for a second time the shock of Elizabeth's departure through narrated monologue. The event ('Miss Kilman feels shock at Elizabeth's departure') is narrated repeatedly. This repetition, combined with the repetitions of Miss Kilman's thoughts, contributes to the expansion of the brief scene.

Analytical techniques

Examining 'speeds' using Genette's terms for duration. This technique is especially useful for establishing the differences and similiarities in technique as used by different writers. Here I treat just a single passage, from chapter 14 of Jane Austen's *Pride and Prejudice* (1813), in order to show how the analysis of narrative pace can be integrated into close reading. The passage occurs during a visit to the Bennets of the odious cousin Mr Collins, who serves his mistress Lady Catherine De Bourgh with extreme obsequiousness. The extract opens towards the end of a speech made by Mr Collins, who has just related how he flatters Lady Catherine:

> '... These are the kind of little things which please her ladyship, and it is a sort of attention which I conceive myself peculiarly bound to pay.'
> 'You judge very properly,' said Mr. Bennet, 'and it is happy for you that you possess the talent of flattering with delicacy. May I ask whether these pleasing attentions proceed from the impulse of the moment, or are the result of previous study?'
> 'They arise chiefly from what is passing at the time, and though I sometimes amuse myself with suggesting and arranging such elegant little compliments as may be adapted to ordinary occasions, I always wish to give them as unstudied an air as possible.'
> [Thus far, Austen employs the pure *scene* of dialogue.]
> Mr. Bennet's expectations were fully answered. His cousin was as absurd as he hoped, and he listened to him with the keenest enjoyment, maintaining at the same time the most resolute composure of countenance, and except in an occasional glance at Elizabeth, requiring no partner in his pleasure.
> [Austen breaks to *summary* of Mr Bennet's feelings and behavior rather than detailing the rest of the conversation.]
> By teatime however the dose had been enough,
> [Summary has verged into *gap* here, as unnarrated time has clearly passed.]
> and Mr. Bennet was glad to take his guest into the drawing room again; and when tea was over, glad to invite him to read aloud to the ladies.

[Austen moves back to *summary*, with another comical scene soon intervening.]

The alternation of summary and scene, with occasional gaps inserted for the sake of economy, characterizes one of Austen's main strategies for handling scenes of social interactions. She also employs dilation to excellent effect for her more inward scenes, as when Elizabeth Bennet reads a letter and thinks about its contents.

The preceding sets of terms and strategies represent the agreed-upon elements of narrative timing. However, theories of narrative time have been subject to re-evaluation in response to the challenges posed by postmodern and nonmimetic fiction. Brian Richardson points out that there are 'several significant varieties of temporal construction' for which Genette's framework cannot account ('Beyond Story and Discourse,' 47). Richardson enumerates the following six types: *circular narratives*, which return to their own beginnings, thus challenging temporal linearity and frequency (if the loop has no ending); *contradictory narratives*, in which more than one 'incompatible and irreconcilable' version of the story appears; *antinomic narratives*, which tell backwards stories prospectively; *differential narratives*, in which a character ages at a different rate than the surrounding people, thus creating two different implicit chronologies; *conflated narratives*, in which two different represented time periods run together; and *dual* or *multiple narratives*, in which narratives that begin and end at the same time contain narratives of different temporal lengths ('Beyond Story and Discourse, 47–52). Richardson's work provides a salutary reminder that narrative theoretical methods often take a small canon of narratives to be exemplary, while many exceptions to the models of structuralist narratology can be found, especially in postmodern writing.

Keywords

Chronotope.   Mikhail Bakhtin emphasizes the interdependence of represented time and space by theorizing what he calls the 'chronotope' of the novel. He writes that the chronotope describes the 'intrinsic connectedness of temporal and spatial relationships ... expressed in literature' ('Chronotope,' 84). The chronotope strongly correlates with the narrative's genre, and most of Bakhtin's essay is dedicated to describing types of novelistic chronotope through a generic survey of ancient fiction, the adventure novel of ordeal, the adventure novel of everyday life, and the biographical novel. From Bakhtin's observations some speculations about modern genres can be made. For instance, a picaresque fiction in which the protagonist is often 'on the road' invokes a set of temporal assumptions about the plot structure of chance encounters, as well as calling up the physical characteristics of the path traveled upon. A fairy tale transpires in the less specific temporal location of 'once upon a time,' though its spatial locale may be quite specific. Historical fiction persuades its reader by a thorough invocation of both a specific place and time. Without the chronotope, as Bakhtin understands, the events of narrative would be impossible to represent: the chronotope 'provides the ground essential for the showing forth, the representability of events. And this is so thanks precisely to the special increase in density and concreteness of time markers—the time of human life, of historical time—that occurs within well-delineated spatial areas' ('Chronotope,' 250).

Gaps.   While narrative theorists use 'gaps' or the synonymous 'ellipses' to indicate jumps in the discourse over implicit story time, reception theorist Wolfgang Iser uses the term to indicate the fundamental asymmetry between text and reader. For Iser, a gap is a productive feature of the reading experience, for as a 'blank' or a 'negation' or a 'place of indeterminacy,' it provokes the reader to project, fill in, and revise in order to complete the reading process (*Act of Reading*, 165–9). Iser's gap overlaps with narratology's use of the term, as he notes that within a scene of pure dialogue, all that is left out (about accompanying thoughts, actions, setting, or interpretations of the characters' speech) invites the reader to fill in gaps. Iser's reading of a page of fiction would find far more gaps than a Genettian reading would allow. (Genette does describe paralipsis, a side-stepping or an omission in the narration that cannot be explained as a temporal omission, in *Narrative Discourse*, 51–3.) The gaps, for Iser, do more than leave out events; they drive the reading and interpretive process by provoking the reader to fill in with details that are not part of the discourse. As Iser writes, 'the asymmetry between text and reader stimulates a constituent activity on the part of the reader; this is given a specific structure by the blanks and the negations arising out of the text, and this structure controls the process of the interaction' (*Act of Reading*, 169–70). Iser's account of the reader's response to gaps is based on a psychoanalytic understanding of the mechanisms of communication and social interaction, with the caveat that text and reader cannot be 'face to face.' This difference accounts for the 'fundamental asymmetry' between text and reader.

Further reading

Bakhtin, Mikhail, 'Forms of Time and of the Chronotope in the Novel: Notes towards a Historical Poetics,' in *The Dialogic Imagination: Four Essays,* ed. Michael Holquist, trans. Caryl Emerson and Michael Holquist (University of Texas Press, 1981), 84–258.

Genette, Gérard, *Narrative Discourse: An Essay in Method*, trans. Jane E. Lewin (Cornell University Press, 1980). The classic treatment of the handling of time by narrative artists, with an emphasis on Proust.

— *Narrative Discourse Revisited* (1983), trans. Jane E. Lewin (Cornell University Press, 1988).

Iser, Wolfgang, *The Act of Reading: A Theory of Aesthetic Response* (Johns Hopkins University Press, 1978). Iser's account of the role of 'gaps' in narrative differs from Genette's use of the term.

Ricoeur, Paul, *Time and Narrative* (1983–85), vol. 1, trans. Kathleen McLaughlin and David Pellauer (University of Chicago Press, 1984); vol. 2, trans. Kathleen McLaughlin and David Pellauer (University of Chicago Press, 1985); vol. 3, trans. Kathleen Blamey and David Pellauer (University of Chicago Press, 1988).

Richardson, Brian, 'Beyond Story and Discourse: Narrative Time in Postmodern and Nonmimetic Fiction,' in Brian Richardson (ed.), *Narrative Dynamics: Essays on Time, Plot, Closure, and Frames* (Ohio State University Press, 2002), 47–63.

Rimmon-Kenan, Shlomith, *Narrative Fiction: Contemporary Poetics* (Methuen, 1983). See her useful explanation and expansion of Genette's ideas in 'Text: Time.'

7
Order and Disorder

Order and disorder in the storytelling can have a significant impact on how a reader receives, comprehends, and interprets a story. In the most orderly narration, the unfolding of time in the story may appear to be quite natural, and its analogy with 'clock time' or 'calendar time' gives it a good claim to be normative. However, in casual oral storytelling, people often loop back or flash forward to introduce salient information. A certain degree of disorderliness (as in, 'by the way, this had happened earlier,' or, 'did I forget to tell you that ...') is also natural and normative. Purely chronological narration may be less 'natural' than it looks at first. Few people would argue that extremely disorderly narration proves more challenging to follow, and experimental writers have often exploited disorder (at the end of this chapter, I describe an influential case of such an experiment, William Faulkner's 'A Rose for Emily'). Some kinds of disorder, however, are quite conventional and even traditional, as in the *in medias res* opening of classical epic, as described by Horace. While modernist fiction often exploits the effects of disorder, the *Bildungsroman* and fictional autobiography typically follow a chronological pattern.

Any generalization about a typical use of order should be questioned: 'realism' does not necessarily require orderly narration, for some kinds of psychological realism depend on representing a character's disorderly 'thoughts,' and experimental fiction may achieve its effects without rearranging the events of a plot line. While some accounts of narrative suggest a development from naive chronological narration (for instance in folklore) to more sophisticated disordering in modernist or postmodernist texts, a broader view of order discovers what theorists call anachronies, or disturbances to chronology, in many periods and kinds of fiction. This chapter provides vocabulary for the assessment of a narrative's handling of chronology.

When approaching questions of narrative order, students of form ask, Do the events of the plot get narrated in the order that they occur, or not? Once again we rely on the structuralist distinction between *story time*, the time that transpires within the imaginary world projected by the text, and *discourse time*, the time implied by the quantity of discourse, in its linear arrangement of elements in the text (sometimes called text time). As a beginning point for the discussion of order, we ask, when is the 'now' of the narrator? And when is the 'now' of the story? What is the relationship of these times to one another? When story time and discourse time run along in neat parallel to one another, with a plot that mimics clock or calendar chronology in its straight-ahead telling, we say that the discourse is orderly. When, as is often the case, some bits of a story time that occur 'before' or 'earlier' than the main stream of the narrative interrupt orderly telling, the discourse has become disorderly, which is not a term with negative connotations, though it may well make a text more challenging to understand. Disorder can be manipulated with great artfulness. In order to discuss disorder in a manageable fashion, narrative theorists describe the relationship of the order of the telling with respect to the order of the happening. The discussion of order and disorder in the narration is thus much more a matter of spatial arrangements within the text than of time, for which reason I have separated it from Chapter 6, on 'Timing.' Here, as in the previous chapter, the major theorist upon whose insights I draw is Gérard Genette.

Terms

Nearly all narratives have a forward-moving direction, with 'and then and then and then' logic dominating the narration. This quality dominates most narrative even when the writer employs a hypotactic style. (*Hypotaxis* makes use of subordination, dependent clauses and connectives suggesting consequence, whereas *parataxis* employs sequences with simple conjunctions and loose implicit connections.) Though complex, subordinated, intricate sentences may slow the reader's progress through a narrative, the momentum of storytelling still usually proceeds forwards in time.

As we will see, even extremely disorderly narratives often employ forwards narration for each narrative unit or episode. This is true even for some stories told in reverse. For instance, Christopher Nolan's 2001 film *Memento* proceeds backwards, exploiting a plot device in which the focal character has lost his short-term memory. The film begins at the end, and each (color) scene plays out what occurred before the previous scene (though, to complicate matters, the backward progression is itself interrupted with conventional flashbacks and a set of scenes in a different palette featuring the main character talking about the deeper past that he does remember). However, within each scene marked as 'before' the previous one, the narration moves forwards. Completely backward-moving narrative in prose fiction is extremely uncommon. Martin Amis's novel *Time's Arrow* (1991) moves backwards more consistently, in the fashion of a video run on rewind, so eating is represented as beginning with regurgitation and working forward to the full plate, and so forth. These unusual experiments in prose fiction and film only suggest the unusual demands a purely backward-moving narrative places on writer, reader, and viewer. Brian Richardson names the temporality of a backward-moving narrative that proceeds prospectively 'antinomic narrative' ('Beyond Story and Discourse,' 49–50), which suggests the logical contradiction or contrariness to natural laws inhering in such a strategy.

Turning to the much more prevalent forward-moving narratives, in which the direction of narration and plot are more or less matched, readers still find a great deal of variety in the handling of chronology. The more conventional uses of disorder are called *anachronies* by narrative theorists following Genette. This does not suggest the use of historical *anachronisms*, as when Benjamin Franklin chats on the phone during an episode of the television series *Bewitched*. Employment of anachrony indicates the use of disorderly (*anachronous*) narration, and it includes a whole range of devices from flashbacks to flash-forwards and extreme disordering that resists reconstitution into a straight-ahead plot.

To discover whether a particular instance of anachrony refers to events 'before' or 'after' the core events of the plot, one must first ascertain what sort of relationship the telling has to the happening. *Ulterior narration*, the most common situation, reports on events after they happen, and is often marked by the use of the past tense. In an ulterior narration, anachrony can refer to an event quite a bit closer to the time of the narration than the rest of the story, or quite a bit further back than the announced 'beginning' of the story. It can also refer to events in a time beyond the narrator's present. *Anterior narration*, marked by future or conditional tenses, is located before the narrated events occur. This kind of narration is used for prophecy, predictions, or the offering of possible outcomes. (When a small pocket of anterior narration occurs within an otherwise ulterior narration, we call that 'flash forward' a *prolepsis*.) On-the-spot reporting and diary entries could be described as ulterior reporting quite close to the events narrated, but common sense dictates a difference between a story told 'as the events unfold' and one told retrospectively. Thus we have a third category, *simultaneous narration*. Even in simultaneous narration, the duration of the storytelling always lags behind the events, as Sterne's narrator Tristram Shandy discovers to his chagrin. Like ulterior narration, simultaneous narration can contain anachronies reaching either into the past or the future. *Intermittent narration*, often applicable to epistolary fiction or diary entries, produces bursts of narration relating events that transpire in between moments of writing. Finally, alternating segments with different relationships to the time of events, as in the overlapping times of two sides of a correspondence in novels of letters, is called *intercalated narration*.

There are many variations on intercalated narration, especially in fiction with complex narrative situations. These examples, which often occur in postmodern or nonrealistic fiction, can prove the trickiest when one is attempting to identify anachronies. As critics of Genette's scheme have pointed out, the terms 'order' and 'disorder' make the most sense when anterior narration and the chronology of past, present, and future are considered normative. This means that certain subgenres of narrative, such as the usually orderly *Bildungsroman*, or the traditional historical novel, can be more readily described using Genette's terms, as Brian Richardson observes.

Given a narrative whose relationship to the time of the events can be established, however, Genette's terms for anachronies can be used to describe breaks in the chronological norm, referring to the past (in *analepses*) or to the future (in *prolepses*). (References to events that cannot be placed in relation to the plot's fundamental chronology are called *achronies*. Obedience to ordering principles other than chronology, for instance a spatial ordering, Genette calls *syllepsis*.) In the case of both analepses and prolepses, the sense of pastness or future location depends upon establishing a central extent of time, the narrative 'now' or present, which may in fact be narrated in past, present, or future tense. All descriptions of analepses or prolepses depend upon their relation to the plot's extent of narrated time, between beginning and ending. Thus some of the qualities of analepses and prolepses described below cannot be assessed until the reading of the narrative is finished.

Analepses/flashbacks

Nothing formally limits the content of an analepsis (or in film, a flashback): it can have a lot to do with the story at hand (providing background on a character, for instance) or it can seem entirely disconnected.

A flashback or an analepsis can narrate past events about something or someone already brought up in the story (the *backstory*), or it can introduce something or someone not already mentioned in the story. When an analepsis turns out in retrospect not to have had any bearing on the finished story, it may also be considered a *digression*. A single narrative can combine multiple analepses of a variety of different types. The *external analepsis* begins and ends before the starting point of the plot, what Genette called the first narration. Clearly, a novel with multiple plot lines should be differentiated from a single plot with an analepsis. When dual or multiple plot lines run according to different chronologies, a break from one plot line's temporal situation to another's does not constitute an analepsis, though certainly each plot line in a multiple narrative can have its own analepses. (In romance these shifts from plot to plot are sometimes called *intrelacement*, a term borrowed from textiles or basketry.) To the first-time reader of a complex multi-plot narrative, the shift to a second plot line set earlier may be indistinguishable from an external analepsis; in the absence of clear labeling, little differentiates the two kinds of breaks formally (see Chapter 8). The *internal analepsis* begins after the start of the narrative's main chronology, and the *mixed analepsis* begins earlier than the plot's beginning but ends within the extent of the plot's chronological extent. Analepses come in a variety of different sizes, so we speak of their *reach*, to indicate how far in time they lie from the 'present' of the main plot, and their *extent*, to suggest the duration of the out-of-order event. The function of analepses varies dramatically from instance to instance. An analepsis can return to a previously omitted event to fill in what happened earlier (Genette calls this a *'completing' analepsis*), or it can recall an event already narrated at least once (Genette calls this kind of internal analepsis *'repeating' analepsis*). The content of analepses can also contribute to their evaluation; for they can appear factual and *objective*, or *subjective* (as in memories and dreams). As with any formal device, the description of an anachrony initiates an interpretive process that can also include these questions: Why was this information introduced out of order? What effect does the return or recall have on the reader's perception of the characters, the story, and the narrator?

Prolepses/anticipations/flashforwards

Like analepses, which reach into the past, forward-reaching *prolepses* can also be characterized according to a set of traits enumerated by Genette and others. *External prolepses* begin and end after the endpoint of the main plot; *internal prolepses* begin and end before the temporal conclusion of the story, and a very common type in the summary wrap-up of characters' later lives, the *mixed prolepsis*, begins before the conclusion but stretches forward into the future. Prolepses, too, have *reach* (measured from the end of the main plot's time) and *extent* (they are often quite brief in terms of text, but can contain lifetimes' worth of events in compressed form). They differ from analepses in that they may fill in, give advance notice, or repeat, but they do not recall or return. (A prolepsis may of course prompt recollection in a reader.) Though a prolepsis may also be evaluated according to its apparent objectivity (providing facts about the subsequent lives of characters) or subjectivity (containing an unverifiable vision of a future otherwise unrecorded), prolepsis as a narrative mode has often been employed to make a special claim of authority. Prophecy narrates future events that can only be called into question after their future has become an experienced past. Narrative fiction borrows the authoritative quality of the prophet's prolepsis to endow the narrator with powers beyond the normal human ability to know, record, and remember.

Analytical strategies

Anachronous texts require that readers attempt to rearrange events to reconstitute the plot. When this is possible (as in most cases), a mystery may be solved or an implicit problem may be revealed. Gaps in time or in the telling may be discovered. The repetition of plot events through recalls rewards critical attention and may suggest key passages for analysis. Many orderly texts contain disorderly episodes, as in a straight-ahead narration of a journey peppered with a sequence of flashbacks. Resolutely straightforward narration rarely does without internal references to the 'past,' and as in all formal analysis, deviations from the prevailing norms of the text demand interpretation. Posing basic questions about the handling of order can yield valuable insights in the characterization of the teller(s), who may offer contrasting views of the same events, or may reveal areas of unreliability. Asking why the discourse is arranged the way it is, or (alternately) wondering how the story would differ if its events were presented in a more or less orderly fashion, can lead to more substantive discoveries about the effect chronology has on readers. It is just as important to notice the craft of ordering events in chronologically arranged mimetic texts, as in those that present actions in deliberate disarrangements.

Reading all the way first.   The discussion of order and disorder can be handled provisionally during a first reading, but a thorough and accurate analysis of narrative chronology requires that the text be read through all the way, then (if it is disorderly) reconsitituted into the order of occurrence (if the text allows that). Next, the text must be broken down into component episodes, usually anchored by kernel plot events, for purposes of labeling. Genette applies alphabetic labels to the units, but names characterizing the action work just as effectively. (When achrony or syllepsis occur, the narrative structure may resist the kind of reconstitution that many disordered narratives permit. Omission of temporal indicators and contradictory time schemes can impede reorganization into a tidy forward-moving plot, and that discovery is itself an opportunity for interpretation.)

As Dorrit Cohn demonstrated in her classroom teaching of anachrony,[1] William Faulkner's 'A Rose for Emily' can be reordered into narrative sub-units bearing the following labels:

Anachronies in 'A Rose for Emily': reorganized in order

  (1) life with Father
  (2) Father's death
  (3) Barron affair
  (4) poison purchase
  (5) end of Barron affair
  (6) smell
  (7) tax remission
  (8) painting lessons (Sartoris' death)
  (9) tax dispute (Commission visit)
(10) Emily's death
(11) discovery of body

The text itself presents these narrative units in an extremely disorderly fashion:

Anachronies in 'A Rose for Emily': as they appear

I.   (10) Emily's death
           (7) tax remission
           (9) tax dispute (Commission visit) (go inside)
II.   (6) smell
           (1) life with Father
           (2) Father's death (ladies call)

III.	(3)	Barron affair
	(4)	poison purchase (cousins)
IV.	(3)	Barron affair (minister's visit)
	(5)	end of Barron affair
	(8)	painting lessons (Sartoris' death)
	(10)	Emily's death
V.	(10)	Emily's death
	(11)	discovery of body

The juxtaposition of these two lists show that Faulkner depends heavily on internal analepses, and raises several questions that bear on interpretation, such as, Why does the narrator (a plural first-person narrator) tell the story out of order, when the corporate voice clearly has access to all but one of the events as they happened? Perhaps the original shock of comprehension experienced by the community can be passed on and shared by using anachronies that replicate their confusion—a straight-ahead telling would make it too easy for the reader to be wiser than the corporate narrator. This is only one possibility for describing the motives of a narrator who generalizes and obstructs by telling in a disorderly fashion. Perhaps the disorderly telling compels re-reading in the way that a more orderly narration would not. The suspenseless narration does not invite a reader to look for clues, but Faulkner has embedded them to be recognized upon re-reading. Perhaps most importantly, the central shock of the story implies an event, or sequence of events, occurring between (5) end of the Barron affair, and (10) Emily's death. The omission of direct narration of Miss Emily's behavior is a significant gap that Faulkner never completes with an analepsis. The reader fills that gap with comprehension that only comes after reading the story all the way through. In a disorderly narrative employing many anachronies, a significant gap may at first be disguised by the expectation that reordering will complete the plot. On the other hand, the invitation to re-order and thus restore the plot events may only invite the application of the *post hoc ergo propter hoc* fallacy (see Chapter 5). Just because events follow one another does not mean that they are causally linked, and the restoration of order to a disorderly text may reveal the lack of relationship among a chain of events just as readily as a completed whole. For instance, B. S. Johnson's experimental novel *The Unfortunates* (1969) comes in a box containing 27 sections, temporarily wrapped in a loose paper slip. The first and last fascicle are labeled as such, but the others are supposed to be read in random order. Indeed, only by comparing notes with another first-time reader of a pristine copy of *The Unfortunates* would a reader be able to verify whether the original set of fascicles appears in the same order from box to box of the edition.

Keywords

Ambiguity.   A disorderly narration that employs achrony can generate narrative ambiguities, and interpretive cruxes may depend upon the lack of temporal information that allows for a certain reconstruction of the order of plot events. Using the term 'ambiguity' points back to New Critical interpretive practices, but the New Critics were especially interested in ambiguities in poetic language rather than in narrative.

Enigma.   Disorder of a type that defers or postpones narration in favor of a later analepsis can contribute to the process of generating narrative enigmas, which Roland Barthes elegantly demonstrates in the post-structuralist classic, *S/Z*. There, Barthes introduces the hermeneutic code, through which enigmas can be 'distinguished, suggested, formulated, held in suspense, and finally disclosed' (*S/Z*, 19). Though enigmas can be introduced without narrative disorder, a combination of disordering and elision (gaps) frequently produces enigmas. Anachronies can also be used to resolve enigmas through their filling-in function.

Spatial form.   Joseph Frank's influential 1945 essay 'Spatial Form in Modern Literature' wedded the notion of a disorderly text to modernism. He saw modernist poetry as breaking up the 'time-flow' in order to attempt to suspend logical, orderly reading practices. A legacy of Frank's idea appears in the common assumption that a disorderly narrative is more subversive than an orderly one.

Further reading

Barthes, Roland, *S/Z: An Essay* (1970), trans. Richard Miller, preface by Richard Howard (NY: Hill & Wang, 1974).

Genette, Gérard, *Narrative Discourse: An Essay in Method*, trans. Jane E. Lewin (Cornell University Press, 1980), chapter 1, 'Order,' 33–85.

Richardson, Brian, 'Beyond Story and Discourse: Narrative Time in Postmodern and Nonmimetic Fiction,' in *Narrative Dynamics: Essays on Time, Plot, Closure, and Frames*, ed. Brian Richardson (Ohio State University Press, 2002), 47–63.

Rimmon-Kenan, Shlomith, *Narrative Fiction: Contemporary Poetics* (Methuen, 1983).

8
Levels: Realms of Existence

Every narrative invites the creation of a story world[1] in the reader's or listener's mind. The characters and events of the story transpire within this imagined space, which may be lightly sketched or elaborately described in the text. Some theorists characterize the story world as a projection implied by the action and characters, some as a bounded set of possibilities strongly guided by and partially constituting genre, and some as a fictional level, surrounded by nonfictional apparatus (and at times containing additional layers of fiction within it). Bakhtin's chronotope (discussed as a keyword in Chapter 6) combines the time/place of the narrative level in order to characterize a genre's and story's possibilities. The details of place and space that contribute to the imagining of the story world are ordinarily referred to as the setting. The elements of setting resemble fictional characters, the other 'existents' inside story worlds, in that they provide the particulars out of which readers create fictional worlds in their minds. Sometimes narratives demand that readers imagine worlds inside worlds, not always in conformity with the laws of physics. Theories of fictional worlds and spatiality in literature are discussed in the next chapter, where I consider the fictional worlds that are designed to contain other worlds, as in some fantasy fiction. This chapter takes on a more limited task, the description of the manipulation of stories within stories that occurs when a character becomes a narrator, or when a story is presented inside another story. The precise description of narrative levels allows a critic to describe how different zones of story relate to one another and opens up their layering for interpretation.

Terms

The analysis of narrative levels includes and goes beyond analysis of *setting*, the specific time(s), place(s), and social realms in which characters move and plot actions transpire. Establishing *narrative level* involves characterizing the story world in relation to the textual apparatus that surrounds it, and in relation to the stories it may frame or surround.[2] Considering the position of the narrator as 'inside' or 'outside' the story world relies upon the idea of narrative level. All narrative fiction has a discourse or textual level and a story world. These distinctions reflect a basic division within narrative level, as comprised of (at least) a *discourse level*, a realm of narrated words-in-order, and the *story level*, a realm of imagined actions and agents.[3] Narrators are described according to their relationships to the other figures in these levels. Narrative situation, treated in Chapter 3, describes where the narrator is located, how overtly or covertly the narrator makes his or her presence felt, and what relationship the narrator has to the characters, in one or more of whom perspective may be invested. Depending on the narrative situation, the discourse level and the story level may overlap: a self-narrating narrator who describes his or her experiences consonantly and chronologically creates a story world that very closely resembles the level of the narration. Despite exceptions like this one, narrative theorists have found it useful to retain the idea of a level 'outside' the story. Perhaps only the operations of book production and textual arrangement reside there, but this level mediates between our real world of active reading and the imagined projected world that we create as we read. In addition, many narratives have plural narrative levels beyond the necessary discourse level and story level. Each narrative level has its own story world and setting(s), however sketchily supplied.

To take a famous example, Geoffrey Chaucer's *Canterbury Tales* (c.1387) take place in a story world that could be labeled 'the pilgrimage.' This primary narrative level contains several settings since the pilgrims travel during the story, but setting becomes more attenuated as it only appears in the links between tales or in brief references in some of the tales' prologues. The story world is defined as much by its action as by its setting: the characters gather at an inn and set off on a journey towards Canterbury together, agreeing to pass the time by telling one another tales. This primary story world acts as a frame, in places very lightly invoked, in which Chaucer embeds the tales of the various Canterbury pilgrims. Each of these tales has its own story world, sometimes more than one, and sometimes quite complex in its own right (as for instance in *The Knight's Tale*).

The analysis of narrative level takes in large-scale frame tales such as Chaucer's *Canterbury Tales* or Boccaccio's *Decameron* (c.1350), both of which organize copious stories narrated by different tellers into coherent overarching storytelling situations, but it also includes examples where stories occur within stories (within stories), like the narrative equivalent of a matryoshka doll. Italo Calvino's *If on a Winter's Night a Traveller* (1979) is a frequently cited example of the latter technique, sometimes called 'the Chinese box narrative.' Thus to follow the spatial metaphor implied by narrative level, fictions can present complications in level that result in a deeper set of levels, or variation can occur in a more horizontal fashion. Mary Shelley's *Frankenstein* (1818) illustrates some of the possible complications. The entire novel is made up of letters, in which accounts by a secondary narrator (Victor) are embedded. Inside Victor's narrative many other stories are embedded, including the monster's self-narrated story.

Narrative level can be strictly adhered to or invoked to be violated, by breaking what appear to be ontological boundaries between story worlds in logic-defying *metalepses* (singular form: metalepsis). Indeed, a great deal of the interest in discussions of narrative level has been generated by postmodern or experimental narrative which defies, or plays games with, the conventions of level. Brian McHale describes *frame-breaking*, another term for metalepsis, as a characteristic feature of postmodernist fiction (McHale, 197). One of the great postmodern artists of narrative level, John Barth, is the author not only of 'Menelaiad,' a seven-layered story in *Lost in the Funhouse* (1968), but also of one of the founding essays in the theory of narrative levels, 'Tales within Tales within Tales' (1981). *Metafiction*, a kind of fiction that draws attention to the fictionality of narrative texts, often calls attention to conventions of narrative level and sometimes plays games in which border violations occur.

The metaleptic play of frame-breaking assumes some familiarity with the conventions of narrative level. These conventions are closely tied to narrative situation. As I discuss in Chapter 3, narrators can be located outside the story world, within the story world, or they can narrate stories with their own story worlds from inside an articulated story world. A caveat: an established narrative situation can change during the course of the text without actually violating the conventions of level. In an example I have mentioned before, Iris Murdoch's *The Philosopher's Pupil*, the narrator appears throughout the text to narrate from outside the story world. However, the last page of the novel reveals that 'N' lives inside the story world, with the characters. The readjustment of narrative situation teases a reader who assumes that a narrator who behaves omnisciently must be located outside the story world, and it challenges the reader to go back and check the narrator's consistency, but it does not in fact violate narrative level. Some examples of frame-breaking are flagrant, as in Martin Amis's novel *Money* (1984), when a character named Martin Amis walks into a bar. There, the existence of the author inside his own obviously fictional world defies logic. It has been reported that Kingsley Amis threw his son's novel down in exasperation when he read that metaleptic joke. Other metaleptic violations of level can occur horizontally, as when a character the reader 'knows' to be the inhabitant of one story world shows up in defiance of historical conventions in another story world.

In most cases, narrative level operates according to conventions that separate a teller's realm of existence from the teller's own story world. Whenever a character in a narrative begins telling a story, not only has the character become a secondary narrator, but a secondary story world has also been created. The metaphor of nested levels allows the critic to label and characterize each narrator and level separately, for each level can employ a different set of conventions. For instance, it is quite common for a third-person externally narrated fictional world to contain characters who pause to tell stories in the first person about their own experiences, or in third person about other characters and events, real or imagined. We distinguish the two layers of story as belonging to primary and secondary narrators, and the narrative levels they create can also be enumerated, as primary, secondary, or tertiary narrative levels.[4] Barth's 'Menelaiad' takes the experiment to the seventh level, and famously ends with a set of quotation marks asserting the conclusion of all the layers.

The story thus told by a secondary narrator is referred to as an *embedded story* (*inset story*) or an *interpolated tale*, though the latter term implies that the inner text has been put in between primary plot events. Though the terms are often used interchangeably, 'interpolation' suggests narration that occurs during a pause or a gap, whereas 'embedded story' clearly signals the initiation of a new narrative level. It is important to note that embedded texts can be non-narrative objects, such as a reprint of a newspaper advertisement within a story. This use of embedding signals that the embedded text is to be regarded as 'real' to the characters of the fictional world; the embedded text functions as a thing in an imagined world of things. When the embedded text includes narration that invokes a distinct story world, then a secondary level exists.

Embedded narratives have a variety of functions when they are considered in relation to the framing level in which they occur. They can, as in the frame tales discussed above, comprise the main narratives, each embedded text possessing its own full-fledged fictional world, setting, characters, plot and resolution. The use of the term 'frame tale' indicates that the secondary level, the level of the embedded texts, is of primary interest, as in Chaucer's *Canterbury Tales*. Within primary narratives not helpfully described as frame tales, embedded narratives can advance the action or explain *backstory* (like an analepsis, but with a new narrator doing the telling). They can predict (like a prolepsis), establish thematic relationships through narrative analogies, or serve persuasive or revelatory purposes. Though it is a dramatic example, the play within the play in *Hamlet* is a famous case. The staging of 'The Mousetrap' makes an attempt to reveal and entrap by startling the guilty within the play's primary world into a reaction. Embedded narratives can distract from the plot line in the primary level, obstruct the progress of the plot, or divert the reader into the beginning of a set of steps down a *staircase narrative* (this term suggests a narrative that takes the reader down into a nested set of levels without bringing them to closure back at the primary level at the end).

Finally, an embedded narrative may serve the special function of mirroring the text in which it appears. Called *mise en abyme*, and sometimes known in English as *the mirror in the text*, this kind of embedding invites interpretation of a small part of a narrative as a focused representation of the whole in which it appears. Andre Gide suggested the term *mise en abyme*, apparently in reference to a heraldic design, in which in one quadrant of a shield an image of the entire shield appears. That image would itself contain a miniature version of itself, and so on, creating the optical illusion (at least in visual arts applications) of an infinite regress into space. The French term alludes to the vertiginous invitation of such an image, meaning 'thrown into the abyss.'[5] The verbal, narrative form of *mise en abyme* necessarily differs from visual embedding. Though limitations of space demand that the embedded *mise en abyme* be shorter and less detailed than the surrounding text it replicates, it presents an image of enough aspects of the whole to be seen as mirroring it. This can be achieved through titling, reduplication of a story line, or through a vivid analogy. Some critics consider episodes at the same narrative level as the primary fictional world instances of *mise en abyme*, but most theorists describe *mise en abyme* as a kind of embedded text, which opens a secondary narrative level. Because the use of *mise en abyme* draws attention to a text's fictionality, the device is associated with metafiction, modernist, and some postmodern fiction, but examples from earlier narratives, including medieval dream visions, can be usefully compared to contemporary examples.

Analytical strategies

Focus on the narrator's character.   When a secondary narrator appears as a character in a primary fictional world before taking up the task of narration, the tale may contribute to the understanding of the narrator as a character or as a representative type. This traditional method has enjoyed enduring popularity in the study of *The Canterbury Tales*, where the relationship of the teller to the tale is a perennial question. Chaucer's text provides an array of alternative answers to such questions. In some cases, the kind of tale (for instance, the bawdy fabliaux told by the Miller) seems to suit what we know of the personality and social status of the teller. In other cases, critics have found ironic relationships between the narrators and the stories they tell. (Textual scholarship has also raised questions about which tales were written for which characters.) This strategy takes an interest in the way a story reveals a narrator's psychology, or in the associations of particular genres with appropriate (or unlikely) tellers, understood as social types.

A more recent application of this kind of reading occurs whenever a detective fiction (or modernist novel) presents testimony that must be judged in light of its teller's reliability.

Focus on formal traits.   It is not uncommon for a text with multiple levels to include complications of order as well. The anachronies described in the previous chapter can occur within or surrounding embedded texts, and the contents of embedded texts can in some circumstances function as anachronies do, though with the difference of an altered narrative source. In addition, the interest in narrative levels within narrative theory has focused some attention on what Genette calls 'paratexts,' those elements of the text that surround the actual narration and presentation of the primary fictional world. Genette sees the paratexts as liminal features comprising the threshold a reader passes through on the way into the fictional world. Paratexts include titles, epigraphs, dedications, and afterwords. Paratexts can be usefully interpreted, particularly as they condition the state of mind in which a reader enters a fictional world, and they can also be the subject of much fun under the guise of 'laying bare the device,' drawing attention to established but often ignored conventions. A recent example of a work that plays with the norms of the paratext is Dave Eggers' *A Heartbreaking Work of Staggering Genius* (2000), where Eggers tinkers with even the publisher's formal presentation of the book; the *locus classicus* for such fun is of course Sterne's *Tristram Shandy*. Though defamiliarization (making strange) and laying bare the device are often associated with self-referential texts and frame-breaking, the Russian Formalists who introduced these concepts advanced them as traits of literariness more generally construed.

Keywords

Frame, framing.   Even within narrative theory, 'frame' has a variety of meanings. In this chapter I have recommended using it for the primary narrative of the frame tale, but it is sometimes often used as a synonym for the primary level. Framing in narrative form can be paratextual (circumtextual). It can refer to the 'frame of reference' in which a reader places the text (extratextual). It can operate within a text, without necessarily creating a new narrative level, when narrative fictions surround particular discrete episodes or passages with boundaries that act like frames in drawing attention to the difference of the materials within (see the account of narrative annexes in Chapter 5). In addition, genre, literary period, or historical context may create a frame that renders a work legible or especially meaningful (intertextual or contextual frames). This brief list only begins to suggest the valences of frames and framing. Narrative itself is sometimes described as a frame. The disciplines of art history, law, cognitive science, and artificial intelligence theory also use the idea of frames and framing in ways that can augment or conflict with the meaning with respect to narrative form. Thus, frame is one of the many formal terms that should be situated explicitly in order to avoid confusion.

Interpellation.   Sometimes mistaken for interpolation because the two words are homonyms, interpellation has nothing to do with narrative level. Instead, it suggests the work of the Marxist theorist Louis Althusser or his interpreters. According to Althusser, ideology hails or calls (interpellates) subjects as subjects—in simple terms, we know who we are because we are told who we are by ideology. Interpellation has entered narrative theory by way of considerations of a reader's identification with a reflecting character, or resistance to that invitation of the narrative structure.

Further reading

Barth, John, 'Tales within Tales within Tales,' *Antaeus* 43 (1981) 45–63. A writer's view of embedding.
Dällenbach, Lucien, *The Mirror in the Text* (University of Chicago Press, 1989). On *mise en abyme*.
Furedy, Viveca, 'A Structural Model of Phenomena with Embedding in Literature and Other Arts,' *Poetics Today* 10:4 (1989), 45–69. On embedding.
Genette, Gérard, *Narrative Discourse: An Essay in Method*, trans. Jane E. Lewin (Cornell University Press, 1980), 227–37. On narrative levels.

Lemon, Lee T. and Marion J. Reis (ed. and trans.), *Russian Formalist Criticism: Four Essays* (University of Nebraska Press, 1965). See Victor Shklovsky on defamiliarization (13–21) and Boris Tomashevsky on 'laying bare the device' (84).

Nelles, William, 'Stories within Stories: Narrative Levels and Embedded Narrative,' *Studies in the Literary Imagination* 215:1 (1992), 79–96. Nelles believes that all embedded narratives involve to some degree the effects of metalepsis.

Reid, Ian, *Narrative Exchanges* (Routledge, 1992). Reid treats four different sorts of framing in narrative: circumtextual, extratextual, intratextual, and intertextual.

Ron, Moshe, 'The Restricted Abyss: Nine Problems in the Theory of Mise en Abyme,' *Poetics Today* 8 (1987), 417–38.

9
Fictional Worlds and Fictionality

Long before there were theories of the novel, there were robust theories of fiction and fictionality. The fact that some of them appear to refer to poetry may have presented an obstacle to seeing their connection to narrative fiction. The philosophical interest in possible worlds, in the use of world-making as a mode of thought and experimentation, and in questions about the distinctiveness of fictional world-making provoke a look back at early theorists. Perhaps the most well-known statements in Philip Sidney's *Defense of Poesie* (*c*.1579–80)[1] are those in which Sidney claims that *poesy*, the fiction of poets, constructs an alternative world. While practitioners of all the arts (by which Sidney means disciplines) are based on 'the works of nature,'

> Only the poet, disdaining to be tied to any such subjection, lifted up with the vigor of his own invention, doth grow in effect another nature, in making things either better than nature bringeth forth, or quite anew, forms such as never were in nature, as the Heroes, Demigods, Cyclops, Chimeras, Furies and such like; so as he goeth hand in hand with nature, not enclosed within the narrow warrant of her gifts, but freely ranging only within the zodiac of his own wit.
>
> Nature never set forth the earth in so rich tapestry as divvers poets have done, neither with pleasant rivers, fruitful trees, sweet smelling flowers, nor whatsoever else may make the too much loved earth more lovely. Her world is brazen, the poets only deliver a golden. (14–15)

This unlimited, alternative Nature, invented by an imagination that is as well organized and as vast as the zodiac, honors 'the heavenly Maker of that maker' (17) who has created the fictional world. Thus, poesy offers a special kind of imitation, not just a mirror held up to nature. Further, poesy (fiction) attempts to bridge the gap between God and fallen humanity, 'sith our erected wit maketh us know what perfection is, and yet our infected will keepeth us from reaching unto it' (17). It works by making manifest an Idea (this is Sidney's term for a general concept) that provides a superior moral example, such as a true lover, a constant friend, a valiant soldier, a right prince, an excellent man, or a just and magnanimous ruler. For Sidney, the consequences of representation lie in the judicious reader, for that reader is not only to imitate these characters, but also to 'learn aright why and how that maker made him' (16). Though the purposes of fiction have certainly expanded beyond the idealizing role that Sidney the romancer describes, the method employed to create characters still depends upon the creation of a fictional world.

Fiction in Sidney's terms enacts a double action: it prepares the reader's wits to receive heart-ravishing knowledge (10) in speaking pictures and it enjoins the reader to move beyond delight and the reception of knowledge to interpret. Sidney describes the poet's invitation of readers into fictional worlds through narration as 'an imaginative ground-plot of a profitable invention' (58). This architectural metaphor of a ground-plot has a long history after Sidney's use, for many narrative artists have employed similar spatial metaphors for their creations. Spatial language for the actions of fiction does not arise first from critics and theorists; it has a prehistory in writers' comments and readers' ways of understanding their experiences in reading fiction.[2]

Sidney emphasizes the role of the maker, but he also imagines readers or auditors. Using words arranged 'in delightful proportion' and a story ('a tale which holdeth children from play and old men in the chimney corner'), the poet, characterized here as a narrative artist, invites readers into a fictional world: 'For he doth not only show the way, but giveth so sweet a prospect into the way, as will entice any man to enter into it' (38). This practice makes poesy the 'most fruitful knowledge' (56) because it goes beyond the precepts or definitions of the moral philosopher and the examples of the historian, to bring the general and particular together in a perfect picture.

The poet succeeds because 'he yieldeth to the powers of the mind an image of that whereof the philosopher bestoweth but a wordish description, which neither strike, pierce, nor possess the sight of the soul so much as that other doth' (28). To put it positively, in reading fiction the reader's mind's eye will be struck, pierced, and possessed by an image that yields 'true lively knowledge' (28). Fiction here is conceived as a technique of visualization which 'illuminate(s) or figure(s) forth' by using 'the speaking picture of poesy' (28). These speaking pictures make up the rich tapestry of the golden world. Sidney's own definition of poesy incorporates the term: 'poesy therefore is an art of imitation ... that is to say, a representing, counterfeiting, or figuring forth—to speak metaphorically, a speaking picture— with this end, to teach and delight' (18). Sidney's metaphor describes not only representation, but also the reader's apprehension of a fictional world, in the form of a mental image, in which characters speak—and out of which a reader may derive the Idea. To the attacks made by 'dispraisers' of fiction, the claim that poetry is 'the mother of lies' is the most famous, as is Sidney's reply that 'the poet nothing affirms, and therefore never lieth' (57). Infamously, according to Plato, the poets lie. Sidney defends fiction that claims (untruthfully) to be true. It makes things up without deceiving: it delivers an alternative, golden world which differs from the brazen world of our experience.

Sidney's claims about fiction show world-making to be an important ingredient of fiction (poesy) and fictionality. They were made at a time in the Renaissance when both artists and scientists embraced world-making as a powerful way of posing questions, producing alternative political visions, and imagining experiments. To be sure, not all world-making creates fictional worlds, but narrative fiction engages in world-making in order to function. Sidney's ideas make a good starting point for understanding the importance of fictional worlds to conceptions of fictionality. As we shall see in this chapter, the nature of fictionality has often been defined by its impossible truth claims, by its creation of alternative possible worlds, and by its exhibition of narrative strategies that do not appear in other narrative texts. It has also often been defined, as Sidney defines it, by contrast to related forms of narrative, such as history. This chapter takes up some of these old problems, which Sidney is neither the first nor the only one to state, in order to suggest the entangelement of fictionality, fictional worlds, and aspects of narrative form. The next chapter, on 'Disguises,' considers the special case of narrative fiction which presents itself in the formal guise of nonfictional texts. Here, I discuss the way in which narrative fiction invites the building of simple and complex fictional worlds, and how certain traits of these fictional worlds, including their narration, may distinguish fiction formally from other world-making narratives, such as history.

Terms

Fictional worlds are comprised of the set of imagined materials presented by a text for re-imagining by the reader. Since the materials of fictional world-making are presented through narrative discourse, the reception and creation of a fictional world is a dynamic process. Narrators and their fictional auditors; characters and their actions, speeches, and thoughts; the duration and order of represented time, the dimension and details of settings; levels of story; and all the items or accessories denoted or implied by the words of a narrative come together in a reader's mind to form an imagined world. Though theorists and philosophers of possible worlds have demonstrated that this process also occurs in nonfictional narratives and in disciplines far afield from fiction-making,[3] for the purposes of this chapter, I focus on fictional world-making. It should be clear from this opening definition that fictional world-making is an effect of both writing and reading narrative. Even quite scanty cues from a writer can set a reader's world-making process in motion.

Fictional worlds may resemble the real world, but the world-making of narrative fiction takes place whether a text is realistic or not. Each fictional world both opens up and limits the possibilities for representation, since no fictional world, no matter how committed to verisimilitude, can refer to more than an infinitesimal fraction of the actual world. Thomas Pavel has written well about how fictional worlds are created and limited by their borders, their size, their complexity, their distance from the implied reader (remoteness), their conventions, and their relationship to the surrounding culture. For Pavel, incompleteness is a key feature of fictional worlds, and coherence, though sometimes a quality of fictional worlds, need not be present. Pavel makes the point that human beings have long lived in 'notoriously incongruous universes' without needing unity and cohesiveness (*Fictional Worlds*, 50). Fictional worlds, according to Pavel, are as various as fictional practices, and they include 'salient' worlds with no corresponding references to verifiable existents in the actual world.

Fictionality thus encompasses fictional worlds that pretend to be representations of the real world and fictional worlds that make highly improbable, even impossible, *truth claims*. Some definitions of narrative fiction hinge on the presence of truth claims, though it is usually recognized that these truth claims are imbued with a high degree of indeterminacy, as Sidney noted when he said that the poet is not a liar, because he affirms nothing about the real (brazen) world. Michael Riffaterre writes in *Fictional Truth* that, 'Fiction is a genre whereas lies are not' and 'A novel always contains signs whose function is to remind readers that the tale they are being told is imaginary' (*Fictional Truth*, 1). (The objection that some early fictions and a minority of contemporary narrative fictions present themselves in the guise of the nonfiction genres I take up in Chapter 10.) The invitation to understand a narrative's claims as imaginary initiates world-making: as Wolfgang Iser suggests, it invites the creation of an 'As If' world. That world may resemble the actual world or not. Realistic fiction asserts its reflection of the actual world in a way that may render its fictionality transparent, but realistic narratives rely on the reader's capacity to generate a sense of wholeness and actuality out of a finite set of references, the reader's world-making. Realistic fictions are as separate from the everyday world of a reader as the most flagrant make-believe. Wolfgang Iser argues that the reader's consciousness of a gap between actual and fictional worlds is instigated by the existence of the imaginary. He describes the fictional world as 'bracketed off' from the reality within which it exists, but he focuses on the 'oscillation' between these separated realms. The bracketed fictional world thus reveals what has been hidden in the real world and brings about the comparison of worlds (*Prospecting*, 272). Bringing to mind the implicit values and explicit contents of a fictional world can thus provoke thought about a reader's experience of the real world: one does not need to concur with the truth claims of a fiction to experience fictional world-making as a process that leads to understanding.

A reader attentive to the construction of a fictional world will notice both differences and similarities between it and the reader's real world. Examining inclusions and omissions of fictional worlds, together with their truth claims, provides rich opportunities for interpretation of narrative as cultural and time-bound artifacts. Thomas Pavel's procedure of examining fictional worlds' borders, their size, their complexity, their distance from the implied reader (remoteness), their conventions, and their relationship to the surrounding culture meshes well with a variety of contextualist interpretive practices. The fictionality that concerns Pavel is, as he puts it, a 'historically variable property.' Separated on one side from myth and on the other from actuality, fictional worlds can undergo changes in status in time: 'Fictional realms sometimes arise through the extinction of the belief in a mythology; in other cases, conversely, fictionalization originates in the loss of the referential link between the characters and events described in a literary text and their real counterparts' (*Fictional Worlds*, 80–1). With this sort of fluidity in the notion of fictionality and the possibility that texts may migrate from one category to another over time, come possible extensions of fictionality into other realms of discourse and understanding. Gerald Graff attacks this view, often attributed to post-structuralists and postmodernists, in his *Literature against Itself*: 'critics now sometimes suggest, by a kind of tautology, that literary meanings are fictions because all meanings are fictions, even those of nonliterary language, including the language of criticism. In its most extreme flights, this critical view asserts that 'life' and 'reality' are themselves fictions' (*Literature against Itself*, 151).[4] It is useful in responding to cautions such as Graff's to distinguish between the view that all meanings are fictions and the view that meanings of both fictional and nonfictional kinds have often been expressed in narrative formats.

Thus, complicating the spread of fictionality beyond traditionally defined fictional texts is a second factor, that of nonfiction's and fiction's shared quality of *narrativity*. Because of a wave of interest in narrative in various disciplines other than fiction, the difference of fictional narrative from other nonfiction narratives has sometimes been blurred. What these types of texts have in common is their narrativity. Narrativity is the set of qualities marking narrative and helping a reader or viewer perceive the difference between narrative and non-narrative texts: possessing a narrator, suggesting a temporal arrangement, mentioning events, characterizing active agents would all be qualities of narrativity. Narrativity can, of course, be a trait of nonfictional narratives, as Hayden White and others have observed of historical narrative. A text or other representational object may possess a degree of narrativity without being fully narrative. White uses the term 'narrativize' to distinguish those texts that are merely narrated from those that, being 'narrativized,' have the form of a story. He describes a difference between a historical discourse that 'openly adopts a perspective that looks out on the world and reports it and a discourse that feigns to make the world speak itself and speak itself as a story' ('Value of Narrativity,' 2–3). The latter example possesses narrativity. Narrativity does not necessarily imply fictionality, but simply the adherence to a set of very basic conventions suggesting a temporal structure, a plot (conflict; beginning, middle, end), and agents. Because formal analysis of narrative fiction has provided the implicit standard elements of narrativity, however, a slippage towards a position that sees nonfictional narrative and fictional narrative as no different from one another can sometimes be observed. Indeed, Käte Hamburger argues in *The Logic of Literature* that narrative itself suggests fictionality, particularly in its allusions to movements in imagined spaces and in its use of a past tense to suggest a present situation.[5] Neither of these qualities can be used as a formal test of fictionality without external information: Does the represented space exist? Does the 'past' that is put before the reader's eyes refer to a reconstruction of actual events, or to an imagined sequence of actions that never happened?

The student of narrative form may reasonably hope to know if one can tell the difference between fictional and nonfictional narrative by examining the formal traits of the texts. Dorrit Cohn argues in 'Signposts of Fictionality' that three formal features distinguish fictional narrative from nonfictional narratives. First, the explanatory model of story and discourse levels works for fiction but not for nonfiction narratives, because these refer to what she describes as a prior existence, a level of reference (or the zone of external documentation to which citations refer). Secondly, the representation of characters' consciousness demonstrates what Cohn calls freedom from referential constraints: in history, for instance, writing what a figure 'thought' would require reference to documentary evidence. In fiction, the minds of characters can be known in a way no one can know another's mind in life or through historical research. Thirdly, narrative fiction employs a narrator separable from the author, and it is normal to discover differences between the narrator's views and the implicit views of the author. This would be considered an abnormal rift in nonfictional writing, where the narrator represents the author's views. The scandal among historians and opinion-makers about *Dutch: A Memoir of Ronald Reagan* (1999) arose, in part, from author Edmund Morris laying bare the device of the narrator in history by personifying the voice of the narrator and placing a fictionalized version of his narrating self inside the story world. The fact that such a move can cause controversy in history but passes without notice in fiction emphasizes an epistemological difference that is embodied in certain conventions of narrative form.

The difference between history and fiction can also be understood by thinking about the kinds of possible worlds they permit. As Lubomír Dolozel has observed, both kinds of narrative employ possible worlds, but historical worlds are subject to restrictions that do not pertain to fictional worlds. This corresponds to what Cohn notices when she argues that narrative fiction shows a freedom from referential constraint. Dolozel's observations supplement Cohn's formal distinctions. He points out that as possible worlds, historical worlds correspond to actual worlds, whereas fiction may posit impossible worlds which violate the laws of the physical universe. In fiction, as in myth, supernatural beings may possess agency; in history, all the agents are natural (though not necessarily human). The invention of agents or actors belongs to fiction; history is confined to those actors who existed. Dolozel observes that historical fiction's typical mixture of actual and invented actors is a defining feature of its fictionality. The persons (and other features) of historical worlds, according to Dolozel, must bear documented properties: this corresponds to Cohn's positing of an additional level, the level of reference, but from the other direction. Dolozel sees the existence of sources as a perpetual challenge to historical world-making, which must always be in a state of revision and refinement, to catch up with the state of newly discovered or newly interpreted sources. Fiction, with the freedom to create logically impossible worlds, is under no such pressure, though of course it often participates in revisionist narrative projects. Finally, fictional gaps are ontological, and as a result, in Dolozel's worlds, are 'irrecoverable lacunae that cannot be filled by legitimate inference'; statements about gaps in fiction are always undecidable ('Fictional and Historical', 258). Historical gaps, by contrast, are epistemological; they arise from missing information or limitations in knowledge or strategies that blind the historian to relevant data. Gaps in historical narrative can be filled by a change in approach or as a result of the discovery of hitherto unknown documents. Dolozel's four observations about the macrostructural differences of fictional and historical worlds support Cohn's contention that freedom from referential constraints separates the makers of narrative fiction from the historian writing a narrative reconstruction of past events. Dolozel concludes, 'From the viewpoint of possible-worlds semantics, this formulation is unobjectionable as long as we understand that historical reconstruction does not recreate the past in actuality, but in represented possibility' (Dolozel, 'Fictional and Historical Narrative,' 261).

Analytical techniques

For those who prefer to focus on the internal details of narrative form, attention to fictional world-making is also rewarding. Limit-cases can be fascinating: one can ask, with possible worlds theorists, what traits or characteristics are necessary to a fictional world's formation (for instance, that a child holding a ring in his or her hand can move between universes), and which traits can be considered incidental? This approach permits a specialized form of comparison of narrative worlds and the extravagance of their truth claims.[6] Alternatively, examining the complexity of some fictional worlds can be an intriguing subject. The manipulation of narrative level, discussed in the previous chapter, can account for the presence of stories within stories through the presence of more than one teller who narrates an additional layer of story. Another set of alternatives, represented by the world-making of fantasy fiction, dream visions, postmodern historiographic metafictions, and other varieties of romance, occurs when narrative deploys fictional worlds that contain other worlds within them.[7] When a single narrator carries the reader over the ontological boundaries marking the differences between these story realms, as in Neil Gaiman's *Neverwhere*

(1996), then a complication of fictional worlds which cannot be explained by the language for narrative levels has occurred.

Some formal issues that have often attracted the attention of critics interested in fictionality and fictional worlds include the examination of front matter and what Genette calls *paratexts*; the role of naming in establishing the existence of characters within fictional worlds, or in characterizing the worlds themselves; the use of settings and representations of places and spaces in fictional worlds; and the relationship between settings and plot functions, following Vladimir Propp on plot functions and Mikhail Bakhtin on the chronotope.

Recently, Franco Moretti has called for the practice of 'distant reading' of fictional worlds, using methods of analysis that result in the creation of maps, trees, and graphs of fictional worlds and the texts in which they are contained. Moretti is most interested in the mainstream realistic texts of the European tradition, although his call to use maps as a method of reaching new kinds of literary understandings can be extended well beyond that field. His methods, demonstrated in his *Atlas of the European Novel 1800–1900* (1998) and in three lectures, entitled 'Maps,' 'Graphs,' and 'Trees,' not only call for the collection of evidence about places (settings) and character movements (plots and directions), but also the rises and falls of novelistic genres within nations. For Moretti, the identification of a fictional world's basic traits is the starting point of an analysis that takes in large numbers of instances and proceeds from quantified observations. Among the results of Moretti's 'distant reading' are the confirmation of Raymond Williams's insights about residual, emergent, and dominant forms, and a significant elaboration of Bakhtin's concept of the chronotope.

Keyword

Metanarratives.   In narrative theory, the term 'metanarrative' indicates the self-referential acknowledgement in a narrative of its embedded stories, contributing to a metafictional effect that calls attention to the text's fictionality. (This use of metanarrative may or may not entail an instance of metalepsis, discussed in Chapter 8.) For narrative theorists, metanarrative means a narrative that acknowledges narrative itself as one of its topics.

However, metanarrative also sometimes refers to the grand narratives or overarching stories embodying ideologies and beliefs as well as implying certain plot lines and resolutions. For instance, the Whig version of history employs a metanarrative that describes progress towards parliamentary democracy; the Christian story of corruption, redemption, and salvation is a metanarrative, as is the epic story of decline and fall. These metanarratives are also sometimes called master narratives (or grand narratives). This meaning of metanarrative is associated with Jean-François Lyotard's influential essay, *The Postmodern Condition* (1979), in which Lyotard interchanges 'grand narratives' implying philosophies of history with the term 'metanarrative,' and defines the postmodern as 'incredulity towards metanarratives.'

This move resembles Hayden White's adoption of an ironic mode for his own historiography in *Metahistory* (1973). Though no means identical, the similarity of White's tropes, plot structures, and genres and Lyotard's metanarratives has resulted in a current meaning of metanarrative that is quite different from its more specialized meaning within narrative theory. This broader sense of metanarrative as an implicit governing story, either of a genre or an ideology or a nation, is the more common usage of the two. White's role in the development of this sense of metanarrative is complex. Though he does not actually use the term, historian Hayden White is often associated with this sense of the word, for his *Metahistory,* a study of the deep structure of the historical imagination, reveals the governing archetypal plot structures (Romance, Comedy, Tragedy, and Satire) and tropes (Metaphor, Synecdoche, Metonymy, and Irony) that underlie and justify historians' explanatory strategies. These archetypal plot structures and tropes possess the governing power of Lyotard's metanarrative, for White argues that the choice of a particular mode of 'emplotment' in the narration of history governs the story that can be told about the events. White does not require self-consciousness about narrativity on the part of the narrative historians whose work he discusses, so the story shape possesses an unusual power. As White indicates, he is indebted to the generic model offered in Northrop Frye's *Anatomy of Criticism* (1957), but in *Metahistory* he does not elide the distinction between fiction and history. In later work White moves towards the equation of representation and fiction, though he retreats from that position with respect to the famous Holocaust test posed to postmodern historians and historiographers. Then, White concedes that certain governing tropes would be inappropriate vehicles for the narration of some kinds of historical events.

A loose use of metanarrative to mean something like an implicit story that can be perceived through interpretation of events or unselfconscious narration thus differs markedly from its narratological meaning.

Further reading

Auerbach, Erich, *Mimesis: The Representation of Reality in Western Literature*, trans. Willard R. Trask (Princeton University Press, 1953).

Berger, Harry, Jr., 'The Renaissance Imagination: Second World and Green World,' *Centennial Review of Arts and Sciences* 9 (1965), 36–78. Berger argues that early modern thinkers in a variety of disciplines used the techniques of world-making to accomplish intellectual tasks in a second world separate from the confusing everyday world.

Cohn, Dorrit, *The Distinction of Fiction* (Johns Hopkins University Press, 1999). See the chapter, 'Signposts of Fictionality: A Narratological Perspective,' 109–31.

Coste, Didier, *Narrative as Communication*, foreword by Wlad Godzich, Theory and History of Literature, vol. 64 (University of Minnesota Press, 1989).

Dolozel, Lubomír, 'Fictional and Historical Narrative: Meeting the Postmodernist Challenge,' in *Narratologies*, ed. David Herman (Ohio State University Press, 1999), 247–73.

— 'Truth and Authenticity in Narrative,' *Poetics Today* 1:3 (Spring 1980), 7–25. A lucid introduction to possible world semantics of narrative fiction.

Eakin, Paul John, *How Our Lives Become Stories: Making Selves* (Cornell University Press, 1999). A psychological approach to self-perception and self-narration.

Goodman, Nelson, *Ways of World Making* (Hackett, 1978). This philosopher's views on world-making pertain to fictional and nonfictional worlds.

Lehman, David W., *Matters of Fact: Reading Nonfiction over the Edge* (Ohio State University Press, 1997). Lehman argues that truth (accuracy) matters in the evaluation of nonfiction, pointing up the difference between nonfiction and fiction, despite the significant overlap in narrative techniques used by fiction and nonfiction writers.

Lyotard, Jean-François, *The Postmodern Condition: A Report on Knowledge*, 1979, trans. Geoff Bennington and Brian Massumi, Theory and History of Literature, vol. 10 (University of Minnesota Press, 1984).

Pavel, Thomas G., *Fictional Worlds* (Harvard University Press, 1986).

Riffaterre, Michael, *Fictional Truth* (Johns Hopkins University Press, 1990).

Ryan, Marie-Laure, *Narrative as Virtual Reality: Immersion and Interactivity in Literature and Electronic Media* (Johns Hopkins University Press, 2001).

— 'Possible Worlds and Accessibility Relations: A Semantic Typology of Fiction,' *Poetics Today* 12:3 (Fall 1991), 553–76.

— 'Stacks, Frames, and Boundaries,' rpt. in *Narrative Dynamics: Essays on Time, Plot, Closure, and Frames*, ed. Brian Richardson (Ohio State University Press, 2002), 366–86. Ryan's work draws on computer science to offer sophisticated alternatives to standard narratological descriptions of narrative levels.

Sidney, Philip, *A Defense of Poesy*. Also known as *An Apology for Poetry*, ed. Forrest G. Robinson (Macmillan/Library of Liberal Arts, 1970).
White, Hayden, 'The Value of Narrativity in the Representation of Reality,' in *On Narrative*, ed. W. J. T. Mitchell (University of Chicago Press, 1981), 1–23.
— *Metahistory: The Historical Imagination in Nineteenth-Century Europe* (Johns Hopkins University Press, 1973).

10
Disguises: Fiction in the Form of Nonfiction Texts

If narrative fiction differs formally from nonfiction narrative in the ways that Dorrit Cohn outlines in *The Distinction of Fiction*, then what is the critic to do with texts that so perfectly mimic nonfictional texts formally that these qualities cannot be observed?[1] Fiction disguised as another form of discourse has an important place in the history of the development of fictional narrative genres, especially the novel in English.[2] The purpose of this chapter is not to revisit the question of the shared narrativity of fictional and nonfictional discourse, and the controversies about whether all narration is thus in some way fictive, but to investigate whether traits of fictiveness might persist in spite of presentation in the form of nonfictional discourse. If not, then what other habits of readers and critics might matter to formal analysis?

Cohn writes that unlike fiction, which employs a story level and a discourse level, nonfiction has an additional level, that of reference to an area of events or documents that can be cited about happenings in the past. Without contesting this description, I can still easily imagine fictional narratives mimicking this quality, and not only in the hybrid genre of historical fiction. What if a novelist sets out to imitate history and does so fully imitating the forms of reference (with footnotes in formal citation style, as in Lawrence Norfolk's *In the Shape of a Boar* (2000))? If the footnotes check out, then perhaps the existence of a 'level of reference' has been verified. If the novelist also chooses, as narrative artists such as Ivy Compton Burnett have done, to eschew the representation of characters' thoughts, focusing instead only on their actions, speech, and recorded words, then adoption of referential constraints common in historical writing would make fictionality harder to detect. If the fiction also employs an uncontroversial, external, apparently neutral and omniscient narrative perspective (Stanzel's authorial narrative), of the kind that would lead a history reader to equate the narrator's views with the author's, then only external knowledge about the actual author's views and other writing might lead to the discovery of the fiction. If, using the fictional licence to make truth claims about invented material, the writer creates an entirely plausible but in fact totally made-up character, then research into the putative history may go so far as to cast doubt, but can hardly be assured of 'disproving' the fiction's truth claims. Nonetheless, this imaginary narrative would still be a fiction, just a formally undetectable one.

I have used just one imaginary example to introduce the problem of disguises. One could do the same, quite easily, with other possibilities, and the history of narrative provides many examples of famous misunderstandings, in which fictional autobiographies are taken to be real memoirs, and so forth.[3] This history dovetails with another literary history, that of willful fakes and forgeries, where the 'feigning' of fiction turns into the crime of fraud. Between fraud or forgery and out-and-out fiction lies another curious case, that of the satire mistaken for the real thing. Literary history provides enough examples of fictions with satirical intention being read straight (sometimes with dire consequences for their authors) to raise substantive questions about the formal mechanisms that supposedly distinguish fiction from nonfiction. If a reader cannot tell the difference, then where does the difference lie? Indeed, the expectations brought by the reader to the text have a powerful role in its reception as fiction, nonfiction, or a work in a particular subgenre.

Terms

Ordinarily, the package in which we receive narrative fiction prevents our confusion: we see the label 'FICTION' on the back cover of *The Autobiography of Miss Jane Pittman*; perhaps we have heard of Ernest Gaines already (we are more likely to have that knowledge than the readers who were confused in 1971). We know that the text that masquerades as 'real' is just that, a fiction in disguise. What Lennard Davis calls its 'presentational context,' making up the 'pre-structure' an informed reader brings to the task of interpretation helps to identify and place the text before we even begin reading it (*Factual Fictions*, 12).

The elaborate set of conventions publishers employ in presenting texts, including fictional narratives, has received extensive witty commentary from Gérard Genette in his book *Paratexts* (1987). As the French title (*seuils*) suggests, Genette is interested in the liminal or threshold qualities of the conventions that mediate among author, reader, book, and publisher. These *paratexts*, as Genette names them, include items that appear both within and outside the physical book. Paratexts are of two kinds, the *peritexts*, which appear within or on the book itself, and the *epitexts*, which exist entirely outside the physical book.

The publisher's peritexts include the cover, the title page, the publisher's information, the blurb, and the typesetting. The author's peritexts include the author's name (including anonymous and pseudonymous names); the title and intertitles of sub-units such as volumes, chapters, or running titles; the printed dedications and written inscriptions; the epigraphs, prefaces, notes. Epitexts can be the documents created by the author or publisher about the text for public consumption (these would include catalog copy and publicity materials for reviewers), or private epitexts such as correspondence, work diaries, or notes made in the process of composition. Much scholarly work depends upon recovery of and interpretation of undervalued or ephemeral epitexts. This seemingly exhaustive list omits, as Genette himself announces, the epitexts of translations, the peritexts marking the serial format of publication, and the visual peritexts of illustrations accompanying the text. Each paratext plays a role in announcing the intentions of the text, the status of the author or publisher, and the generic expectations that the reader should activate to be prepared for the reading experience (a subject Genette treats in more detail in another work, the *Architext* (1979), discussed in Chapter 11). The status of the paratexts—both epitexts external to the book itself, and part of its history as an object, and peritexts, those that appear on or in the book—Genette treats with sensitivity to their in-between status, their covert powers, and their pragmatic functions.

For the present purpose of considering fiction which appears in disguise, paratexts take on special significance. If the title, a peritext, declares that the work is history, but the publisher's catalog or materials prepared for the book reviewer announce the opposite, that the work is a fiction, then the external epitext commands the informed reader's trust and the (contrary) title does not disappoint, but confirms the reader's sense of the work's feigning by making an impossible truth claim. The preparation that readers bring to these nearly unnoticed interpretive acts to a large extent determines how competently they can receive the writer's and publisher's signals. Writer and publisher may, of course, act either in cooperation with one another, or discordantly. A novelist who finds her adult fiction about child abuse marketed as juvenile fiction because the main character is 10 years old may find her own peritexts clashing with the publisher's epitexts. A work that has reached publication in a system of state or unofficial censorship may rely upon the protections offered by a publisher's paratexts, while covertly subverting their reassuring messages. In this circumstance, as in the interpretation of parable, the reading audience may be tacitly divided into those in the know and those in the dark, who will most likely fail to detect the clues that would signal an alternate way of reading a text.[4]

To return to the subject at hand, the problem presented by fictional texts which are presented in the guise of nonfictional discourse, it should be clear that the deployment of paratexts plays a significant role in the attitude with which a reader engages in reading. The paratexts, such as the back-cover labeling or the book reviews in the Sunday paper, may be the crucial details that guarantee a reading of an apparently nonfictional text as a work of fiction. The process by which readers make the judgments that will result in a better informed or a more misguided reading of such a text is a common, everyday occurrence. Its ordinariness and its apparent belonging to the realm of reader response may make this process seem far afield from issues of narrative form.

The literary theorist Peter J. Rabinowitz offers several very useful concepts for bringing this process and problem into focus, though his scope in *Before Reading: Narrative Conventions and the Politics of Interpretation* is considerably broader than my use of his ideas here suggests. Rabinowitz distinguishes between the *authorial audience*—to which we belong when we know that a fictional text is not real—and the observer position readers occupy within the reading experience, the *narrative audience*—to which we belong when we are 'suspending disbelief' to accept the truth claims of a fiction. Readers may belong to both audiences at the same time, knowing that a text is fictional while fully engaging with the illusion of reality that it offers. Rabinowitz uses these concepts to offer a test for realism. If the only difference between the narrative audience position and the authorial audience position is the belief in the actuality of the characters and events (necessary to the narrative audience position, and ruled out by the authorial audience position), then the text must be seen as realistic. If other differences in beliefs between the two audiences can be cataloged (for instance, if the narrative audience is asked to accept that the planet has two moons orbiting around it, something the authorial audience will reject), then the text is not realistic. In the case of disguised fictions, the beliefs of the narrative audience may possess peculiar powers. In some instances, they may override the usual situation of the authorial audience, where we know at the outset that the text at hand is fictional. When narrative audience and authorial audience hold identical beliefs about the truth of a text that happens to be fictional, then all the formal qualities that are supposed to distinguish fiction from nonfiction have failed to be discerned. This calls into question the very project of cataloging fiction's ostensibly distinctive traits, or makes a value judgment about the authority and expertise of audiences necessary.

Dramatists and satirists sometimes run into trouble because of this kind of conflation of audience belief. Infamously, the realism of the 1938 broadcast of Orson Welles's version of H. G. Wells's *The War of the Worlds* caused panic among some radio listeners, who were taken in by its pastiche of the conventions of news announcements. If the listeners had missed the opening assurances that the broadcast was a radio play, they had to wait though 40 minutes of the broadcast before clarification occurred. In the interim, some people went to their cellars, got out their weapons, and fled into the streets. Though Orson Welles was not jailed or reprimanded, doubts were expressed about the dangerous qualities of simulations that could take in a mass audience. Print texts may seem less threatening because they reach fewer individuals than radio or television broadcasts, but breaches in the supposedly fixed boundary between truth and fiction are common in the history of the reception of satire. Eighteenth-century satirist Jonathan Swift wrote a parody called *Prediction for the Ensuing Year by Isaac Bickerstaff*, in which he predicted the death of a real man, the cobbler and astrologer John Partridge. In March 1708, Swift announced that his prediction of Partridge's death had come true, though the real man in fact was still alive. Partridge complained that his business had been ruined because his customers all thought he was dead; mercilessly, Swift insisted on proving Partridge's decease. Though the humor of the satire depends on the recognition of the fictiveness of Swift's claims, at the time of the original publication some readers clearly failed to discern the difference between the two roles, in the narrative audience and the authorial audience. They simply believed, and the fiction was taken for the truth.

When Thomas Carlyle's *Sartor Resartus* (1833–34) was reviewed as if it were an actual memoir, no one came to any harm. Yet damage can occur. The most pernicious use of the powers of simulation and disguise occurs when dishonest individuals create fakes whose disguise as the real thing may benefit the forger economically, politically, or personally, but in any case illegally. Had the Hitler Diaries been presented to the world as the fictional constructions they were, no scandal would have occurred, and historians who authenticated the forgeries would have suffered no disgrace.[5] The fact that so much money was to be made, not only by the forger but also by the magazine that announced the discovery, might suggest that such a case should be treated with suspicion. Surely, we may feel, ordinary readers come better prepared to detect fictions masquerading as nonfiction. The remote date of many famous examples of literary forgeries (the poems of Ossian, the forgeries of Chatterton) might suggest that such confusions of fictional works with nonfiction are things of the past, or common only in the substrata of unscholarly websites.

One might imagine that the methods of peer review employed by academic presses ostensibly guard against misrepresentations. This is not the case. As recently as 1976, the University of Arizona Press published a fictional autobiography by the novelist and amateur historian Glenn Boyer. Entitled *I Married Wyatt Earp*, the first published edition (1976) and subsequent reprintings through the 1990s represented the text as the 'recollections' of Josephine Earp, the third wife of the frontier lawman. A paratext that appears on the copyright page explains:

GLENN BOYER, as a youth, was captivated by the dramatic portrayal of Wyatt Earp in Stuart Lake's popular book. The desire to discover the true man behind his boyhood hero embarked him upon more than thirty years of library and field investigation regarding the facts of life of Wyatt Earp. He became a close friend of the descendents of Wyatt's second wife and the family of the lawman's sister. Eventually these associations led to his obtaining the two Josephine Earp manuscripts upon which this book is based.

While with hindsight the critical reader might recognize this brief romance of the archive[6] as the announcement of a fictive research quest, it was taken as a claim of nonfictionality, a claim that was no doubt subtly reinforced by its appearance on the official space of the copyright page, where the ISBN number and other matters of fact reside. The publisher thus tacitly represented the text as a nonfiction source, edited by Glenn Boyer, and it was used accordingly by historians, though some had their doubts. The two manuscript sources were inaccessible and unverifiable.

As a result of the work of two investigative journalists, Allen Barra and Tony Ortega, the publisher responded in 1999 (23 years after first publishing the book) by announcing its intention to redesign the cover, alter the declaration of authorship, and add a publisher's note about sources. In other words, adjustment of external paratexts were to be made in order to avoid the appearance of fraud. Barra wonders, 'How can you say for 23 years that a book is a memoir, let it be used as a primary source for historians, and then say all of a sudden that it is fictional and that every-one should have known it was fictional all along? Can anyone offer any parallel for this?'[7] In fact there are many parallels, when one considers the history of historical fiction since Walter Scott. Many historical novelists represent themselves as the discoverers and editors of collections of hith-erto unknown documents. Boyer's truth claims do not differ formally from those of Walter Scott's antiquarian editors, but perhaps the assent of his publisher to the representation of nonfictionality differs.

Boyer and his new publishers, Historical Research Associates, now charac-terize the text as 'creative nonfiction,' adding that it thus participates in a tradition including 'The Iliad of Homer, Macaulay's History of England, Stanley Vestal's Sitting Bull, all of Gore Vidal's American history series, etc.' The new publishers assert through Amazon.com that 'Boyer has never claimed to be anything but a "storyteller" who tried to preserve some history he'd stumbled onto, then investigated further with remarkable tenacity and luck, to bring it to the public.' The emphasis on Boyer's border performances as the act of a 'master-storyteller' is balanced in the pub-lisher's assertions with a new set of claims regarding documentation: 'Of interest regarding the controversy surrounding the sources of this book, since the co-author had lost many of them, and in addition refused to divulge others that were confidential, most of the documentation on which this book is based was recently (2002) discovered in—of all places—the Special Collections of the University of Arizona Library where Glenn Boyer had forgotten he left them years ago.'[8] I am not aware of any attempts to follow up on this tantalizing clue or to have the manuscripts verified by independent historians.

An interesting parallel case to consider is George MacDonald Fraser's original Flashman novel, which appeared in 1969 as *Flashman: From the Flashman Papers 1839–1842*, edited by Fraser. The only difference from the Earp/Boyer text was its paratextual apparatus. *Flashman* was not repre-sented by its publisher Herbert Jenkins as nonfiction; indeed, the American edition was explicitly marked as fiction. Nonetheless, as many as ten reviewers of the first edition were taken in.[9] The formal difference between *trompe l'oeil* and forgery may exist only in the external epitexts generated by the publisher. If a disclaimer sent to the *New York Times* is the only firm evidence that *Flashman* is a novel, and not a fraudulent scam, then how can fictionality be seen as inhering in internal formal characteristics? John R. Searle has argued the opposite, asserting that there is 'no textual prop-erty, syntactical or semantic, that will identify a text as a work of fiction' ('Logical Status,' 325). In Searle's view, the 'illocutionary stance' that the author takes towards the work, embodying the complex intentions that the author brings to the writing of the text, defines a fictional text as fictional. (Illocutions are speech acts such as statements, assertions, asking questions, descriptions, characterizations, apologies, identification, explanations, and so on.) A writer of fiction pretends to perform illocutionary acts, according to Searle (325). The complications in cases such as Fraser's *Flashman* or Boyer's *I Married Wyatt Earp* arise when the author's intentions are misunderstood, not known, or are willfully misrepresented.

Searle suggests that what makes fiction possible is a set of conventions that allow a writer to use words with their literal meanings without taking on the commitments usually entailed by those meanings (326). The distinction of fiction then lies not in the formal traits of language, but in the suspension of the usual rules concerning illocutionary acts: 'there is no textual property that will identify a stretch of discourse as a work of fiction' (327). Narratives that we take to be fictions have often appeared in the guise of existing nonfictional genres of story, and it is only our literary historical framing of these texts as 'fictions' or as 'proto-novels' that announces their fictionality. The gallows confessions of condemned criminals, autobiographies, travel narratives, histories, collections of letters or other documents, depositions and the reports of early journalism all provided models for narrative fiction in the Renaissance. These models have long been considered sources for various aspects of what is represented as the development of the novel, but it is useful in this context to note what Lennard Davis has influentially argued in *Factual Fictions* (1983). Davis holds that the novel in its early phases has more to do with journalism than with the already existing narrative genre of romance. In other words, Renaissance authors had an option if they wanted to present their stories in a format that announced its fictiveness—they could write romances, as many did. The novel, according to Davis, arises when the writer makes the pretense of the illocutionary act of truthful assertion that typifies fiction according to Searle. The common claim that a fictional work is a history, a true story, and so forth reflects not the deceptiveness of the fraud, but early modern attitudes about fact and fiction quite different from ours. As any student of Shakespeare knows, early modern people tolerated the admixture of history and invention, and had very different attitudes towards intellectual property: borrowing and close imitation were not considered plagiarism. However, early modern prose fiction was strongly associated with the criminal lives it often depicted, so the taint of criminality, vice, and lying clung to the early novel with its urgent truth claims.

Narrative fiction before the novel often presented itself in the guise of history, autobiography, confession, or travel narrative (as well as in romance forms). This disguising feature of narrative fiction does not disappear with the success of romance and more realistic novels (and their combinations). It persists in narrative of both sorts, in works that imitate actual documents or collections, such as Walter Scott's historical fictions that appear in antiquarian frame, purporting to surround a discovered set of documents, or in books such as Wilkie Collins's *The Moonstone* (1868), which masquerades as a set of legal depositions. The history of the epistolary novel makes a prominent part of this formal story, whereby fiction takes its form from an existing form of communication or record making. Throughout the nineteenth and twentieth centuries, the fictional autobiography has exploited its formal similarity to real memoirs by actual living persons. Though most of these novels have not been mistaken for nonfiction, some exceptions have occurred. Though few postmodern fictions would be mistaken as nonfictional texts, postmodern novelists have played a significant role in resuscitating through pastiche of earlier forms of writing the novel's earlier imitative history. It has often been observed that in its fondness for pastiche, postmodern fiction imitates the forms of earlier narrative in metafictional play. This does not mean that modern readers have completely suspended the activity of sorting out 'truth' from 'fiction.' Quite the contrary: these category distinctions often seem urgent to readers, and postmodernism's freewheeling use of historical materials can still provoke outrage on the part of readers expecting firmer boundaries between documented factual narrative and fiction.

According to Davis, the use of framing pre-structures differentiates novels from romances. While romances freely mix fact and fiction, Davis sees the early novel's pre-structures as asserting their factuality. However, the news, ballad broadsheets, and histories that provide the models for factual narration were full of fabrications and were often anything but new. In a Foucaultian argument, Davis asserts that legal pressure arose in when truthfulness, proofs, and documentation came to be more highly valued; then novels were gradually separated from the news on the one hand and from history on the other, as these genres became more dedicated to fact. The Glenn Boyer case shows that recourse to lawsuits can still be used to help articulate generic boundaries. The notion that a press's labeling a work 'historical fiction' constitutes 'defamation of character' heightens the importance of generic labels. The author believes he has created a work of nonfiction from documentary sources and names it 'creative nonfiction.' The press markets the work in a nonfiction line, implying its value to historians as a documentary source. Journalists reveal the truth of the text's fabrications through investigative reporting in the news. The negative publicity and the imputation of fraud may have been factors in the University of Arizona Press's decision to let Boyer's text go out of print (in 2000).[10] Some 300 years after the period studied by Davis, the process of separation of fiction from history is still being worked out through real and threatened lawsuits.

Barbara Foley extends Davis's observations about the movable boundary between fiction and fact, a boundary that was articulated during the seventeenth century through the application of libel law. In her work on the documentary novel, Foley argues that factual and fictional forms of writing are not 'immutable essences' but should be understood instead as 'historically varying types of writing, signaled by and embodied in, changing literary conventions and generated by the changing structures of the historically specific relations of productions and intercourse' (*Telling the Truth*, 27). Foley explores those shifting boundaries, and the material conditions of authorship and historical contexts that help to move them, in her study of the documentary novel, a hybrid form of narrative. Foley describes the documentary effect generated by these narratives, which purport 'to represent reality by means of agreed-upon conventions of fictionality, while grafting onto [their] fictive pact some kind of additional claim to empirical validation' (25). For Foley, the pseudo-factual fiction of the eighteenth century invites an ironic reading and employs pastiche and parody in order to take over the turf occupied by prose romance. Foley sees these early novelists as extending the range of their assertions (in Searle's terms, their feigned illocutionary acts) by using pseudo-statements of fact (*Telling the Truth*, 108). Further, she sees the documentary novel as a major tradition within realism, modernism, and contemporary African-American writing.

The recognition that no immutable boundary between nonfiction and fiction can be fixed; that the categories interpenetrate from the earliest period of the novel; that legal pressures and the economic incentives of the marketplace often work to shift a particular narrative's placement; and that the commonsense recognition of a work as fiction or nonfiction depends heavily on contexts and paratexts all make the absence of surefire formal tests for fictionality much more understandable. Yet the experiential fact remains that most readers usually feel that they 'know' whether a particular narrative is meant to be 'true' or 'fictional.' Readers are certainly capable of expressing dismay when they feel that they have been misled, or when they recognize that a narrative (often a film) makes historical claims with which they disagree. The use of Peter Rabinowitz's concept of authorial reading to describe the way an individual reader rises to the expectations projected by the text's implied, hypothetical reader, can assist in understanding why such intensity of feeling surrounds category issues. If a reader cooperates with the text's projection of a 'reader interested in an historical account,' and later finds that he ought to have been reading as a 'reader who enjoys subversion of conventions,' he may reasonably feel as if he has read the text 'the wrong way.' Though readers are flexible, they bring expectations and knowledge with them when they read. Their experience and judgment of a narrative in part stems from their successfully recognizing the position that the text asks them to assume, whether they collaborate by joining the authorial audience, or whether they dissent by deliberately reading against the grain. The interpretation of paratexts is thus one of the most important activities a reader undertakes, even when it is done automatically and rapidly.

Analytical strategies

Paratexts.   As this chapter has already suggested, strictly formal analysis of discourse is not likely to result in a way of recognizing the fictionality of a narrative. This does not preclude fascinating close work with the texts. Indeed, research into the history of paratexts is an especially promising area for new work. Anthony Grafton's book, *The Footnote: A Curious History* (1997), Kevin Dunn's *Pretexts of Authority: The Rhetoric of Authorship in the Renaissance Preface* (1994), and George Bornstein and Theresa Tinkle's edited volume *The Iconic Page in Manuscript, Print, and Digital Culture* (1998) suggest some promising directions for formal and contextual analysis of paratexts. Collections of essays such as D. C. Greetham's *The Margins of the Text* (1997) suggest how the study of paratexts can bring the concerns of textual scholarship and editing into play with cultural studies.

History of the book.   Closely related to the approaches mentioned above, but not limited to the study of paratexts, are methodologies that consider literature as a cultural institution. The practices of printers, publishers, collectors, and editors, as well as of authors change over time and bear the traces of changing notions of textual authority. The growing interest in periodicals and publishing houses, in reception history of texts, in the nuts and bolts of the book trade, and in contemporary alternatives to traditional publishing through electronic means all promise to be rich areas for scholarly and theoretical inquiry.

Keywords

Mimesis.   Mimesis is an extremely tricky term, for it has meant many
   different things to different critics since Plato and Aristotle. (See the
   brief definitions of mimesis and diegesis in Chapter 1.) Mimesis
   means imitation, and it has been influentially used to mean 'the representation of reality,' as in Erich Auerbach's broad-ranging study.
   Often equated with literary 'realism' (though 'realism' has a more
   recent history, dating from the mid-nineteenth century), mimesis
   can be used to mean 'showing' over the diegesis of 'telling.' Mimetic
   critics are those who, following Plato, judge a work with respect to
   its success in representing reality truthfully. Mimesis can also mean
   the disguising discussed in this chapter, in the sense that it can be
   an imitation of an existing kind or subgenre of writing. Barbara
   Foley sees mimesis as a mode of cognition. For Foley, its salient qualities (for prose fiction) lie in its construction of characters and
   actions in relationships that suggest the analogous configuration of
   the reader's reality. Thus mimesis employs particular textual features
   to invoke a fictional contract in relation to the reader's experiences
   and knowledge. It should go without saying that this understanding
   of mimesis allows for shifts over time in what is regarded as
   mimetic.

Pastiche.   Used in this chapter simply to mean an intentional close imitation of the style and traits of a work, pastiche has a second sense
   deriving from its French meanings, that is, an imitation with a
   parodic or satirical intention. Fredric Jameson's influential use of
   pastiche in his 1991 *Postmodernism; or, The Cultural Logic of Late
   Capitalism* suggests that pastiche has taken parody's place: 'Pastiche
   is, like parody, the imitation of a peculiar or unique, idiosyncratic
   style, the wearing of a linguistic mask, speech in a dead language,'
   Jameson writes. With disapproval of its rhetorical emptiness,
   Jameson characterizes pastiche as 'a neutral practice of such
   mimicry, without any of parody's ulterior motives, amputated of the
   satiric impulse, devoid of laughter and of any conviction that along-
   side the abnormal tongue you have momentarily borrowed, some
   healthy linguistic normality still exists' (*Postmodernism*, 17). Thus,
   the use of the term pastiche can be charged with an extremely negative implication, if it suggests to the reader the 'imitation of dead
   styles, speech through all the masks and voices stored up in the
   imaginary museum of a now global culture' (18).

Further reading

Auerbach, Erich, *Mimesis: The Representation of Reality in Western Literature*, trans. Willard R. Trask (Princeton University Press, 1953).

Cohn, Dorrit, *The Distinction of Fiction* (Johns Hopkins University Press, 1999).

Davis, Lennard J., *Factual Fictions: The Origins of the English Novel*, 1983, rpt. (University of Pennsylvania Press, 1996).

Dolozel, Lubomír, 'Fictional and Historical Narrative: Meeting the Postmodernist Challenge,' *Narratologies*, ed. David Herman (Ohio State University Press, 1999), 247–73.

Elam, Diane, *Romancing the Postmodern* (Routledge, 1992).

Foley, Barbara, *Telling the Truth: The Theory and Practice of Documentary Fiction* (Cornell University Press, 1986).

Genette, Gérard, *Palimpsests: Literature in the Second Degree*, 1982, trans. Channa Newman and Claude Doubinsky (University of Nebraska Press, 1997). This work treats imitation, adaptation, parody and pastiche.

— *Paratexts: Thresholds of Interpretation*, 1987, trans. Jane E. Lewin (Cambridge University Press, 1997).

Hutcheon, Linda, *Narcissistic Narrative: The Metafictional Paradox* (Wilfred Laurier University Press, 1980). See Hutcheon on parody.

Jameson, Fredric, *Postmodernism; or, The Cultural Logic of Late Capitalism* (Duke University Press, 1991). See Jameson on pastiche.

Rabinowitz, Peter J., *Before Reading: Narrative Conventions and the Politics of Interpretation*, 1987, 2nd ed., foreword by James Phelan (Ohio State University Press, 1998).

Searle, John R., 'The Logical Status of Fictional Discourse,' *New Literary History* 6 (Winter 1975), 319–32.

11
Genres and Conventions

'Narrative form,' the subject of the preceding chapters, often means something entirely different from the tools and techniques described in most of this text. To the question 'What form is this narrative?' an interlocutor may expect an answer that names a genre. It is an epic in twelve books. It is a mystery novel, with a gathering of characters in an English country house, one of whom will be revealed to be the murderer. It begins as a psychological thriller and halfway through turns into a farce. It is a space opera. It is the third and climactic part of a fantasy trilogy. These forms (or kinds, types, or subgenres) have often been left out of theoretical discussion of narrative form, as the undignified sub-literary cousins of 'serious fiction' which obey no formulas, as the irrelevant impingements of ancient traditions on up-to-date narratives, or as the too-contingent categories that confute the premise of structuralist ahistoricity.[1] The rejection of the idea of genre often implies that genre impedes originality, that it imposes form onto an artist's ideas, and that it is the enemy of innovation. Yet as Claudio Guillén observes, genre is but an 'invitation' to combine matter and form in ways that resemble previously achieved combinations (*Literature as System*, 109). Neither a strict recipe nor an exclusionary tradition, genre can thus be seen as Guillén recommends, as a problem-solving model, whose usefulness is demonstrated when real writers match matter and form (*Literature as System*, 110–11). The result of this process may in fact be the creation of an innovative narrative in a never-before-seen form. This chapter seeks to reintegrate the discussion of forms in narrative with narrative form. It does so by introducing in summary fashion the complex area of genre theory, as it pertains to narrative.

Terms

The pertinence of genre to the analysis of narrative, particularly in its prose fiction forms, does not always appear obvious to the critic confronting the ancient divisions of literature, often described as 'the three genres.'[2] Where does the novel go among epic, drama, and lyric? There is something extremely unsatisfactory about placing novels, short stories, and novellas as subdivisions of 'epic,' and not only because of the hierarchical relation implied by the family tree. Genre theorists have proposed many alternative versions of this triad, sometimes revising it to include many subdivisions, and sometimes simplifying it to fewer categories. Narrative fits more easily in the contemporary version of 'the genres,' replicated in introductory literature courses and textbooks as poetry, drama, and fiction (film and nonfiction jostle at the edges). These categories do not sustain much scrutiny. Never mind that poetry can be fictional and narrative, that drama and fiction can be in verse, and that fiction need not take the form of prose narrative. Though these broad, tripartite divisions are often called 'the genres,' or even 'the three genres,' I avoid that usage here. They are also often called *modes*, a term which suggests their special differences of approach to representation, sometimes seen as inhering in their typical grammatical person, their implicit relations to the audience, or their fundamental subjects. Few critics take the task of dividing literature into intrinsic and mutually exclusive modes seriously these days, though a preoccupation with forms that blend modes suggests that the modes themselves retain some significance. For the student of narrative form it is sufficient to know that from the Renaissance and the Romantic periods, highly elaborated genre systems, some claiming descent from the classical theorists, gave pride of place to one exemplary kind of narrative, the epic poem.

Following Wellek and Warren in their *Theory of Literature*, I set these modes, or 'ultimate' genres, aside and use the term *genre* to mean 'historical genre.'[3] That is, a genre means the name by which we recognize a group of texts dynamically linked through shared formal, stylistic, and thematic features. Typically, a genre persists through more than one literary period, though a period may be characterized by the efflorescence of a particular genre or related kinds. A single writer may be seen, in hindsight, to have inaugurated a genre, but to become a full-fledged genre, the cluster of qualities must appear in texts by different authors. Though genres overlap with one another in various different ways, through historical developments, shared techniques, and as a result of thematic similarities, they are often perceived as articulating 'boundaries' between those of their group and those of another grouping (the sets vary according to the system of generic classification in use). While these very systems of classification may appear to impose from above artificial separations into classes or families whose differences define them, genre as it operates within and among texts often invokes metaphors of boundary, border regions, and the notion of crossing over from one literary realm to another. This aspect of genre is explored below.

Genre in narrative fiction can be conceived as a list of what are variously known as types, kinds, or subgenres. From among these synonyms the advanced student can select a term to indicate subdivisions of narrative; none of them is without drawbacks. *Kind*, a venerable term with roots in Renaissance genre taxonomies, can sound casual or breezy to a contemporary reader. *Type* carries an implication of typicality that a student may not intend. The term *subgenre*, my own choice, unfortunately suggests lowness in a hierarchy, but it has the advantage of containing the word 'genre' within it, which helps avoid confusion. Narrative subgenres include: adventure; allegory; ballad; *Bildungsroman;* comic novel; detective fiction; dime novel; domestic fiction; epic; fable; fairy tale; fantasy; fictional auto-biography; gothic; historical fiction; horror story; industrial novel; metafiction; multi-plot novel; mystery; naturalist novel; novel of ideas; parable; postmodern novel; pulp fiction; realistic fiction; romance; satire; short story; science fiction; social problem novel; thriller.

Telling these subgenres apart depends on recognizing the sort of plot lines, character types, settings, time periods, tones, broad themes, and a number of other particular conventions shared by works bearing their labels. Gérard Genette cautiously observes, 'The properly (sub)generic categories are apparently always connected to thematic specifications. But that question requires closer examination' (*Architext*, 75 n. 79). Theme alone does not account for generic grouping or generic difference, for some markedly different subgenres share themes, but it can be an important portion of a generic category. Individual works may possess combinations of themes that suggest different subgenres, and many narratives belong to more than one subgenre simultaneously—a dime novel can be a thriller; a mystery can be a metafiction; an historical novel can be a novel of ideas. Because themes, those ideas that connect literary representations and the broader world of human concerns and experience, have often been interpreted as elements of ideology, an emphasis on the thematic components of genre may lead to useful discoveries about the ideology of particular subgenres. Especially when a narrative genre is handled with attention to historical contexts, questions about implicit and/or explicit beliefs embedded in its themes can help explain why certain formal strategies become associated with ideological positions. For instance, the detective's revelation of the murderer at the end of a detective story, a conventional kind of closure, is sometimes read as politically conservative, embedding as it does assumptions about the accessibility of truth, analogies with religious ideas about guilt and judgment, and the consoling social wish fulfillment of the apprehension of criminals.

The defining features of some categories can be formal: the triple-decker novel comes in three volumes; the novella is a work of intermediate length; epistolary fiction is comprised of letters. More commonly, qualities of the fictional worlds separate works in one genre from another, as in the chronotope, the space/time coordinates, of picaresque (featuring episodic events on the road) or historical fiction (located in the past). Generic labels are themselves slippery: their meanings change over time, or they describe quite different kinds of works in different national traditions. Even when the terms are agreed upon, generic identification or classification of a work can be a matter of controversy, as the previous chapter suggests, and placing a text generically may not in itself yield useful insights. Further, many narratives defy generic placement, combine genres in unconventional ways, or invoke generic conventions only to subvert them.

Natural as it is to want to know where a narrative belongs in a taxonomic scheme of types, this sort of classification only takes the advanced student so far. Not to be despised, a knowledge of commonly used labels can provide a handy shortcut to more related texts, and one somewhat more precise than Amazon.com's rubric: 'Customers who bought this book also bought ...' Many bibliographies, most bookstores and library catalogs, and more than a few academic studies of narrative rely on generic labels to sort out the vast and diverse array of fiction into manageable categories.

This in itself, however, does not make a compelling case for the advanced student's attention to genre. An alternative case can be made for the significance of genre from the perspective of the reading experience, as it is shaped and guided by the recognition of conventions. *Conventions* are the particular traits of formal arrangement, setting, character types, narrative situation, plot, and theme which can be identified in more than one work, and which activate expectations in the reader who has encountered them before. According to Raymond Williams, the 'coming together' of conventions suggests an agreement about an implicit method: 'all forms of art contain fundamental and often only implicit conventions of method and purpose' (*Keywords*, 80). The power of implication inhering in form matters here. Plot conventions can cue the reader to expect a particular train of events and not another one. Conventions of character can sketch with economy a stock figure and his associated role. Conventions of setting, of time/place or chronotope, contribute to atmosphere as well as to the trajectory of plots that traverse fictional worlds. Knowledge of and reaction to conventions shape the fictional world-making of the reader. A reader baffled by the generic demands of a time-shift fantasy fiction's nested time settings may not be able to do his or her part in the creation of a fictional world. Familiarity with conventions effects the degree to which a reader can rise to the challenge of belonging to what Rabinowitz calls the text's authorial audience; indeed, generic signals embedded in paratexts often play a deciding role in whether a text gets read at all by a particular reader.

If the text is read all the way through, genre then plays an important role in the account a reader makes, after the fact, of its qualities and the label assigned to it. Generic labeling often frames a reading experience: expectations are formed at the outset on the basis of external knowledge, context, or paratextual cues; then judgments about the text follow until reading ceases. From this perspective, generic conventions are of greatest interest as features signaling to the reader during the as yet unfinished reading experience. Michael Goldman puts the strange double powers of genre beautifully in his book *On Drama*: 'We experience it as something looming or fading, definite or disruptive, something more like expectation or occasion—a weather, an attitude, a mood. Yet, as such, it involves a sensation like that of classification, of boundaries anticipated and apprehended' (*On Drama*, 5). For the critic of narrative form, attention to genre can be a powerful component of an analysis of the dynamic processes of recognition, co-creation, comprehension, and interpretation that stories set in motion.

As Gary Saul Morson observes, '*genre does not belong to texts alone, but to the interaction between texts and a classifier*' (*Boundaries*, p. x; emphasis original). The classifier of Morson's conception is a reader well versed in the alternatives that might be invoked to describe a text, and who might well have a specific purpose in mind when choosing to place a text in a particular category. The attainments necessary to the exercise of such skill have sometimes given generic criticism a reputation for pedantry. But genre operates on, and with the cooperation of readers and viewers who employ no specialized vocabulary. Knowledge of genres and convention can of course be acquired through formal study of a particular narrative subgenre,[4] but it more fundamentally depends on a reader's exposure to a wide range of narratives in prose, verse, and film. Most readers possess a large stock of generic knowledge, though it may be latent. Some ways in which readers employ that knowledge include the recognition of a kind of narrative from a short sample (such as a film trailer), the supplying of familiar examples of a particular kind (for example, cyberpunk?—William Gibson's *Neuromancer*), and the distinguishing of 'serious' or 'literary' works from 'popular' products of the mass market (though some kinds cut across the social lines of high-brow, middle-brow, and low-brow fiction).

Generic sorting operates every time a reader decides, often on the basis of paratextual cues, that a work suits her mood, or answers her hankering for a particular kind of reading experience. Naturally, the text taken up after such a generic recognition confirms, qualifies, or alters the reader's sense of what was expected. Preliminary recognition of clusters of conventions, and the experience of having their promises fulfilled or broken, then becomes part of the equipment a reader brings to subsequent reading or viewing experiences. Many factors, not only matters of form or type, contribute to this dynamic of reading. Heather Dubrow writes, 'we should acknowledge and scrutinize the ways generic expectations may interact with other expectations and hence be intensified or undercut—or even both at once—by a whole series of signals that have nothing to do with genre directly' (*Genre*, 108). Those other expectations may belong to areas of form already discussed in this book, or they may derive from social, political, or other contextual features of the reader's position in relation to the text.

The analogies or metaphors that often accompany generic theories deserve at least brief notice. David Fishelov enumerates four deep metaphors that encapsulate approaches to genre. These are the analogy with biology (employing the metaphor of evolution), the family analogy (in which family traits, resemblance, and relations among family members figure), the institutional analogy (in which norms, conventions, and social functions loom large), and the speech act analogy (in which genres represent speech acts). Each analogy, Fishelov demonstrates, has its limitations as well as its likely emphases; he recommends a pluralistic approach to genre rather than the choice and imposition of a single metaphor.

Recent work on genre often employs a geopolitical analogy, in which borders, boundary crossing, contested territory, and other spatial metaphors figure.[5] Structuralist anthropology's interest in liminality, threshold spaces, or in-between phases of life gives to genre theory a set of metaphors borrowed from understandings of life cycles, social dramas, and mechanisms for cultural change. Benedict Anderson's study of the novel and nationalism, *Imagined Communities* (1983), has had a role in the dissemination of geopolitical analogies, as has postcolonial theories' interest in migrancy (and hybridity, a biological metaphor). As Susan Stanford Friedman observes in *Mappings* (1998), routes and roots overlap

in metaphors for identity. Our contemporary preoccupation with globalization shows in our contemporary concerns and in our metaphors for
genre.[6] This adoption of spatial metaphors to articulate a sense of
generic limitation or representational norms is not new, however; I
argue in *Victorian Renovations of the Novel: Narrative Annexes and the
Boundaries of Representation* (1998) that novelists, taste-makers, and book
reviewers in the Victorian period commonly referred to borders, boundary lines, and realms in order to create and police representational
norms for the novel. Violations of the social norms that constituted
informal censorship of narrative representation were noticed as incur-
sions into forbidden territory or crossing the line. Indeed, negative criticism of generic admixture often employs another set of analogies,
culinary or medical in nature. Unpalatable mixtures on a plate, strange
juxtapositions of flavor, and infectious diseases provide the metaphors
for deploring texts that startle the reader with unexpected generic combinations. Attitudes towards genre have histories as rich and interesting
as genres themselves.

Analytical strategies

Interpreting genres and narrative conventions as cultural artefacts. The historical study of genres, or the tracking of the use of particular narrative conventions over time, need not be a matter of dry-as-dust
  bibliography. It can contribute to interdisciplinary cultural studies,
  following models such as Greg Urban's *Metaculture: How Culture
  Moves through the World* (2001). Urban writes that the 'new cultural
  object ... can only be fully evaluated in relationship to the objects
  that have come before it. Hence, the new object will become, in its
  turn, part of the past against which some subsequent object will be
  judged.' Urban's description of temporal position of cultural objects
  closely resembles what many literary theorists have said about genre:
  'it is a once and future thing, predicting or foreseeing future objects,
  and contributing to the metacultural framework—the precipitated
  past—through which those future objects will be judged'
  (*Metaculture*, 236). It stands to reason that the analysis of newness,
  responsiveness to cultural stimuli, and the self-understanding of narrative genres can become part of the accumulation of social learning
  that Urban calls for in *Metaculture*. While Urban's work suggests
  through various scaled down and minutely detailed case studies how
  anthropology, linguistic analysis, and film criticism can contribute

an understanding of how culture moves through the world, a renewed genre criticism has something to offer as well.

Distant reading.   The interpretation of bibliographic data by graphing opens up new areas in literary history and cultural studies for synthetic, summary insights based on large pools of information about the history of the book. Franco Moretti argues in his lecture 'Graphs' that a great deal can be discerned about a culture and its reading by graphing (for instance) the publication dates of particular genres within nations or national literary traditions. Moretti's method, which he describes as a more rational literary history than the usual sort (which tracks the careers of representative texts), produces graphic evidence based on large numbers of narrative texts ('Graphs,' 1). Moretti's graphs demonstrate with admirable empiricism the gist of Raymond Williams's theory of dominant, residual, and emergent forms of expression in culture, discussed in Chapter 6.[7] Having graphed the publication dates of what he calls 'super-genres' (epistolary fiction, gothic, historical fiction) in eighteenth-century and early nineteenth-century Britain, Moretti then provides commentary on his graph that supports Williams's insight. The decline of epistolary fiction appears to be a precondition for the rise of gothic, which in turn yields to historical fiction. Moretti observes that his graph suggests 'the decline of a super-genre is a sort of necessary precondition for the take-off of its successor' ('Graphs,' 6). What Williams would have called the dominant form, Moretti's hegemonic form, coexists with the earliest instances of the emergent genre. These texts hover in a 'latency period' before the decline in popularity of the dominant form makes room for the new form's take-off. The historical specificity yielded by this method transcends the usual list of dates of selected publications by locating take-offs and declines of large numbers of texts. This in turn opens up the possibility of making historically specific arguments about hierarchies of taste, changes in offerings in the marketplace, the attraction of 'newness' or of 'retro' fashions, and the influence of external contexts on narrative forms.

The compilation and graphing of publication data from different nations makes Moretti's project a truly comparative and collaborative endeavor. An advanced student with the language skills to study the national bibliographies and graph the appearance and success of successor subgenres of the novel can make a substantive contribution to the study of the novel spearheaded by Moretti. See the website, The

Center for the Study of the Novel, at <http://novel.stanford.edu/> for details about ongoing scholarship in this area.

Analyzing the migration of conventions.   If Moretti's 'distant reading' does not appeal to the advanced student, a more precise study of a particular convention, set of conventions, or generic configuration of traits can be carried out within a more limited set of texts. Applying the methodology of motif-tracing on a larger scale than the individual work, this sort of work on conventions can demonstrate the obscured relations among writers who transmit and alter clusters of conventions, or among genres that are thought to be mutually exclusive. The journal *New Literary History* provides many examples of critical work focusing on the reasons for literary change, the definitions of periods, and the evolution of styles, conventions, and genres, not only narrative genres. An exemplary book-length critical work of this kind is Ian Duncan's *Modern Romance and Transformations of the Novel: The Gothic, Scott, Dickens* (1992). Duncan traces the revival of romance during the period of the rise of the novel in a study rich with detailed analysis of specific conventions and tropes.

Noticing the repetitions and alterations in the career of a literary convention may at first appear daunting, and Duncan's comprehensive range of reference does nothing to diminish that impression, but this sort of work can be accomplished with the assistance of other wide readers. Reaching those readers has never been easier: the excellent digital archives of specialized discussion lists such as VICTORIA-L make good starting points for crafting an informed query to a group of scholars.[8] For instance, a quick search of the VICTORIA archives for prior discussion of 'blood transfusions' results in dozens of hits from discussion of *Dracula* and nineteenth-century medical texts. A thread on serial publications of novels interrupted by the death of the author provides a number of examples and discussion of the strengths and weaknesses of standard reference books. Other lists do not maintain public archives, but any scholar with access to email can subscribe to a list in order to post a query and receive replies, unsubscribing when finished.

Of particular interest to readers of this book will be the 'listserv' discussion run by the Narrative Society.[9] It is 'for all people interested in narrative,' not just members of the Society. A note about etiquette for interacting with scholars in their specialized online discussions: it's best to do your best to find preliminary information before you place your request in hundreds or even thousands of email boxes around the world. Once you know enough to have a sense of where the gaps in your knowledge lie, then you should introduce yourself, explain the nature of your project, and politely request the assistance of the list members. Each person who writes to you, either privately, or for distribution to the whole list, should be thanked with an individual email from you (and names should be recorded for future acknowledgements pages). You should keep in mind that some of the most influential scholars and theorists in the field will see your question; this is a wonderful benefit to scholarship and a truly democratic development, but it is also an incentive not to appear a dunce. Finally, make every effort not to send private messages out to all the members of a listserv. This is at the least annoying, and at the worst, very embarrassing indeed.

Literary recovery work.   Though it need not be organized in terms of narrative subgenres, the area of literary recovery of forgotten or neglected texts has augmented our knowledge of important subgenres such as slave narratives. Feminist critics in the 1980s achieved some of their revisionist work by redefining the significance of subgenres and questioning unexamined hierarchies that undergirded literary historical accounts of past periods of literature. Narrative subgenres that had been undervalued because of their female authorship and readership were brought to light, re-evaluated, and reissued in teachable editions. Scholars of African-American literature have searched archives and sources such as old newspapers to locate African-American autobiographies, sermons, and epics. The gain in knowledge about works by women and minorities thus results in a better understanding of the dominant, residual, and emergent forms of a particular period, as well. This sort of work promises surprises as well as confirmation of hunches. Laura Browder's *Slippery Characters: Ethnic Impersonators and American Identities* (2000), for instance, describes a fascinating subgenre of autobiography (or of narrative fiction), in which the writers (mis)represent their life stories in order to claim false ethnic identities. Though some of Browder's texts were bestsellers in their time, her project undertakes the recovery of a tacit generic tradition.

Discovering emergent genres.   The study of contemporary narrative permits a wide reader to discern new, unprecedented, or recently revived subgenres. Though this task may seem impossibly daunting in the face of the huge unsorted output of contemporary writing, scholars who pursue thematic links through large numbers of texts may in the process sometimes discover those combinations of formal attributes and theme that create a new subgenre. I argue as much in my *Romances of the Archive in Contemporary British Fiction* (2001), in which I hold that research narratives have become a characteristic vehicle for British novelists to express their fascination with and anxieties about history, heritage, and the uses of the past. This sort of work can supplement thematic or theoretical projects, or it can contribute to literary history, if the student has the time and energy to collect sufficient instances of the emergent genre to make a case for its significance.

Keywords

Intertextuality.   Its classical description by Julia Kristeva identifies intertextuality as the presence within one text of traces of another text. Kristeva's semiotic approach sees a text (and a self) as a sign system shot through with the markers of other signifying practices.[10] Some of the features of genre are clearly a form of intertextuality, and conventions certainly deserve notice as intertexts, but the adoption of a 'restricted' intertextuality between literary texts has been criticized as a retreat to philology or as a repackaging of old-fashioned sources and influences study. Gérard Genette distinguishes among the generic architext; the allusions, quotations, and plagiarism that for him constitute intertexts; the intratexts that occur within the works of a single writer; and the relationship of hypotext and hypertext (as for instance in the *Odyssey* and *Ulysses*). Intertextuality has meant such a startling variety of things in the past several decades of use, and in different theoretical schools, that the advanced student should approach the complex of concepts implied by its use with caution.

Modes and mythoi.   Northrop Frye played an influential role in revising genre theory to include the prose fictional forms that had often been omitted in earlier centuries' models, but he did so by creating an idiosyncratic genre system of his own, not often followed today. Many of his terms, however, retain some of the meaning with which he imbued them. According to *An Anatomy of Criticism*, the five 'modes' are myth, romance, the high mimetic, the low mimetic, and irony. It should be noted that this use of 'modes' is particular to Frye, and the items he lists would in several cases ordinarily be called genres. (Other critics have named different modes: satiric, elegiac, epideictic, to mention a few.) Frye's modes correlate to his *mythoi*, or archetypical generic plots, and they play a role in his Jungian criticism. In the third essay of *An Anatomy of Criticism*, he proposes four narrative categories prior to literary genres: romance, irony, tragedy, and comedy. Each of these *mythoi*, or generic plots, makes up a portion of an all-encompassing conceptual map of the possible stories. Frye offers the categories of introverted-person fiction (romance), extroverted-personal fiction (realistic novels), introverted-intellectual fiction (the confession), and extroverted-intellectual fiction (the anatomy). Some narrative texts—Joyce's *Ulysses*—combine these alternatives. Most important for students of genre in the novel is Frye's endorsement of the opposition of romance and realism, a concept that has had staying power, despite the persistent intertwining of these supposed opposites in actual novels since the eighteenth century.

Topoi (singular: *topos*).   A term often used by genre critics and theorists. For rhetoricians 'topoi' means the general topics of rhetoric as well as formal qualities of the arguments that contain them. Topoi differ from genres and kinds, because they indicate content (phrasings, metaphors, concepts, stock characters) that have become associated with a genre. Thus, when used in reference to a particular genre, 'topoi' usually indicates the commonplaces or typical situations associated with that genre. Because these commonplaces suggest a tendency towards the formulaic, the term 'topoi' is sometimes linked with oral culture, or with strong traditions offering implicit models against which individual texts are measured, though they may or may not conform to those models. The use of the term 'topoi' may suggest a critic's belief in cultural continuity, the importance of continuous literary traditions, and even universal values. The critique of each of these attitudes by Marxist and post-structuralist critics does not invalidate the observation that genres tend to accrue, over time, somewhat standardized sets of conventions and expressions, but it does imply the need for carefully contextualized handling of topoi, when they are invoked. It should go without saying that a writer may deliberately choose to employ topoi associated with a particular genre in fresh mixtures with the topoi of other genres, or that topoi may be invoked for satirical or subversive purposes.

Further reading

Bakhtin, Mikhail, 'Forms of Time and of the Chronotope in the Novel,' in *The Dialogic Imagination: Four Essays by M. M. Bakhtin*, ed. Michael Holquist, trans. Caryl Emerson and Michael Holquist (University of Texas Press, 1981).

Burke, Kenneth, *Counter-Statement*, 2nd ed. (Hermes Publications, 1953). See 'Lexicon Rhetoricae,' 123–83.

— *The Philosophy of Literary Form: Studies in Symbolic Action*, 2nd ed. (Louisiana State University Press, 1967). See the title essay, 1–137.

Colie, Rosalie, *The Resources of Kind: Genre-Theory in the Renaissance*, ed. Barbara Kiefer Lewalski (University of California Press, 1973).

Derrida, Jacques, 'The Law of Genre,' trans. Avitall Ronell, in *On Narrative*, ed. W. J. T. Mitchell (University of Chicago Press, 1981), 51–77. A playful look at the madness of the law of genre, particularly the 'law' that says 'genres are not to be mixed.'

Dubrow, Heather, *Genre: The Critical Idiom* (Methuen, 1982). This provides a very concise run-down of genre theory.

Fishelov, David, *Metaphors of Genre: The Role of Analogies in Genre Theory* (Penn State University Press, 1993). Fishelov makes a compelling case for a pluralistic approach to genre, in which no one conceptual framework (implicit in analogies for genre) overrides the potential usefulness of the others.

Fowler, Alastair, *Kinds of Literature: An Introduction to the Theory of Genres and Modes* (Harvard, 1982). Renaissance focus; very useful.

Frye, Northrop, *Anatomy of Criticism: Four Essays* (Princeton University Press, 1957). The first and fourth essays are the most relevant, though parts of the third essay also contribute to our understanding of Frye's conception of genre.

Genette, Gérard, *The Architext: An Introduction*, 1979, trans. Jane E. Lewin (University of California Press, 1992).

Goldman, Michael, *On Drama: Boundaries of Genre, Borders of Self* (University of Michigan Press, 2000).

Guillén, Claudio, *Literature as System: Essays toward the Theory of Literary History* (Princeton University Press, 1971). See especially essays 4 and 5, 'On the Uses of Literary Genre' and 'Genre and Countergenre,' 105–58.

Hernadi, Paul, *Beyond Genre: New Directions in Literary Classification* (Cornell University Press, 1972).

Hirsch, E. D., *Validity in Interpretation* (Yale University Press, 1967). See especially chapter 3, 'The Concept of Genre,' 68–126.

McKeon, Michael (ed.), *Theory of the Novel: A Historical Approach* (Johns Hopkins University Press, 2000). See especially 1–69 for a selection of readings from genre theory.

Moretti, Franco, 'Graphs,' a lecture (Sept. 2002). Forthcoming (2003) in *New Left Review*.

Morson, Gary Saul, *The Boundaries of Genre: Dostoevsky's* Diary of a Writer *and the Traditions of Literary Utopia* (University of Texas Press, 1981).

Rabinowitz, Peter J., *Before Reading: Narrative Conventions and the Politics of Interpretation* (1987), 2nd ed., foreword by James Phelan (Ohio State University Press, 1998).

Todorov, Tzvetan, *Genres in Discourse*, trans. Catherine Porter (Cambridge University Press, 1990).

Urban, Greg, *Metaculture: How Culture Moves through the World* (University of Minnesota Press, 2001).

Appendix A
Terms Listed by Chapter

Scanning this appendix helps readers locate discussions of terms by their context.

Preface: Studying Narrative Form

narrative form
formalism: uses of its insights
structuralist and culturalist approaches
narratology
jargon, use of

1. Major Approaches to and Theorists of Narrative

definitions of narrative and fiction
narrator and narratee
plot
description and narration
fabula (story) and *sjuzet* (discourse)
characters, actants

Major schools of thought

classical theorists (Plato, Aristotle)
Renaissance theories of fictions (Philip Sidney)
writer-critics from Romanticism to present (Henry James, E. M. Forster)
Russian Formalists (Shklovsky, Tomashevsky, Propp)
Mikhail Bakhtin
New Critics (Cleanth Brooks and Robert Penn Warren; Rene Wellek and Austin Warren)

role of the reader
   Chicago school
   speech act theory
   reception theory
   reader response criticism
structuralism and post-structuralism
   narratology and narrative poetics (Todorov, Barth, Genette)

Recent developments

the narrative turn in other disciplines
contextual narratology

narrative ethics
feminist narratology
cognitive approaches to literary study

2. Shapes of Narrative: A Whole of Parts

Narrative

its subdivisions

Components of narrative

story and discourse
plots

Forms of narrative

short short story
short stories
novel
epic
ballad
romance
novella

Sections within narratives

books
chapters
volumes, as in the three-volume novel or triple-decker
serial installments
   monthly numbers
   magazine or newspaper installments
sequences
episodes
letters (epistolary fiction)

Series, sequences, or cycles

genre fiction
short story collections
story sequences
volume of short stories (unified)
short story cycle
anthologies

Keywords related to the concepts in Chapter 2

- epic and novel (Bakhtin)
- loose baggy monsters (Henry James)

- textual editing/textual criticism (a discipline: the principles for scholarly editing of texts)

3. Narrative Situation: Who's Who and What's its Function

Narrative situation

characters
   reflectors, focalizers, filters
narrators
narrative levels
   discourse level
   story level

Paradigm of 'participants' in narrative

author
implied author
narrator
narratee
implied reader
real readers

First-person narrators

self-narration
fictional autobiographies
narrating self and experiencing self
consonant narration and dissonant narration
plural first-person narration
   communal voice

Third-person narrators

limited and omniscient
authorial and figural narration
   authorial narrative situation
   figural narrative situation
external and internal narration

Overt and covert narrators

Unreliable narrators

discordant narration

Perspective (point of view)

Reflectors (focalizers, filters)

single (fixed perspective)

multiple perspectives
variable perspectives
interior and exterior perspectives

Second-person narration

Multi-personed narration

polyphony
dialogic form
heteroglossia

Keywords related to concepts in Chapter 3

- author: author function, death of the author, authority (Foucault, Barthes, Kristeva)
- discourse (Foucault and Bakhtin)
- voice (Genette, lyric voice, post-structuralism)

4. People on Paper: Character, Characterization, and Represented Minds

Character and plot

Characters as 'people' or 'word masses'

Character traits

Representation of fictional consciousness

psycho-narration
quoted monologue (interior monologue)
narrated monologue (free indirect discourse)

Characterization

traits and habits
internal and external characterization
names
description
block characterization

Types

flat and round characters
defined by plot functions (Propp)
defined by structural roles (Greimas)
    subject, object, sender, helper, receiver, and opponent
defined by rhetorical roles (Phelan)
    synthetic, mimetic, thematic
taxonomy by trait (Hochman)

stylization and naturalism
coherence and incoherence
wholeness and fragmentariness
literalness and symbolism
complexity and simplicity
transparency and opacity
dynamism and staticism (rigidity or inertness)
closure and openness

Keywords related to concepts in Chapter 4
- Aristotelian character (agent [pratton] and character [ethos])
- stream of consciousness

5. Plot and Causation: Related Events

plot
causation
story and plot
fabula and *sjuzet*
story world, story level
discourse level
events
causal relations and consequences
beginning, middle, and end
plot line
multi-plot narratives
plot summary (synopsis)
subplot
events
  kernels and satellites
  snares
episodes
digressions
narrative annexes
plot turns (peripety)
post hoc ergo propter hoc fallacy
plot types
plot functions
actants
  subject, object
  sender, receiver
  helper, opposer

Keywords related to the concepts in Chapter 5
- dialogic form
- grammar of narrative/story grammars
- masterplots

6. Timing: How Long and How Often?

story time
discourse -time
timing
duration/speeds
   scene/showing/mimesis
   summary/telling/diegesis
   ellipses/gaps
   pauses
   expansion, dilation, stretching

Pace

Frequency

   normative frequency
   repetitive frequency
   iterative frequency

Challenges to Genette's model for narrative time (Richardson)

   circular narratives
   contradictory narratives
   antinomic narratives
   differential narratives
   conflated narratives
   dual or multiple narratives

Keywords related to the concepts in Chapter 6

- chronotope
- gaps

7. Order and Disorder

Forward-moving narration

Hypotaxis and parataxis

Backward-moving narration

Story time and discourse time

ulterior narration
anterior narration
simultaneous narration
intermittent narration
intercalated narration

Anachronies

analepses
prolepses
syllepses
achronies

Analepses/flashbacks

backstory
digression
external analepsis
internal analepsis
mixed analepsis
reach and extent
return (completing)
recall (repeating)
objective or subjective

Prolepses/anticipations/flashforwards

external prolepses
internal prolepses
mixed prolepses
reach and extent
fill in, advance notices, repetitions
objective or subjective

Keywords related to the concepts in Chapter 7

• ambiguity
• enigma
• spatial form

8. Levels: Realms of Existence

Story world

setting
chronotope

Narrative level

discourse level, textual level
story level
narrative situation

Framing

frame tale
stories within stories
    Chinese box narrative

metalepses/frame-breaking
  metafiction

Primary, secondary, and tertiary narrative levels

embedded story/Inset
  staircase narrative
interpolated tale
mise en abyme

Metafictionality

paratexts
'laying bare the device'
defamiliarization

Keywords related to the concepts in Chapter 8

- frame
- interpellation

9. Fictional Worlds and Fictionality

poesy as fiction
world-making
fictional worlds
  fictionality
  truth claims
  'As If' worlds (Iser)
narrativity
formal distinctiveness of fiction (Cohn)
worlds within worlds: ontological use of levels
chronotope
distant reading (Moretti)

Keyword related to the concepts in Chapter 9

- metanarratives

10. Disguises: Fiction in the Form of Nonfiction Texts

formal distinctiveness of fiction revisited
presentational context
pre-structure
paratexts
  epitexts
  peritexts
authorial audience and narrative audience (Rabinowitz)

satires, forgeries, fakes
parody
illocutionary stance
documentary novel
pseudofactual fiction
authorial reading
history of the book

Keywords related to the concepts in Chapter 10

- mimesis
- pastiche

11. Genres and Conventions

narrative form as generic form
the 'three genres' or universal modes
genre as historical genre
types, kinds, subgenres
conventions
Raymond Williams's dominant, emergent, and residual forms
Franco Moretti's 'distant reading'

Keywords related to the concepts in Chapter 11

- intertextuality (Julia Kristeva and others)
- modes and mythoi (Northrop Frye)
- topoi, topos.

Appendix B
Representative Texts: A List of Suggested Readings

Forms of narrative by length

minimal narrative	Russell Edson, stories in *The Very Thing that Happens*; *Short Shorts*, ed. Irving Howe and Ilana Wiener Howe
short short story	Jamaica Kincaid, 'Girl,' in *At the Bottom of the River*; numerous works by Russell Edson
short stories	Ring Lardner, 'Haircut'; William Faulkner, 'A Rose for Emily'
novel	Jane Austen, *Pride and Prejudice*; Margaret Atwood, *The Handmaid's Tale*
epic	Homer, *The Odyssey*; John Milton, *Paradise Lost*; Derek Walcott, *Omeros*
ballad	'Sir Patrick Spens'; Sterling A. Brown, 'Slim in Hell'
romance	*Sir Gawain and the Green Knight*; Edmund Spenser, *The Faerie Queene*; Nathaniel Hawthorne, *The House of the Seven Gables*; A. S. Byatt, *Possession*
novella	Joseph Conrad, *Heart of Darkness*; Doris Lessing, *The Fifth Child*

Illustrations of sectioning within narratives

books or parts	Henry Fielding, *Tom Jones*
chapters	Jane Austen, *Emma*
volumes, as in the three-volume novel	Charlotte Brontë, *Jane Eyre*
serial installments	Thomas Hardy, *Tess of the D'Urbervilles*; Charles Dickens, *Hard Times*
monthly numbers	William Thackeray, *Vanity Fair*; George Eliot, *Middlemarch*; Stephen King, *The Green Mile*
letters (epistolary fiction)	Laclos, *Dangerous Liaisons*; Samuel Richardson, *Pamela*; Ring Lardner, *You Know Me Al*; Alice Walker, *The Color Purple*

Series, sequences, or cycles

in genre fiction	J. R. R. Tolkien, *The Lord of the Rings*; Patricia Cornwell, the Scarpetta mysteries
in literary fiction	Anthony Powell, *A Dance to the Music of Time*; C. P.

	Snow, *Strangers and Brothers*; John Updike, *The Rabbit Tetrology*; Doris Lessing, *The Children of Violence* sequence
story sequences	Arthur Conan Doyle, Sherlock Holmes stories
volume of short stories (unified)	Sherwood Anderson, *Winesburg, Ohio*; James Joyce, *Dubliners*; Ernest Hemingway, *In Our Time*; Harriet Doerr, *Stones for Ibarra*; Margaret Laurence, *A Bird in the House*
short story cycles	Jean Toomer, *Cane*; Jamaica Kincaid, *Annie John*; Amy Tan, *The Joy Luck Club*

Illustrations of different kinds of narrative situation

narratees	Laurence Sterne, *Tristram Shandy*; Italo Calvino, *If on a Winter's Night a Traveler*; Kazuo Ishiguro, *The Remains of the Day*; Charlotte Brontë, *Jane Eyre*; Tillie Olson, 'I Stand Here Ironing'
first-person narrators	Charles Dickens, *David Copperfield*; Ernest Gaines, *A Lesson before Dying*; Anthony Burgess, *A Clockwork Orange*; Margaret Atwood, *A Handmaid's Tale*; Evelyn Waugh, *Brideshead Revisited*; Ford Madox Ford, *The Good Soldier*
plural first-person narrators	Joyce Carol Oates, *Broke Heart Blues*; William Faulkner, 'A Rose for Emily'
first-person consonant narration	Seamus Deane, *Reading in the Dark*; Roddy Doyle, *Paddy Clarke Ha Ha Ha*
first-person dissonant narration	Salman Rushdie, *Midnight's Children*; Jamaica Kincaid, *The Autobiography of my Mother*; Charles Dickens, *Great Expectations*; Daphne DuMaurier, *Rebecca*
third-person narrators	Opal Palmer Adisa, *It Begins with Tears*; Arundhati Roy, *The God of Small Things*; A. S. Byatt, *Possession*; Margaret Drabble, *The Radiant Way*; Rumer Godden, *Black Narcissus*; Walter Abish, *How German Is It?*; Paul Auster, *The New York Trilogy*; George Eliot, *The Mill on the Floss*
third-person authorial narration	Harriet Beecher Stowe, *Uncle Tom's Cabin*; Jim Crace, *Being Dead*; Salman Rushdie, *The Satanic Verses*; Anita Desai, *Fire on the Mountain*
third-person figural narration	James Joyce, *A Portrait of the Artist as a Young Man*; John Le Carré, *Tinker, Tailor, Soldier, Spy*; Nadine Gordimer, *July's People*
mixed, multiple, and variable narrators	Gloria Naylor, *Mama Day*; William Faulkner, *As I Lay Dying*; Ali Smith, *Hotel World*; Andre Brink, *A Chain of Voices*; Margaret Atwood, *Alias Grace*; Barbara Kingsolver, *The Poisonwood Bible*

second-person narration	Helen Dunmore, *With Your Crooked Heart*; Jay McInerney, *Bright Lights, Big City*; Lorrie Moore, stories in *Self Help*; Frederick Barthelme, 'Shopgirls' in *Moon Deluxe*
unreliable narrators	Ring Lardner, 'Haircut'; Kazuo Ishiguro, *The Remains of the Day*; Ian McEwan, *Atonement*; Edgar Allan Poe, 'The Tell-Tale Heart'; William Faulkner, *The Sound and the Fury*

Modes for representation of characters' consciousness

psycho-narration	Thomas Mann, *Death in Venice*; James Joyce, *A Portrait of the Artist as a Young Man*; Iris Murdoch, *The Philosopher's Pupil*; Jane Austen, *Emma*; D. H. Lawrence, *Women in Love*; Elizabeth Bowen, *The House in Paris*
quoted monologue	James Joyce, *Ulysses*; Virginia Woolf, *Mrs. Dalloway*; Keri Hulme, *The Bone People*; Ann Quin, 'Motherlogue'
narrated monologue	Gustave Flaubert, *Madame Bovary*; Jane Austen, *Pride and Prejudice*; Henry James, *A Portrait of a Lady*; Michael Ondaatje, *Anil's Ghost*

Handling of story-lines, pace, order, and levels

multi-plots	Anthony Trollope, *The Way We Live Now*; Opal Palmer Adisa, *It Begins with Tears*; Vikram Seth, *A Suitable Boy*; Leo Tolstoi, *War and Peace*; Rohinton Mistry, *A Fine Balance*; Salman Rushdie, *The Satanic Verses*
speeds	Nicholas Baker, *The Mezzanine*; Virginia Woolf, *Between the Acts*; Jim Crace, *Being Dead*; James Joyce, *Ulysses*; V. S. Naipual, *A House for Mr. Biswas*; Emily Brontë, *Wuthering Heights*; Doris Lessing, *The Fifth Child*; Laurence Sterne, *Tristram Shandy*
orderly, chronological narration	Charlotte Brontë, *Jane Eyre*; Charles Dickens, *David Copperfield*; Michael Chabon, *Summerland*; Salman Rushdie, *Midnight's Children*; Kazuo Ishiguro, *The Unconsoled*
disordered (anachronous or achronous) narratives	Toni Morrison, *Beloved*; Diana Wynne Jones, *Hexwood*; Kazuo Ishiguro, *Remains of the Day*; Margaret Atwood, *The Handmaid's Tale*; Martin Amis, *Time's Arrow*; Paul Scott, *The Raj Quartet*
narrative levels and embedding	Peter Carey, *Jack Maggs*; Bram Stoker, *Dracula*; A. S. Byatt, *Possession*; Italo Calvino, *If on a Winter Night a Traveler*; Joseph Conrad, *Heart of Darkness*; Opal Palmer Adisa, *It Begins with Tears*; Peter Ackroyd, *Hawksmoor*; Nick Hornby, *High Fidelity*

Limit cases

disguised fiction	Daniel Defoe, *Moll Flanders*; Walter Scott, *Waverley*; George MacDonald Fraser, *Flashman*; Ernest Gaines, *The Autobiography of Miss Jane Pittman*
narrative but not necessarily fiction	Nicholson Baker, *U and I*; Art Spiegelman, *Maus*; Maxine Hong Kingston, *The Woman Warrior*; Dave Eggers, *A Heart-Breaking Work of Staggering Genius*; V. S. Naipaul, *The Enigma of Arrival*
novels but not necessarily prose	Tom Phillips, *The Humument*; Vikram Seth, *Golden Gate*; Bernardine Evaristo, *The Emperor's Babe*; Neil Gaiman, *The Books of Magic*; Nick Bantock, *Griffin and Sabine*

Notes

Preface: Studying Narrative Form

1 Monika Fludernik, *The Fictions of Language and the Languages of Fiction*: *The Linguistic Representation of Speech and Consciousness* (Routledge, 1993), and especially *Towards a 'Natural' Narratology* (Routledge, 1996).
2 Mary Louise Pratt, Barbara Herrnstein Smith, and Susan Snaider Lanser all, in different ways, emphasize the situation of the narrative act, and authorize questions about motives, contexts, and responses. See Pratt's *Towards a Speech Act Theory of Literature* (Indiana University Press, 1977), Smith's 'Narrative Versions, Narrative Theories,' in W. J. T. Mitchell (ed.), *On Narrative* (University of Chicago Press, 1981), 209–32, and Lanser's *The Narrative Act: Point of View in Fiction* (Princeton University Press, 1981).

1   Major Approaches to and Theorists of Narrative

1 E. S. Dallas, Roman Jakobson, and Käte Hamburger have in various ways advanced theories of linguistic person as intrinsic to generic functions. Dallas and Jakobson are cited in René Wellek and Austin Warren, *A Theory of Literature* (Penguin, 1963), 228, 307 nn. 11, 13.
2 Susan Onega and and José Ángel García Landa, *Narratology: An Introduction* (Longman, 1996), 3. By semiotic representations, Onega and García Landa mean the use of sign systems, including visual images and gestures, so their definition of narrative contains drama, comic strips, chronicles, and scientific narrative. Strictly speaking, it could describe certain statements in mathematics.
3 Brian Richardson extends the critique in 'Recent Concepts of Narrative and the Narratives of Narrative Theory,' *Style* 34:2 (Summer 2000), 168–75.
4 Brooks and Warren's influence continues by means of many textbooks and anthologies, through secondary school teaching of literature, and through creative writing handbooks. The Appendix 'Technical Problems and Principles in the Composition of Fiction—A Summary' contains advice for the aspiring writer under the headings 'Beginning and Exposition,' 'Description and Setting,' 'Atmosphere,' 'Selection and Suggestion,' 'Key Moment,' 'Climax,' 'Conflict,' 'Complication,' 'Pattern or Design' (treating repetition), 'Denouement,' 'Character and Act,' 'Focus of Interest,' 'Focus of Character,' 'Focus of Narration: Point of View,' 'Distance' (treating the position of the narrator), 'Scale,' and 'Pace.' Decades later, the critical vocabulary in works such as Richard M. Eastman's *A Guide to the Novel* (Chandler, 1965) and Hallie and Whit Burnett's *Fiction Writer's Handbook* (Harper & Row, 1975) remains substantially unchanged from Brooks and Warren, though by the 1960s, the historical context unpopular with the New Critics comes back in. In the late 1960s and

1970s, the intervention of French structuralism and the revival of interest in Russian Formalism of the 1920s begin a sharp separation of narrative theory from creative writers' handbooks and basic literature texts. The latter two preserve much of Brooks and Warren's vocabulary and methodology intact, updating by adding more recent examples or newly relevant themes. Thus one can find in works published in the 1980s and 1990s advice for writers relying on the same terms and concepts popularized over 50 years earlier by Brooks and Warren. (See Leonard Bishop's *Dare to be a Great Writer* (1988) and Evan Marshall's *The Marshall Plan for Novel Writing* (1998), both published by Writer's Digest Books.) Many literature anthologies for first and second year students contain the same vocabulary. Exceptions to this phenomenon include M. H. Abrams's *Glossary of Literary Terms*, now in its 7th edition (Harcourt Brace, 1999), and assiduously updated; Janet Burroway's *Writing Fiction: A Guide to Narrative Craft*, 5th ed. (Longman, 2000); and Seymour Chatman's *Reading Narrative Fiction* (Macmillan, 1993). This last, an anthology for university students, is a rare cross-over text that introduces narrative theory methodologically and with a sparing use of narratological vocabulary. Unlike Abrams and Burroway, who layer some of the insights of narratology onto a traditional superstructure, Chatman constructs his anthology from the perspective of narrative poetics.

5 Lodge and Barth are unusual in that they are taken seriously by both academic theorists and by novel readers. See David Lodge's *The Art of Fiction* (Penguin, 1992) and Barth's *Friday Book* (Putnam's, 1984) and *Further Fridays* (Little, Brown, 1995). Experimental writers sometimes work in the liminal area between theory and practice. See Ronald Sukenick's *Narralogues: Truth in Fiction* (SUNY Press, 2000), and William Gass's *Fiction and the Figures of Life* (David R. Godine, 1979), as well as Christine Brooke-Rose's *Invisible Author: Last Essays* (Ohio State University Press, 2002). Annie Dillard's *The Writing Life* (HarperCollins, 1989), A. S. Byatt's *On Histories and Stories: Selected Essays* (Chatto & Windus, 2000), John Gardner's *The Art of Fiction: Notes on Craft for Young Writers* (Knopf, 1984), and Madison Smartt Bell's *Narrative Design: A Writer's Guide to Structure* (Norton, 1997) admirably represent the sub-genre of writers' books on their craft. These books can be read with pleasure and illumination by anyone interested in narrative literature.

6 John Guillory asserts that Reuben Brower of Harvard University was responsible for popularizing the term and the practice of 'close reading.' Guillory cites Brower's The *Fields of Light: An Experiment in Critical Reading* (Oxford University Press, 1951). See John Guillory, 'The Very Idea of Pedagogy,' *Profession 2002* (MLA, 2002), 168, 171 n. 4.

7 For instance, compare Roland Barthes's 'Introduction to the Structural Analysis of Narratives' (1966) and his post-structuralist *S–Z: An Essay* (1970).

8 See, for example, Mary Chamberlain and Paul Thompson (ed.), *Narrative and Genre* (Routledge, 1998), for an interdisciplinary collection of essays focusing on life-stories.

9 See for starting points in this rich area, Wayne C. Booth, *The Company We Keep: An Ethics of Fiction* (University of California Press, 1988); Martha Nussbaum, *Poetic Justice: The Literary Imagination and Public Life* (Beacon Press, 1995); Adam Zachary

Newton, *Narrative Ethics* (Harvard University Press, 1995); and Richard A. Posner, 'Against Ethical Criticism: Part Two,' *Philosophy and Literature* 22:2 (1998), 394–412.
10 Warhol cites, among other recent exemplars, Susan S. Lanser's 'Toward a Feminist Narratology' (1986) and her *Fictions of Authority: Women Writers and Narrative Voice* (Cornell University Press,1992), and Sally Robinson's *Engendering the Subject: Gender and Self-Representation in Contemporary Women's Fiction* (SUNY Press, 1991). Warhol's own work in *Gendered Interventions* (Rutgers University Press,1989) demonstrates in a very readable study of Victorian fiction how analysis of narrative strategy (the narrator's address to the reader) can be combined with feminist questions about authority, gender, and readers.

2   Shapes of Narrative

1 Referring to 'a text,' 'a narrative,' or 'a fiction' often signals an intention to convey structuralist or post-structuralist insights about a work. Its generic identity as a novel, a short story, a Renaissance romance, or pulp fiction is de-emphasized by this language.
2 Many critics would add the word 'realistic' to this definition. It may be useful to retain the broader definition, by which romances and other unrealistic prose fictions can be called novels. I accept the argument that Margaret Anne Doody makes in *The True History of The Novel* (Rutgers, 1996) that prose fictions meeting the description of 'novels' antedate the rise of the realistic novel described by Ian Watt and others, but the specific literary history of realistic European prose fiction from its origins is often implied by the standard use of the term 'novel.'
3 M. H. Abrams's definition of 'epic' in *A Glossary of Literary Terms* makes an excellent starting point for a student interested in this influential narrative genre.
4 See for example Derek Attridge, *Poetic Rhythm: An Introduction* (Cambridge University Press, 1995); Lewis Turco, *The New Book of Forms: A Handbook of Poetics* (University Press of New England, 1986); John Hollander, *Rhyme's Reason: A Guide to English Verse* (Yale University Press, 1989); Jack Myers and Michael Simms (ed.), *The Longman Dictionary of Poetic Terms* (Longman, 1989); or, for the most comprehensive treatment of poetic form and world poetry, Alex Preminger and T. V. F. Brogan (ed.), *The New Princeton Encyclopedia of Poetry and Poetics* (Princeton University Press, 1993).
5 See Anthony Trollope, *An Autobiography*, 1883 (Oxford University Press, 1950), 237–8.
6 Anthony Burgess, 'Introduction: A Clockwork Orange Resucked' (1986), in *A Clockwork Orange*, 1962 (Norton, 1987), p. vi.
7 Letters used as building blocks of narrative fiction raise questions treated in two different chapters. Epistolary fiction is just one example of fiction mimicking nonfictional texts; for more, see Chapter 10. More common than the full epistolary fiction is the presentation of letters as secondary texts, written and read by characters within fictional worlds. See Chapter 8 for a discussion of embedded texts.
8 See Hans Walter Gabler, 'Textual Criticism,' in *The Johns Hopkins Guide to Literary Theory and Criticism*, ed. Michael Groden and Martin Kreiswirth (Johns Hopkins University Press, 1994), 708–14.

3   Narrative Situation

1 My treatment of this subject blends the insights of a number of theorists, including Wayne Booth, Seymour Chatman, Wolfgang Iser, Gérard Genette, Susan Lanser, and Dorrit Cohn, but the advanced student can do no better than to begin with Franz Stanzel's seminal work. See *A Theory of Narrative* (1979), trans. Charlotte Goedsche (Cambridge University Press, 1984). See also Dorrit Cohn's useful amendment of Stanzel, 'The Encirclement of Narrative: On Franz Stanzel's *Theorie des Erzählens*,' *Poetics Today* 2:2 (1981), 157–82. I give here a streamlined version of Cohn's amendments of Stanzel.

2 See James Monaco, *How to Read a Film: The Art, Technology, Language, History, and Theory of Film and Media*, rev. ed. (Oxford University Press, 1981), 170–8. For an alternative view, see Celestino Deleyto, 'Focalisation in Film Narrative,' in *Narratology: An Introduction*, ed. Susana Onega and José Angel García Landa (Longman, 1996), 217–33. Seymour Chatman's work makes the effort of accounting for both prose fiction and film fiction: see *Story and Discourse* and *Coming to Terms*.

3 'Reflector' suggests an allegiance to Stanzel; 'focalizer' indicates a Genettian approach; 'filter' comes from Seymour Chatman (*Coming to Terms*, 2). Chatman's usage is preferable when describing strategies used by both prose fiction and film.

4 Not all critics agree on the usefuless of the term 'implied author.' For a good terse summary of the debate, see Ansgar Nünning, 'Implied Author,' *Encyclopedia of the Novel*, vol. 1, ed. Paul Schellinger et al. (Fitzroy Dearborn, 1998), 589–91.

5 See Stewart Garrett, *Dear Reader: The Conscripted Audience in Nineteenth-Century British Fiction* (Johns Hopkins University Press, 1996), and Robyn Warhol, *Gendered Interventions: Narrative Discourse in the Victorian Novel* (Rutgers University Press, 1989), for treatments of direct address to readers.

6 Rabinowitz's dynamic description of authorial audiences is treated in Chapter 10, where I discuss the competency of the reader to recognize the author's (and publisher's) cues. See *Before Reading: Narrative Conventions and the Politics of Interpretation*, 1987, 2nd ed., foreword by James Phelan (Ohio State University Press, 1998).

7 Dorrit Cohn's consonance and dissonance can be fruitfully compared with Roman Ingarden's contrast of a progressively evolving narrative perspective and a retrospective one. See *The Cognition of the Literary Work of Art*, trans. Ruth Ann Crowley and Kenneth R. Olson (Northwestern University Press,1973).

8 In *Fictions of Authority* (1992), the feminist narrative theorist Susan Snaider Lanser argues that communal voices ought to be considered a separate type of point of view, but to make matters more complicated, she finds examples of communal voices whose perspective is represented by a singular first-person narrator.

9 One often reads that 'omniscient narration' has fallen into disuse and disfavor after its nineteenth-century heyday, but I frequently come across *authorial* narration in my reading of contemporary fiction, especially in genre fiction and postmodern writing. Margaret Drabble frequently uses authorial narration, for instance, though her narrators are too sophisticated and self-aware to simply

'know everything.' On the uses and limitations of 'omniscience,' see the essay of that title by Jonathan Culler, forthcoming in *Narrative* (2004).

10 See Dorrit Cohn, 'Discordant Narration,' *Style* 34:2 (Summer 2000), 307–16.

11 David Herman has suggested a useful addition to the traditional model of characters as reflectors/focalizers. He points out that narration often includes 'hypothetical focalization,' or observations about what might be seen were an observer possessing the capacities of a reflector to be present. Herman demonstrates that this form of reflection appears in stronger, weaker, more direct and more indirect forms. For our purposes, hypothetical focalization would be a trait of an overt narrator. See David Herman, 'Hypothetical Focalization,' *Narrative* 2:3 (Oct. 1994), 230–53.

12 Percy Lubbock may have been responsible for some of the vicissitudes of the term 'point of view,' which he popularized in his book *The Craft of Fiction* (1926), but he clearly recognized that even a text like James's *The Ambassadors*, which is limited to a single character's (Strether's) point of view, includes representations that, strictly speaking, cannot be 'viewed' by Strether, such as his own thoughts (*Craft of Fiction*, 161–2).

13 Janet Burroway's *Writing Fiction: A Guide to Narrative Craft* (Longman, 2000) is an exception. She treats second-person narration briefly but with an open mind (202–3).

14 See Monika Fludernik, 'Introduction: Second-Person Narrative and Related Issues,' *Style* 28:3 (Fall 1994), 281–311, for a historical survey of uses of the second-personal narrative situation. See also James Phelan, 'Self-Help for narratee and narrative Audience: How "I"—and "You"?—Read "How",' *Style* 28:3 (Fall 1994), 350–65.

15 On the subjunctive mode in second-person narrative, see Brian Richardson, 'The Poetics and Politics of Second Person,' *Genre* 24:3 (Fall 1991), 319.

16 David Herman, 'Textual *You* and Double Deixis in Edna O'Brien's *A Pagan Place*,' *Style* 28:3 (1994), 380–1.

17 Brian Richardson, 'I etcetera: On the Poetics and Ideology of Multipersoned Narratives,' *Style* 28:3 (Fall 1994), 313.

18 Foucault, 'What is an Author?' in *Language, Counter-Memory, Practice: Selected Essays and Interviews*, ed. Donald F. Bouchard (Cornell University Press, 1977), 133–8. Barthes, 'The Death of the Author,' in *Image–Music–Text*, essays sel. and trans. by Stephen Heath (Hill & Wang, 1977), 142–8.

19 Paul A. Bové, 'Discourse,' in Frank Lentricchia and Thomas McLaughlin, *Critical Terms for Literary Study*, 2nd ed. (University of Chicago Press, 1995), 50–1.

20 See both 'From the Prehistory of Novelistic Discourse' (41–83) and 'Discourse and the Novel' (259–422) in *The Dialogic Imagination: Four Essays by M. M. Bakhtin*, ed. Michael Holquist, trans. Caryl Emerson and Michael Holquist (University of Texas Press, 1981).

4 People on Paper

1 L. C. Knights's 1934 article of this title insists that biographical speculations about fictional characters only result in absurd departures from a literary work's

language and image patterns. Rpt. in L. C. Knights, *Explorations* (Chatto & Windus, 1965).

2 Some theorists have argued that fictional characters are akin to dead people, since we know the dead through stories and textual traces, and because we cannot encounter either the dead or fictional characters in the flesh. See Chatman, *Story and Discourse*, 117–18.

3 Jill Paton Walsh, 'Here are some of the questions I often get asked, and the answers to them.' <http://www.greenbay.co.uk/qanda.html> (accessed 18 Dec. 2002).

4 Briefly, psycho-narration has its first-person correlative in self-narration, quoted monologue becomes self-quoted monologue, and narrated monologue becomes self-narrated monologue. The sense of these distinctions depends on an understanding of first-person narrative situation (see Chapter 3) as either consonant or dissonant (Cohn, *Transparent Minds*, 14, 143–216).

5 Free indirect discourse (*Erlebte Rede*) has been theorized under various names by, among others, Seymour Chatman, in *Story and Discourse*; Gérard Genette, in *Narrative Discourse*; Tzvetan Todorov, in *Introduction to Poetics*; and Mieke Bal, in *Narratology*. For a useful starting point in the company of a host of related terms, see Gerald Prince's entry in *A Dictionary of Narratology*, 34–5. The comprehensiveness of Dorrit Cohn's paradigm, in which she advances the alternative term 'narrated monologue' instead of free indirect discourse, makes it the best choice for the full description of modes of representation of consciousness. David Herman suggests that the narration of hypothetical observations should be included in discussions of focalization. These are reflections that might have been thought by a character were any figure present in the scene. They can take the form of either psycho-narration or narrated monologue. See 'Hypothetical Focalization,' *Narrative* 2:3 (Oct. 1994), 230–53.

6 See David Lodge on Frances Burney's narrative technique, in *Consciousness and the Novel* (46–7).

7 For an alternative view that has had some influence, see Ann Banfield's *Unspeakable Sentences: Narration and Representation in the Language of Fiction* (Routledge & Kegan Paul, 1982).

8 Genie Babb, 'The Body and Theories of Character,' *Narrative* (Oct. 2002), 195–221.

9 Richard A. Posner, 'Against Ethical Criticism: Part Two,' *Philosophy and Literature* 22:2 (1998), 394–412, 403–4.

5   Plot and Causation

1 See Jeremy Hawthorn's lucid but finally inconclusive entry on 'story and plot' in *A Glossary of Contemporary Literary Theory*, 4th ed. (Arnold, 2000), 336–8.

2 Manfred Jahn, *Narratology: A Guide to the Theory of Narrative*, version 1.6 (10 Apr. 2002), English Dept, University of Cologne, primary jump page <http://www.uni-koeln.de/~ame02/pppn.htm N4.6> (accessed 9 July 2002).

3 Some theorists, including Genette, have argued that a minimal narrative occurs with a single event or a single indication of time sequence (one 'and then'). Forster's sample plot provides a more commonly accepted version of a minimal

plot, consisting of two states and one event, chronologically and causally related. See Prince, *A Dictionary of Narratology*, 53. Cf. Gérard Genette, *Narrative Discourse Revisited*, 19.

4 Freytag's pyramid, from Gustav Freytag's *Techniques of the Drama* (1863), is reproduced in many places. See for instance Prince, *Dictionary of Narratology*, 36. Freytag's vocabulary and method for diagramming plot still has currency in secondary education, and many students enter college and university equipped with Freytag's ideas, but not necessarily aware that they do not apply to all plots.

5 Beginnings and endings have been studied by numerous critics and theorists. Some of the most important include: Edward Said, *Beginnings* (Basic Books, 1975); Frank Kermode, *The Sense of an Ending: Studies in the Theory of Fiction with a New Epilogue*, 1967 (Oxford University Press, 2000); Barbara Herrnstein Smith, *Poetic Closure: A Study of How Poems End* (University of Chicago Press, 1968); Marianna Torgovnick, *Closure in the Novel* (Princeton University Press, 1981), D. A. Miller, *Narrative and its Discontents: Problems of Closure in the Traditional Novel* (Princeton University Press, 1981); and Peter J. Rabinowitz, 'End Sinister: Neat Closure as Disruptive Force,' in *Reading Narrative: Form, Ethics, Ideology*, ed. James Phelan (Ohio State University Press, 1989), 120–31. Middles, as such, have attracted less attention than beginnings or endings (and closure), but two very fine studies of the dynamics of the middles of narratives are Peter Brooks, *Reading for the Plot: Design and Intention in Narrative* (Knopf, 1984), and Steven Hutchinson, *Cervantine Journeys* (University of Wisconsin Press, 1992).

6 Porter Abbott, *Cambridge Introduction to Narrative* (Cambridge University Press, 2001), 53.

7 On multi-plot fiction, see Peter K. Garrett, *The Victorian Multiplot Novel: Studies in Dialogical Form* (Yale University Press, 1980).

8 One of the best treatments of the reader's experience of encountering and falling for snares (an essential ingredient in detective fiction) is Roland Barthes's classic of post-structuralist narrative theory, *S/Z: An Essay* (1970), trans. Richard Miller (Farrar, Straus, & Giroux, 1974).

9 See Suzanne Keen, *Victorian Renovations of the Novel: Narrative Annexes and the Boundaries of Representation* (Cambridge University Press, 1998).

10 Hejinian is associated with the avant-garde language poets, but her work has shown an uncommon interest in narrative. Leslie Scalapino and Carla Harryman also explore aspects of narrative in their postmodern poetry.

11 Paul Ricoeur, *Time and Narrative*, 3 vols., trans. Kathleen McLaughlin and David Pellauer (University of Chicago Press, 1984–88).

12 Vladimir Propp, *Morphology of the Folk Tale*, 2nd ed., trans. Laurence Scott (University of Texas Press, 1968).

13 See Margaret Homans's survey of the trend in her essay, 'Feminist Fictions and Feminist Theories of Narrative,' *Narrative* 2:1 (Jan. 1994), 3–16. Some of the most influential essays and books in this field of feminist criticism include: Nancy K. Miller, 'Emphasis Added: Plots and Plausibilities in Women's Fiction,' *PMLA* 96 (Jan. 1981), 36–48; Susan Stanford Friedman, 'Lyric Subversions of Narrative,' in *Reading Narrative: Form, Ethics, Ideology*, ed. James Phelan (Ohio State University Press, 1989), 162–85; and Rachel Blau DuPlessis, *Writing Beyond the Ending:*

Narrative Strategies of Twentieth-Century Women Writers (Indiana University Press, 1985).

14 See both 'From the Prehistory of Novelistic Discourse' and 'Discourse and the Novel' in *The Dialogic Imagination: Four Essays by M. M. Bakhtin*, ed. Michael Holquist, trans. Caryl Emerson and Michael Holquist (University of Texas Press, 1981), 41–83, 259–422.

6 Timing

1 For a comprehensive set of recent essays on this broad topic, see Karen Newman, Jay Clayton, and Marianne Hirsch (ed.), *Time and the Literary* (Routledge, 2002).
2 Raymond Williams, *Marxism and Literature* (Oxford University Press, 1977), 132–4. For influential arguments about narrative form in history and historical writing, see also Fredric Jameson, *The Political Unconscious: Narrative as a Socially Symbolic Act* (Cornell University Press, 1981); Hayden White, *Metahistory: The Historical Imagination in Nineteenth-Century Europe* (Johns Hopkins University Press, 1973); and *The Content of the Form: Narrative Discourse and Historical Representation* (Johns Hopkins University Press, 1987).

7 Order and Disorder

1 Lecture notes from Dorrit Cohn's Literature 102, Forms of Narration, Harvard University (Spring 1987).

8 Levels

1 Narrative theorists often refer to this story world as the 'diegesis.' Because diegesis also means something close to 'telling' in the conventional distinction between 'showing' and 'telling' (mimesis and diegesis), I employ 'story world' instead. Genette's 'extradiegetic,' for instance, I render 'outside the story world.' Genette's 'hypo-diegesis' I render 'secondary story world' or 'embedded story.'
2 I do not follow Mieke Bal in referring to the primary narrative level in which the characters are situated as the 'frame' (*Narratology*, 94). I reserve the use of frame for the special use of a narrative level to contain other narrative levels within it.
3 Patrick O'Neill suggests a four-level model for narrative theory, adding a level for the reader's interaction for the text in time. O'Neill splits the discourse level into two separate levels, text and narration. The former is the words on the page; the latter is the creation of the inferences of text. See *Fictions of Discourse: Reading Narrative Theory* (University of Toronto Press, 1994).
4 Secondary narratives are sometimes called 'second-degree' narratives; I don't like this terminology because it reminds an English-speaking reader of the severity of burns. Who could read of a 'third-degree narrative' without thinking of painful skin grafts?
5 The deconstructionists' use of '*mise en abyme*' refers to something akin to this feeling of vertigo, provoked by the play of unstable meanings. If a critic uses the term and no embedded mirror-text appears to be under discussion, it's a fairly

safe bet that the subject is the effect of the endless play of signifiers, and the approach is deconstructionist, whether or not that has been announced.

9 Fictional Worlds and Fictionality

1 Sidney's *Defense* was published in two editions in 1595, after Sidney's death. One was entitled *The Defense of Poesie* and the other *An Apology for Poetrie*. I use the prior title because it echoes a phrase of Sidney's in the text. The edition cited parenthetically is Sir Philip Sidney, *An Apology for Poetry*, ed. Forrest G. Robinson (Macmillan/Library of Liberal Arts, 1970).
2 Indeed, some cognitive theorists of narrative see the small spatial stories that human beings recognize and execute as prior to literary narrative and even language. See Mark Turner, *The Literary Mind: The Origins of Thought and Language* (Oxford University Press, 1996). For a critique of spatial metaphors in discussion of literature, see chapter 2 of Alexander Gelley's *Narrative Crossings: Theory and Pragmatics of Prose Fiction* (Johns Hopkins University Press, 1987), 35–57.
3 See, canonically, Nelson Goodman, *Ways of Worldmaking* (1978), and for a more recent exposition and application of questions about possible worlds, Marie-Laure Ryan's *Narrative as Virtual Reality: Immersion and Interactivity in Literature and Electronic Media* (Johns Hopkins University Press, 2001).
4 Gerald Graff, *Literature against Itself* (University of Chicago Press, 1979). Graff does not name him here, but he could be referring to ideas like those expressed in Roland Barthes's 1967 essay, 'The Discourse of History,' in which Barthes denies a difference between history and fiction, describing 'the reality effect' of history as a product of its use of narrative. For a version of this essay in English, see *Comparative Criticism: A Yearbook*, vol. 3, ed. E. S. Shaffer, trans. Stephen Bann (Cambridge University Press, 1981), 7–20.
5 Käte Hamburger, *The Logic of Literature*, 2nd ed., trans. Marilynn J. Rose (Indiana University Press), 1973.
6 On possible worlds theory, see for starters, Lubomír Dolozel, *Heterocosmica: Fiction and Possible Worlds* (Johns Hopkins University Press, 1998); Umberto Eco, *The Limits of Interpretation* (Indiana University Press, 1990); David Lewis, 'Truth in Fiction,' *American Philosophical Quarterly* 15 (1978), 37–46; Ruth Ronen, *Possible Worlds in Literary Theory* (Cambridge University Press, 1994).
7 Marie-Laure Ryan distinguishes these two types by contrasting their 'illocutionary' and 'ontological' boundaries. The latter involves crossing into a domain with a new system of reality; the former occurs when a new voice begins to narrate. See 'Stacks, Frames, and Boundaries,' 366–7.

10 Disguises

1 The macrostructural test of difference between fictional and nonfictional texts outlined by Lubomír Dolozel in 'Fictional and Historical Narrative' requires access to knowledge external to the text. Cohn's propositions concern formal traits that can be observed of the text. See Chapter 9.

2 See Lennard J. Davis, *Factual Fictions: The Origins of the English Novel*, 1983 (University of Pennsylvania Press, 1996).
3 In a fascinating inversion of this process of fiction mistaken for real autobiographies, there are also a number of documented cases of fake ethnic autobiographies, written by writers who intentionally represent themselves, and their illustrative life stories, as belonging to assumed ethnicities. See Laura Browder, *Slippery Characters: Ethnic Impersonators and American Identities* (University of North Carolina Press, 2000).
4 On obscurity in narrative literature, see Frank Kermode's superb *The Genesis of Secrecy: On the Interpretation of Narrative* (Harvard University Press, 1979). Kermode brings biblical hermeneutics to bear on the interpretation of puzzling narratives from the Gospel of Mark to James Joyce's *Ulysses* (1922).
5 For a full account, see Robert Harris, *Selling Hitler: The Story of the Hitler Diaries* (Faber, 1986).
6 On romances of the archive as a contemporary genre, see Suzanne Keen's *Romances of the Archive in Contemporary British Fiction* (University of Toronto Press, 2001).
7 Barra quoted in 'Bogus Bride,' by Andrew Richard Albanse, *Salon* (8 Feb. 2000). <http://archive.salon.com/books/feature/2000/02/08/earp/print.html> (accessed 31 Oct. 2002). See Allen Barra, *Inventing Wyatt Earp: His Life and Many Legends* (Carroll & Graf, 1998).
8 'I Married Wyatt Earp Product Details,' <http://www.amazon.com> (accessed 13 Nov. 2002).
9 See David Leon Higdon, *Shadows of the Past in Contemporary British Fiction* (University of Georgia Press, 1985), 86–7.
10 'Out of print publications,' The University of Arizona Press <http://www.uapress.arizona.edu/catalogs/op.htm> (accessed 13 Nov. 2002).

11   Genres and Conventions

1 See Didier Coste, *Narrative as Communication* (University of MinnesotaPress, 1989), 252–4, for an unusual acknowledgment of the eclipse of genre in much narrative theory, and Monika Fludernik, 'Genres, Text Types, or Discourse Modes? Narrative Modalities and Generic Categorization,' *Style* 34:2 (Summer 2000), 274–92, for a strong argument in favor of genre in narrative theory. Ordinarily, one must turn to works in the area of 'theory of the novel,' or to works explicitly concerned with narrative subgenres, to find the integration of genre with narrative form. In his anthology *Theory of the Novel: A Historical Approach*, Michael McKeon explains that 'poststructuralist thought has been unremitting in its efforts to demystify the category of "genre" itself as a superstitious constraint on authorial and readerly innovation, and to replace the arbitrary dogmas of genre theory by the transhistorical sweep of narratology' ('Genre Theory,' 3).
2 See Gerard Genette, *The Architext: An Introduction* (1979), trans. Jane E. Lewin (University of California Press, 1992), for a brief, engaging historical survey of these divisions, and for Genette's recommendation that the intersection of

modes and themes take his name, *architexts*. Unlike many of Genette's coinages, this one has not caught on. Genette's historical treatment of the divisions does suggest that they are anything but 'universal,' 'natural,' and 'essential,' as they are sometimes labeled. See, for instance, the qualified use of these epithets by Claudio Guillén in *Literature as System*, 114ff. Guillén writes that 'one must stress that these essential modes or universals do not coincide with the historically determined, practically oriented, form-conscious categories that we have been calling genres' (*Literature as System*, 114–15).

3 René Wellek and Austin Warren, *A Theory of Literature* (Penguin, 1963), 226–37.

4 The list that follows, though by no means exhaustive, suggests some exemplary studies of subgenres of the novel. See John G. Cawelti's *Adventure, Mystery, and Romance: Formula Stories as Art and Popular Culture* (University of Chicago Press, 1976); Martin Green's *Seven Types of Adventure Tale: An Etiology of a Major Genre* (Pennsylvania State University Press, 1991); Linda Hutcheon's *Narcissistic Narrative: The Metafictional Paradox* (Wilfred Laurier University Press, 1980); Colin Manlove's *The Fantasy Literature of England* (Macmillan/ St. Martin's Press [now Palgrave], 1999); Patricia Merivale and Susan Elizabeth Sweeney (ed.), *Detecting Texts: The Metaphysical Detective Story from Poe to Postmodernism* (University of Pennsylvania Press, 1999); Jerry Palmer's *Potboilers: Methods, Concepts, and Case Studies in Popular Fiction* (Routledge, 1991) and *Thrillers: Genesis and Structure of a Popular Genre* (Edward Arnold, 1978); Dennis Porter's *The Pursuit of Crime: Art and Ideology in Detective Fiction* (Yale University Press, 1981); David Punter's *The Literature of Terror: A History of Gothic Fictions from 1765 to the Present Day* (Longman, 1980); and Tzvetan Todorov's *The Fantastic: A Structural Approach to a Literary Genre* (Cornell University Press, 1975).

5 For instance, see Gary Saul Morson's *Boundaries of Genre* (1981), in which he defines both boundary works (in these it is unclear which of two sets of generic conventions govern a work) and threshold texts (here an author deliberately invokes contradictory generic expectations and sustains double encoding throughout the work). It should be clear that the metaphor of boundary employed by Morson suggests a doubleness (since boundaries lie between two spaces) and generic admixture certainly need not be limited to two ingredients, as Northrop Frye argues in his *Anatomy of Criticism*.

6 Benedict Anderson, *Imagined Communities: Reflections on the Origin and Spread of Nationalism* (1983), rev. ed. (Verso, 1991); Susan Stanford Friedman, *Mappings: Feminism and the Cultural Geographies of Encounter* (Princeton University Press, 1998).

7 Raymond Williams, *Marxism and Literature* (Oxford University Press, 1977), 132–4. For influential arguments about narrative form in history and historical writing, see Fredric Jameson, *The Political Unconscious: Narrative as a Socially Symbolic Act* (Cornell University Press, 1981); Hayden White, *Metahistory: The Historical Imagination in Nineteenth-Century Europe* (Johns Hopkins University Press, 1973); and *The Content of the Form: Narrative Discourse and Historical Representation* (Johns Hopkins University Press, 1987).

8 See e.g. 'Search the VICTORIA archives' at <http://listserv.indiana.edu/cgi-bin/wa?S1=victoria> (accessed 11 Dec. 2002).

9 See 'The Society for the Study of Narrative Listserve,' at <http://www.vander-bilt.edu/narrative/nar-list.htm> (accessed 11 Dec. 2002).

10 See Julia Kristeva, 'The Bounded Text,' in *Desire in Language: A Semiotic Approach to Literature and Art*, ed. Leon S. Roudiez, trans. Thomas Gora, Alice Jardine, and Leon S. Roudiez (Columbia University Press, 1980), 36–63.

Bibliography

Abbot, H. Porter. *Cambridge Introduction to Narrative*. Cambridge University Press, 2001.

Abrams, M. H. *Glossary of Literary Terms*. 7th ed. Harcourt Brace, 1999.

Anderson, Benedict. *Imagined Communities: Reflections on the Origin and Spread of Nationalism*. 1983. Rev. ed. Verso, 1991.

Aristotle. *Aristotle's Poetics*. Trans. and commentary, George Whalley. Ed. John Baxter and Patrick Atherton. McGill-Queen's University Press, 1997.

Auerbach, Erich. *Mimesis: The Representation of Reality in Western Literature*. Trans. Willard R. Trask. Princeton University Press, 1953.

Babb, Genie. 'The Body and Theories of Character.' *Narrative* (Oct. 2002), 195–221.

Bakhtin, Mikhail. *The Dialogic Imagination: Four Essays by M. M. Bakhtin*. Ed. and trans. Caryl Emerson and Michael Holquist. University of Texas Press, 1981.

— *Problems of Doestoevsky's Poetics*. Trans. Caryl Emerson. University of Minnesota Press, 1984.

Bakhtin, M. M. and P. N. Medvedev. *The Formal Method in Literary Scholarship: A Critical Introduction to Sociological Poetics*. 1928. Trans. Albert J. Wehrle. Johns Hopkins University Press, 1978.

Bal, Mieke. *Narratology: Introduction to the Theory of Narrative*. 1980. Trans. Christine van Boheemen. University of Toronto Press, 1985.

Banfield, Ann. *Unspeakable Sentences: Narration and Representation in the Language of Fiction*. Routledge & Kegan Paul, 1982.

Barra, Allen. *Inventing Wyatt Earp: His Life and Many Legends*. Carroll & Graf, 1998.

Barth, John. *The Friday Book: Essays and Other Nonfiction*. Putnam's, 1984.

— *Further Fridays: Essays, Lectures, and Other Nonfiction, 1984–94*. Little, Brown & Co., 1995.

— 'Tales within Tales within Tales' *Antaeus* 43 (1981), 45–63.

Barthes, Roland. 'The Death of the Author.' 1968. *Image–Music–Text*. Essays sel. and trans. by Stephen Heath. Hill &Wang, 1977: 142–8.

— 'The Discourse of History.' 1967. *Comparative Criticism: A Yearbook*, vol. 3, ed. E. S. Shaffer, trans. Stephen Bann. Cambridge University Press, 1981: 7–20.

— 'Introduction to the Structural Analysis of Narratives.' 1966. *Image–Music–Text*. Essays sel. and trans. by Stephen Heath. Hill & Wang, 1977: 79–124.

— *S/Z: An Essay*. 1970. Trans. Richard Miller. Farrar, Straus, & Giroux, 1974.

Bell, Madison Smartt. *Narrative Design: A Writer's Guide to Structure*. Norton, 1997.

Benjamin, Walter. 'The Storyteller.' *Illuminations: Essays and Reflections*. 1955. Trans. 1968. Ed. Hannah Arendt. Trans. Harry Zohn. Schocken Books, 1969: 83–109.

Berger, Harry, Jr. 'The Renaissance Imagination: Second World and Green World.' *Centennial Review of Arts and Sciences* 9 (1965), 36–78.

Bishop, Leonard. *Dare to Be a Great Writer: 329 Keys to Powerful Fiction*. Writer's Digest Books, 1988.

Booth, Alison. *Famous Last Words: Changes in Gender and Narrative Closure*. University Press of Virginia, 1993.

Booth, Wayne C. *The Company We Keep: An Ethics of Fiction*. University of California Press, 1988.

— 'The Ethics of Forms: Taking Flight with The Wings of the Dove.' *Understanding Narrative*. Ed. James Phelan and Peter J. Rabinowitz. Ohio State University Press, 1994: 99–135.

— *The Rhetoric of Fiction*, 2nd ed. University of Chicago Press, 1983.

Bornstein, George and Theresa Tinkle (ed.). *The Iconic Page in Manuscript, Print, and Digital Culture*. University of Michigan Press, 1998.

Bové, Paul A. 'Discourse.' *Critical Terms for Literary Study*. 2nd ed. Ed. Frank Lentricchia and Thomas McLaughlin. University of Chicago Press, 1995: 50–65.

Brooke-Rose, Christine. *Invisible Author: Last Essays*. Ohio State University Press, 2002.

Brooks, Cleanth and Robert Penn Warren, *Understanding Fiction*. 2nd ed. Appleton-Century-Crofts, 1959.

Brooks, Peter. *Reading for the Plot: Design and Intention in Narrative*. Knopf, 1984.

— and Paul Gewirtz (ed.). *Law's Stories: Narrative and Rhetoric in the Law*. Yale University Press, 1996.

Browder, Laura. *Slippery Characters: Ethnic Impersonators and American Identities*. University of North Carolina Press, 2000.

Brower, Reuben. *The Fields of Light: An Experiment in Critical Reading*. Oxford University Press, 1951.

Bruner, Jerome. *Actual Minds, Possible Worlds*. Harvard University Press, 1992.

Burgess, Anthony. 'Introduction: A Clockwork Orange Resucked.' 1986. *A Clockwork Orange*. 1962. Norton, 1987: pp. v–xi.

Burke, Kenneth. *Counter-Statement*. 2nd ed. Hermes Publications, 1953.

— *The Philosophy of Literary Form: Studies in Symbolic Action*. 2nd ed. Louisiana State University Press, 1967.

Burnett, Hallie and Whit Burnett. *Fiction Writer's Hand Book*. Harper & Row, 1975.

Burroway, Janet. *Writing Fiction: A Guide to Narrative Craft*. 5th ed. Longman, 2000.

Byatt, A. S. *On Histories and Stories: Selected Essays*. Chatto & Windus, 2000.

Caserio, Robert. *Plot, Story, and the Novel: From Dickens and Poe to the Modern Period*. Princeton University Press, 1979.

Cawelti, John G. *Adventure, Mystery, and Romance: Formula Stories as Art and Popular Culture*. University of Chicago Press, 1976.

Chamberlain, Mary and Paul Thompson (ed.). *Narrative and Genre*. Routledge, 1998.

Chambers, Ross. *Room for Maneuver: Reading (the) Oppositional (in) Narrative*. University of Chicago Press, 1991.

— *Story and Situation: Narrative Seduction and the Power of Fiction*. Foreword by Wlad Godzich. Theory and History of Literature, vol. 12. University of Minnesota Press, 1984.

Chatman, Seymour. *Coming to Terms: The Rhetoric of Narrative in Fiction and Film*. Cornell University Press, 1990.

— *Story and Discourse: Narrative Structure in Fiction and Film*. Cornell University Press, 1978.

— *Reading Narrative Fiction*. Macmillan, 1993.

Cixous, Hélène. 'The Character of 'Character.' *New Literary History* 5 (1974), 383–402.
Cohn, Dorrit. 'Discordant Narration.' *Style* 34:2 (2000), 307–16.
— *The Distinction of Fiction.* Johns Hopkins University Press, 1999.
— 'The Encirclement of Narrative: On Franz Stanzel's *Theorie des Erzählen.' Poetics Today* 2:2 (1981), 157–82.
— *Transparent Minds: Narrative Modes for Presenting Consciousness in Fiction.* Princeton University Press, 1978.
Colie, Rosalie. *The Resources of Kind: Genre-Theory in the Renaissance.* Ed. Barbara Kiefer Lewalski. University of California Press, 1973.
Coste, Didier. *Narrative as Communication.* Foreword by Wlad Godzich. Theory and History of Literature, vol. 64. University of Minnesota Press, 1989.
Dällenbach, Lucien. *The Mirror in the Text.* University of Chicago Press, 1989.
Davis, Lennard J. *Factual Fictions: The Origins of the English Novel.* 1983. Rpt. with new intro. University of Pennsylvania Press, 1996.
Deleyto, Celestino. 'Focalisation in Film Narrative.' *Narratology: An Introduction.* Ed. Susana Onega and José Angel García Landa. Longman, 1996: 217–33.
Derrida, Jacques. 'The Law of Genre.' Trans. Avitall Ronell. *On Narrative,* ed. W. J. T. Mitchell. University of Chicago Press, 1981: 51–77.
Dickens, Charles. *Oliver Twist.* 1837–9. Ed. Fred Kaplan. Norton, 1993.
Dijk, Teun Adrianus van. *Handbook of Discourse Analysis.* Vol. 1. *Disciplines of Discourse.* Academic Press, 1985.
— and Walter Kintsch. *Strategies of Discourse Comprehension.* Academic, 1983.
Dillard, Annie. *The Writing Life.* HarperCollins,1989.
Dolozel, Lubomír. 'Fictional and Historical Narrative: Meeting the Postmodernist Challenge.' *Narratologies.* Ed. David Herman. Ohio State University Press, 1999: 247–73.
— *Heterocosmica: Fiction and Possible Worlds.* Johns Hopkins University Press, 1998.
— 'Truth and Authenticity in Narrative' *Poetics Today* 1:3 (Spring 1980), 7–25.
Doody, Margaret Anne. *The True History of the Novel.* Rutgers University Press, 1996.
Dubrow, Heather. *Genre. The Critical Idiom.* Methuen, 1982.
Duncan, Ian. *Modern Romance and Transformations of the Novel: The Gothic, Scott, Dickens.* Cambridge University Press, 1992.
Dunn, Kevin. *Pretexts of Authority: The Rhetoric of Authorship in the Renaissance Preface.* Stanford University Press, 1994.
DuPlessis, Rachel Blau. *Writing Beyond the Ending: Narrative Strategies of Twentieth-Century Women Writers.* Indiana University Press, 1985.
Eakin, Paul John. *How Our Lives Become Stories: Making Selves.* Cornell University Press, 1999.
Eastman, Richard M. *A Guide to the Novel.* Chandler Publishing Co., 1965.
Eco, Umberto. *The Limits of Interpretation.* Indiana University Press, 1990.
Elam, Diane. *Romancing the Postmodern.* Routledge, 1992.
Fehn, Ann, Ingeborg Hoesterey, and Maria Tatar (ed.). *Neverending Stories: Toward a Critical Narratology.* Princeton University Press, 1992.
Fishelov, David. *Metaphors of Genre: The Role of Analogies in Genre Theory.* Penn State University Press, 1993.
Fludernik, Monika. *The Fictions of Language and the Languages of Fiction: The Linguistic Representation of Speech and Consciousness.* Routledge, 1993.

— 'Genres, Text Types, or Discourse Modes? Narrative Modalities and Generic Categorization.' *Style* 34:2 (Summer 2000), 274–92.
— 'Introduction: Second-Person Narrative and Related Issues.' *Style* 28:3 (Fall 1994), 281–311.
— *Towards a 'Natural' Narratology*. Routledge, 1996.
Foley, Barbara. *Telling the Truth: The Theory and Practice of Documentary Fiction*. Cornell University Press, 1986.
Forster, E. M. *Aspects of the Novel*. Harcourt, 1927.
Foucault, Michel. *Language, Counter-Memory, Practice: Selected Essays and Interviews*. Ed. Donald F. Bouchard. Cornell University Press, 1977.
— *The Archaeology of Knowledge* [*Archéologie du Savoir*]. Trans. A. M. Sheridan Smith. Pantheon Books, 1972.
Fowler, Alastair. *Kinds of Literature: An Introduction to the Theory of Genres and Modes*. Harvard University Press, 1982.
Frank, Joseph. 'Spatial Form in Modern Literature.' *Sewanee Review* 53 (1945), 221–40, 433–56, 643–53.
Freytag, Gustav. *Techniques of the Drama: An Exposition of Dramatic Composition and Art*. 1863. Trans. from the 6th German ed. by Elias J. MacEwan. S. C. Griggs & Co., 1895.
Friedman, Norman. *Form and Meaning in Fiction*. University of Georgia Press, 1975.
Friedman, Susan Stanford. 'Lyric Subversion of Narrative in Women's Writing: Virginia Woolf and the Tyranny of Plot.' *Reading Narrative: Form, Ethics, Ideology*. Ed. James Phelan. Ohio State University Press, 1989: 162–85.
— *Mappings: Feminism and the Cultural Geographies of Encounter*. Princeton University Press, 1998.
Frye, Northrop. *Anatomy of Criticism: Four Essays*. Princeton University Press, 1957.
Furedy, Viveca. 'A Structural Model of Phenomena with Embedding in Literature and Other Arts.' *Poetics Today* 10:4 (1989), 45–69.
Gabler, Hans Walter. 'Textual Criticism.' *The Johns Hopkins Guide to Literary Theory and Criticism*. Ed. Michael Groden and Martin Kreiswirth. John Hopkins University Press, 1994: 708–14.
Gardner, John. *The Art of Fiction: Notes on Craft for Young Writers*. Knopf, 1984.
Garrett, Peter J. *The Victorian Multiplot Novel: Studies in Dialogical Form*. Yale University Press, 1980.
Gass, William. *Fiction and the Figures of Life*. David R. Godine, 1979.
Gelley, Alexander. *Narrative Crossings: Theory and Pragmatics of Prose Fiction*. Johns Hopkins University Press, 1987.
Genette, Gérard. *The Architext: An Introduction*. 1979. Trans. Jane E. Lewin. University of California Press, 1992.
— *Narrative Discourse: An Essay in Method*. Trans. Jane E. Lewin. Cornell University Press, 1980.
— *Narrative Discourse Revisited*. 1983. Trans. Jane E. Lewin. Cornell University Press, 1988.
— *Palimpsests: Literature in the Second Degree*. 1982. Trans. Channa Newman and Claude Doubinsky. University of Nebraska Press, 1997.
— *Paratexts: Thresholds of Interpretation*. 1987. Trans. Jane E. Lewin. Cambridge University Press, 1997.
Goldman, Michael. *On Drama: Boundaries of Genre, Borders of Self*. University of Michigan Press, 2000.

Goodman, Nelson. *Ways of Worldmaking*. Hackett, 1978.

Graff, Gerald. *Literature Against Itself*. University of Chicago Press, 1979.

Grafton, Anthony. *The Footnote: A Curious History*. Harvard University Press, 1997.

Green, Martin. *Seven Types of Adventure Tale: An Etiology of a Major Genre*. Pennsylvania State University Press, 1991.

Greetham, D. C. *The Margins of the Text*. University of Michigan Press, 1997.

Greimas, A. J. 'Actants, Actors, and Figures.' *On Meaning: Selected Writings in Semiotic Theory*. Trans. Paul J. Perron and Frank H. Collins. University of Minnesota Press, 1987.

— *Structural Semantics: An Attempt at a Method*. 1966. Trans. Danielle McDowell, Ronald Schleifer, and Alan Velie. University of Nebraska Press, 1983.

Griest, Guinevere L. *Mudie's Circulating Library and the Victorian Novel*. Indiana University Press, 1970.

Groden, Michael and Martin Kreiswirth (ed.). *The Johns Hopkins Guide to Literary Theory and Criticism*. Johns Hopkins University Press, 1994.

Gross, Sabine. 'Cognitive Readings; or, The Disappearance of Literature in the Mind.' *Poetics Today* 18:2 (Summer 1997), 271–97.

Guillén, Claudio. *Literature as System: Essays toward the Theory of Literary History*. Princeton University Press, 1971.

Guillory, John. 'The Very Idea of Pedagogy.' *Profession 2002*. MLA, 2002: 164–71.

Hamburger, Käte. *The Logic of Literature*. 2nd ed. Trans. Marilynn J. Rose. Indiana University Press, 1973.

Harris, Robert. *Selling Hitler: The Story of the Hitler Diaries*. Faber, 1986.

Harvey, W. J. *Character and the Novel*. Cornell University Press, 1965.

Hawthorn, Jeremy. *A Glossary of Contemporary Literary Theory*. 4th ed. Arnold, 2000.

— *Studying the Novel*. 4th ed. Arnold, 2001.

Herman, David. 'Hypothetical Focalization.' *Narrative* 2:3 (Oct. 1994), 230–53.

— *Story Logic: Problems and Possibilities of Narrative*. University of Nebraska Press, 2002.

— 'Textual *You* and Double Deixis in Edna O'Brien's *A Pagan Place*.' *Style* 28:3 (1994), 380–1.

Herman, David (ed.). *Narrative Theory and the Cognitive Sciences*. CSLI Publications, 2003.

— *Narratologies: New Perspectives on Narrative Analysis*. Ohio State University Press, 1999.

Herman, David, Manfred Jahn, and Marie-Laure Ryan. *The Routledge Encyclopedia of Narrative Theory*. Routledge, forthcoming.

Hernadi, Paul. *Beyond Genre: New Directions in Literary Classification*. Cornell University Press, 1972.

Higdon, David Leon. *Shadows of the Past in Contemporary British Fiction*. University of Georgia Press, 1985.

Hirsch, E. D. *Validity in Interpretation*. Yale University Press, 1967.

Hochman, Baruch. *Character in Literature*. Cornell University Press, 1985.

Homans, Margaret. 'Feminist Fictions and Feminist Theories of Narrative.' *Narrative* 2:1 (Jan. 1994), 3–16.

Hutcheon, Linda. *Narcissistic Narrative: The Metafictional Paradox*. Wilfred Laurier University Press, 1980.

Hutchinson, Steven. *Cervantine Journeys*. University of Wisconsin Press, 1992.

Ingarden, Roman. *The Cognition of the Literary Work of Art*. Trans. Ruth Ann Crowley and Kenneth R. Olson. Northwestern University Press, 1973.

Iser, Wolfgang. *The Act of Reading: A Theory of Aesthetic Response*. Johns Hopkins University Press, 1978.

— *The Implied Reader: Patterns of Communication in Prose Fiction from Bunyan to Beckett*. Johns Hopkins University Press, 1974.

— *Prospecting: From Reader Response to Literary Authropology*. Johns Hopkins University Press, 1989.

Jahn, Manfred. *Narratology: A Guide to the Theory of Narrative*. Version 1.6 (10 Apr. 2002). English Dept, University of Cologne. Primary jump page <http://www.uni-koeln.de/~ame02/pppn.htm> (accessed 9 July 2002).

Jameson, Fredric. *The Political Unconscious: Narrative as a Socially Symbolic Act*. Cornell University Press, 1981.

Keen, Suzanne. *Romances of the Archive in Contemporary British Fiction*. University of Toronto Press, 2001.

— *Victorian Renovations of the Novel: Narrative Annexes and the Boundaries of Representations*. Cambridge University Press, 1998.

Kermode, Frank. *The Art of Telling: Essays on Fiction*. Harvard University Press, 1983.

— *The Genesis of Secrecy: On the Interpretation of Narrative*. Harvard University Press, 1979.

— *The Sense of an Ending: Studies in the Theory of Fiction with a New Epilogue*. 1967. Oxford University Press, 2000.

Knights, L. C. *Explorations*. Chatto & Windus, 1965.

Kristeva, Julia. 'The Bounded Text.' *Desire in Language: A Semiotic Approach to Literature and Art*. Ed. Leon S. Roudiez. Trans. Thomas Gora, Alice Jardine, and Leon S. Roudiez. Columbia University Press, 1980: 36–63.

Lanser, Susan Snaider. *Fictions of Authority: Women Writers and Narrative Voice*. Cornell University Press, 1992.

— *The Narrative Act: Point of View in Fiction*. Princeton University Press, 1981.

— 'Toward a Feminist Narratology.' 1986. *Feminisms*. Rev. ed. Robyn R. Warhol and Diane Price Herndl. Rutgers University Press, 1997: 674–93.

Lehman, David W. *Matters of Fact: Reading Nonfiction over the Edge*. Ohio State University Press, 1997.

Lemon, Lee T. and Marion J. Reis (ed. and trans.). *Russian Formalist Criticism: Four Essays*. University of Nebraska Press, 1965.

Lewis, David. 'Truth in Fiction.' *American Philosophical Quarterly* 15 (1978), 37–46.

Lodge, David. *After Bakhtin: Essays on Fiction and Criticism*. Routledge, 1990.

— *The Art of Fiction*. Penguin, 1992.

— *Consciousness and the Novel: Connected Essays*. Harvard University Press, 2002.

Lohafer, Susan and Jo Ellyn Clarey (ed.). *Short Story Theory at a Crossroads*. Louisiana State University Press, 1989.

Lubbock, Percy. *The Craft of Fiction*. 1926. Viking, 1957.

Lyotard, Jean-François. *The Postmodern Condition: A Report on Knowledge*. 1979. Trans. Geoff Bennington and Brian Massumi. Theory and History of Literature, vol. 10. University of Minnesota Press, 1984.

Makaryk, Irene R. (ed.). *The Encyclopedia of Contemporary Literary Theory: Approaches, Scholars, Terms*. University of Toronto Press, 1993.

Manlove, Colin. *The Fantasy Literature of England*. Macmillan/St. Martin's Press, 1999.

Marshall, Evan. *The Marshall Plan for Novel Writing: A 16-step Program Guaranteed to Take You from Idea to Completed Manuscript*. Writer's Digest Books, 1998.

Martin, Wallace. *Recent Theories of Narrative*. Cornell University Press, 1986.

Martínez-Bonati, Félix. *Fictive Discourse and the Structures of Literature: A Phenomenological Approach*. Trans. Philip W. Silver. Cornell University Press, 1981.

Matejka, Ladislav and Krystyna Pomorska (ed.). *Readings in Russian Poetics: Formalist and Structuralist Views*. Michigan Slavic Publications, 1978.

Mcttale, Brian. *Postmodernist Fiction*. Methuen, 1987.

McKeon, Michael (ed.). *Theory of the Novel: A Historical Approach*. Johns Hopkins University Press, 2000.

Mcquillan, Martin. *The Narrative Reader*. Routledge, 2000.

Merivale, Patricia and Susan Elizabeth Sweeney (ed.). *Detecting Texts: The Metaphysical Detective Story from Poe to Postmodernism*. University of Pennsylvania Press, 1999.

Miller, D. A. *Narrative and its Discontents: Problems of Closure in the Traditional Novel*. Princeton University Press, 1981.

Miller, Nancy K. 'Emphasis Added: Plots and Plausibilities in Women's Fiction.' *PMLA* 96 (Jan. 1981), 36–48.

Mitchell, W. J. T. (ed.). *On Narrative*. University of Chicago Press, 1981.

Monaco, James. *How to Read a Film: The Art, Technology, Language, History, and Theory of Film and Media*. Rev. ed. Oxford University Press, 1981.

Moretti, Franco. *Atlas of the European Novel 1800–1900*. Verso, 1998.

— 'Graphs.' Lecture (Sept. 2002). Forthcoming in *New Left Review* (2003).

Morson, Gary Saul. *The Boundaries of Genre: Dostoevsky's* Diary of a Writer *and the Traditions of Literary Utopia*. University of Texas Press, 1981.

Nagel, James. *The Contemporary American Short-Story Cycle*. Louisiana State University Press, 2001.

Nelles, William. 'Stories within Stories: Narrative Levels and Embedded Narrative.' *Studies in the Literary Imagination* 215:1 (1992), 79–96.

Newman, Karen, Jay Clayton, and Marianne Hirsch (ed.). *Time and the Literary*. Essays from the English Institute. Routledge, 2002.

Newton, Adam Zachary. *Narrative Ethics*. Harvard University Press, 1995.

Nünning, Ansgar. 'Implied Author.' *Encyclopedia of the Novel*. Vol. 1. Ed. Paul Schellinger et al. Fitzroy Dearborn, 1998: 589–91.

Nussbaum, Martha. *Poetic Justice: The Literary Imagination and Public Life*. Beacon Press, 1995.

Onega, Susana and José Ángel García Landa. *Narratology: An Introduction*. Longman, 1996.

O'Neill, Patrick. *Fictions of Discourse: Reading Narrative Theory*. University of Toronto Press, 1994.

Palmer, Jerry. *Potboilers: Methods, Concepts, and Case Studies in Popular Fiction*. Routledge, 1991.

— *Thrillers: Genesis and Structure of a Popular Genre*. Edward Arnold, 1978.

Pavel, Thomas G. *Fictional Worlds*. Harvard University Press, 1986.

Phelan, James. *Reading People, Reading Plots: Character, Progression, and the Interpretation of Narrative*. University of Chicago Press, 1989.

— 'Self-Help for Narratee and Narrative Audience: How "I" — and "You"? — Read "How",' *Style* 28:3 (Fall 1994), 350–65.

Phelan, James (ed.). *Reading Narrative: Form, Ethics, Ideology*. Ohio State University Press, 1989.

Phelan, James and Peter J. Rabinowitz (ed.). *Understanding Narrative*. Ohio State University Press, 1994.

Poe, Edgar Allan. 'Review of *Twice-Told Tales*.' Charles E. May (ed.) *Short Story Theories* (Ohio University Press, 1976. 45–51.

Porter, Dennis. *The Pursuit of Crime: Art and Ideology in Detective Fiction*. Yale University Press, 1981.

Posner, Richard A. 'Against Ethical Criticism: Part Two.' *Philosophy and Literature* 22:2 (1998), 394–412.

Pratt, Mary Louise. *Towards a Speech Act Theory of Literature*. Indiana University Press, 1977.

Price, Leah. *The Anthology and the Rise of the Novel: From Richardson to George Eliot*. Cambridge University Press, 2000.

Price, Martin. *Forms of Life: Character and Moral Imagination in the Novel*. Yale University Press, 1983.

Prince, Gerald. *A Dictionary of Narratology*. University of Nebraska Press, 1987.

— 'Introduction to the Study of the Narratee.' *Reader-Response Criticism*. Ed. Jane Tompkins. Johns Hopkins University Press, 1980: 7–25.

— 'Narratology.' *The Johns Hopkins Guide to Literary Theory and Criticism*. Ed. Michael Groden and Martin Kreiswirth. Johns Hopkins University Press, 1994: 424–8.

Propp, Vladimir. *Morphology of the Folk Tale*. 2nd ed. Trans. Laurence Scott. University of Texas Press, 1968.

Punter, David. *The Literature of Terror: A History of Gothic Fictions from 1765 to the Present Day*. Longman, 1980.

Rabinowitz, Peter J. *Before Reading: Narrative Conventions and the Politics of Interpretation* (1987). 2nd ed. Foreword by James Phelan. Ohio State University Press, 1998.

— 'End Sinister: Neat Closure as Disruptive Force.' *Reading Narrative: Form, Ethics, Ideology*. Ed. James Phelan. Ohio State University Press, 1989: 120–31.

Reid, Ian. *Narrative Exchanges*. Routledge,1992.

Richardson, Brian. 'Beyond Story and Discourse: Narrative Time in Postmodern and Nonmimetic Fiction.' *Narrative Dynamics: Essays on Time, Plot, Closure, and Frames*. Ed. Brian Richardson. Ohio State University Press, 2002: 47–63.

— 'I etcetera: On the Poetics and Ideology of Multipersoned Narratives.' *Style* 28:3 (Fall 1994), 312–28.

— 'The Poetics and Politics of Second Person.' *Genre* 24:3 (Fall 1991), 309–30.

— 'Recent Concepts of Narrative and the Narratives of Narrative Theory.' *Style* 34:2 (Summer 2000), 168–75.

— *Unlikely Stories: Causality and the Nature of Modern Narrative*. University of Delaware Press, 1997.

Richter, David H. (ed.). *Narrative/Theory*. Longman, 1996.

Ricoeur, Paul. *Time and Narrative*, vol. 1. Trans. Kathleen McLaughlin and David Pellauer. University of Chicago Press, 1984.

— *Time and Narrative*, vol. 2. Trans. Kathleen McLaughlin and David Pellauer. University of Chicago Press, 1985.

— *Time and Narrative*, vol. 3. Trans. Kathleen Blamey and David Pellauer. University of Chicago Press, 1988.

Riffaterre, Michael. *Fictional Truth*. Johns Hopkins University Press, 1990.

Rimmon-Kenan, Shlomith. *Narrative Fiction: Contemporary Poetics*, 2nd ed. New Accents. Routledge, 2002.

Robinson, Sally. *Engendering the Subject: Gender and Self-Representation in Contemporary Women's Fiction*. SUNY Press, 1991.

Ron, Moshe. 'The Restricted Abyss: Nine Problems in the Theory of Mise en Abyme.' *Poetics Today* 8 (1987), 417–38.

Ronen, Ruth. *Possible Worlds in Literary Theory*. Cambridge University Press, 1994.

Ryan, Marie-Laure. *Narrative as Virtual Reality: Immersion and Interactivity in Literature and Electronic Media*. Johns Hopkins University Press, 2001.

— 'Possible Worlds and Accessibility Relations: A Semantic Typology of Fiction.' *Poetics Today* 12:3 (Fall 1991), 553–76.

— 'Stacks, Frames, and Boundaries.' Rpt. in *Narrative Dynamics: Essays on Time, Plot, Closure, and Frames*. Ed. Brian Richardson. Ohio State University Press, 2002: 366–86.

Said, Edward W. *Beginnings: Intention and Method*. Basic Books, 1975.

Scholes, Robert and Robert Kellogg, *The Nature of Narrative*. Oxford University Press, 1966.

Searle, John R. 'The Logical Status of Fictional Discourse.' *New Literary History* 6 (Winter 1975), 319–32.

Sidney, Philip. *A Defense of Poesy. An Apology for Poetry* [1595] Ed. Forrest G. Robinson Macmillan/Library of Liberal Arts, 1970.

Smith, Barbara Herrnstein. 'Narrative Versions, Narrative Theories.' *On Narrative*. Ed. W. J. T. Mitchell. University of Chicago Press, 1981: 209–32.

— *Poetic Closure: A Study of How Poems End*. University of Chicago Press, 1968.

Smitten, Jeffrey R. and Ann Daghistany. *Spatial Form in Narrative*. Foreword by Joseph Frank. Cornell University Press, 1981.

Stanzel, F. K. *A Theory of Narrative*. 1979. Trans. Charlotte Goedsche. Cambridge University Press, 1984.

Stewart, Garrett. *Dear Reader: The Conscripted Audience in Nineteenth-Century British Fiction*. Johns Hopkins University Press, 1996.

Sukenick, Ronald. *Narralogues: Truth in Fiction*. SUNY Press, 2000.

Sutherland, John. *Victorian Fiction: Writers, Publishers, Readers*. St. Martin's Press, 1995.

Todorov, Tzvetan. *The Fantastic: A Structural Approach to a Literary Genre*. Cornell University Press, 1975.

— *Genres in Discourse*. Trans. Catherine Porter. Cambridge University Press, 1990.

— *Introduction to Poetics*. Trans. Richard Howard. Intro. Peter Brooks. University of Minnesota Press, 1981.

— *The Poetics of Prose*. Trans. Richard Howard. Foreword by Jonathan Culler. Cornell University Press, 1977.

Tomashevsky, Boris. 'Thematics.' *Russian Formalist Criticism: Four Essays*. Trans. Lee T. Lemon and Marion J. Reis. University of Nebraska Press, 1965: 61–95.

Tompkins, Jane (ed.). *Reader-Response Criticism*. Johns Hopkins University Press, 1980.

Torgovnick, Marianna. *Closure in the Novel*. Princeton University Press, 1981.

Trollope, Anthony. *An Autobiography*. 1883. Oxford University Press, 1950: 237–8.

Turner, Mark. *The Literary Mind: The Origins of Thought and Language*. Oxford University Press, 1996.

Urban, Greg. *Metaculture: How Culture Moves through the World*. University of Minnesota Press, 2001.

Warhol, Robyn R. *Gendered Interventions: Narrative Discourse in the Victorian Novel* Rutgers University Press, 1989.

— 'Guilty Cravings: What Feminist Narratology Can Do for Cultural Studies.' *Narratologies*. Ed. David Herman. Ohio State University Press, 1999: 340–55.

Watt, Ian. *The Rise of the Novel: Studies in Defoe, Richardson and Fielding*. University of California Press, 1957.

Wellek, René and Austin Warren. *A Theory of Literature*. 1942. New rev. ed. Penguin, 1963.

White, Hayden. *The Content of the Form: Narrative Discourse and Historical Representation*. Johns Hopkins University Press, 1987.

— *Metahistory: The Historical Imagination in Nineteenth-Century Europe*. Johns Hopkins University Press, 1973.

— 'The Value of Narrativity in the Representation of Reality.' *On Narrative*. Ed. W. J. T. Mitchell. University of Chicago Press, 1981: 1–23.

Williams, Jeffrey. *Theory and the Novel: Narrative Reflexivity in the British Tradition*. Cambridge University Press, 1998.

Williams, Raymond. *Keywords: A Vocabulary of Culture and Society*. Rev. ed. Oxford University Press, 1983.

— *Marxism and Literature*. Oxford University Press, 1977.

Woolf, Virginia. 'Mrs Dalloway in Bond Street.' *The Longman Anthology of British Literature*. Ed. David Damrosch et al. Longman/Addison-Wesley, 1999: 2453–61.

Index

Abbott, Porter, 15, 77, 80, 173
Abish, Walter, 164
Abrams, M. H., 169
achrony, 102, 105, 107, 160, 165
Ackroyd, Peter, 165
actants, 68, 84–5, 154, 157, 158
   see also helper; object; opponent;
      receiver; sender; subject
Adams, Richard, 57
Adisa, Opal Palmer, 164, 165
advertisements, 16
Alexander, Lloyd, 24
allusion, 151
Althusser, Louis, 114
Amazon.com, 35, 134, 144
ambiguity, 107, 160
Amis, Kingsley, 111
Amis, Martin, 101, 110–11, 165
anachrony, 77, 85, 99–107, 113,
      160, 165
analepses, 77–8, 81, 102–3, 107,
      112, 160
   completing, 103, 104, 112, 160
   external, 103, 160
   internal, 103, 106, 160
   mixed, 103, 160
   objective, 103, 160
   repeating, 103, 104, 160
   subjective, 103, 160
anatomy, 152
Anderson, Benedict, 146, 177
Anderson, Sherwood, 164
annexes, narrative, 80, 114, 158,
      173
anonymity, 33–4
anonymous, as author, 33–4, 163
antagonist, and protagonist 64
anthologies, 25, 29, 155
anticipations, see prolepses
Appiah, Kwame Anthony, 29
approaches to narrative, x, 1–15,
      154–5
   classical, 154
   cognitive, 5, 7, 12–14, 35, 53,
      155, 175
   cultural studies, xii, 49, 50, 52,
      56, 91, 148, 154

feminist, 11–12, 17, 50–2, 56, 86,
      155
formalist, xi–xii, 10, 26–7, 154
interdisciplinary, xii, 5, 6–7, 11,
      12, 114, 154
modern, 64, 154
narratological, xii, xiii, 6–7,
      11–12, 31–2, 40, 48, 85, 88,
      96, 97, 126, 154, 155, 168,
      172
New Critical, xii, 3–4, 9–10, 51,
      56, 69, 154
post-structuralist, xii, xiii, 11, 12,
      50–2, 56, 64, 69, 72, 120,
      154, 168, 169, 176
reader-centered, xv, 4–5, 10–11,
      12, 35, 50, 56, 82, 131, 154
Renaissance, 8, 116–18, 154
rhetorical, xii, 11, 12, 43, 68, 80,
      152, 154
Romantic, 7, 154
structuralist, xii, xiii, 4–5, 7, 8,
      9, 11, 17, 50–2, 56, 67, 69,
      72, 73, 84, 87, 141, 154, 168,
      169
architext, 151, 176
Aristotelian character, 71, 139, 158
Aristotle, 2, 3, 7, 8, 71, 76–8, 79,
      139, 154, 158
Attridge, Derek, 169
Atwood, Margaret, 20, 163, 164,
      165
audience
   authorial, 54, 131–2, 138, 145,
      161, 170
   narrative, 54, 131–2, 138, 161
Auerbach, Erich, 126, 139, 140
Austen, Jane, 65, 70, 85, 95–6. 163,
      165
Auster, Paul, 164
author, death of the, 50–1,157
author-function, 50–1, 157
authorial audience, 54, 131–2, 138,
      145, 161, 170
authors, 31–5, 38–41, 70, 71, 90–1,
      130, 156, 157
   anonymous, 163

189

implied, 32–5, 38, 40–1, 49, 50, 53, 69, 70, 156, 170
mediation of the voices of, 48
narrators distinct from, 31, 38, 40, 71, 122
pseudonymous, 33–4
real or actual, 32–4, 40–1, 50, 69, 70, 90, 129
authority, 50–1, 52, 157
authorship, material conditions of, xiv, 17, 18, 19, 21, 22–3, 24, 25, 29, 137, 138
autobiographies, fictional, 36, 99, 129, 133, 136, 143, 150, 156, 175–6

Babb, Genie, 66, 172
backstory, 103, 112, 160
Baker, Nicholson, 165, 166
Bakhtin, Mikhail, xiv, 9, 28, 47, 51, 52, 53, 79, 87, 92, 124, 152, 154, 155, 157, 174
Bal, Mieke, 74, 88, 172, 174
ballads, 2, 19, 136, 143, 155, 163
Balzac, Honoré de, 24
Banfield, Ann, 172
Bantock, Nick, 166
Barker, Pat, 24
Barra, Allen, 133–4, 176
Barth, John, 111, 114, 154, 168
Barthelme, Frederick, 165
Barthes, Roland, 11, 33, 50–1, 64–5, 168, 171, 173, 175
beginnings, 3, 18, 75–8, 81, 100, 102, 121, 158, 167, 173
'in medias res' a form of, 77, 99; see also anachrony
Behn, Aphra, 62
Bell, Madison Smartt, 8
Benjamin, Walter, 53
Berger, Harry, 126
Bible, the, 20
Bildungsroman, 36, 68, 92, 99, 102, 143
Boccaccio, Giovanni, 109–10
book, history of the, 130, 138, 148, 162
books, as subdivisions, 16–17, 19–23, 155, 163
Booth, Wayne, 11, 12, 33, 42, 50, 53, 69, 168, 170
Bornstein, George, 138

Bové, Paul, 51, 52, 171
Bowen, Elizabeth, 23, 165
Boyer, Glenn, 133–4, 136
Brink, Andre, 26, 164
Broch, Hermann, 26
Brogan, T. V. F., 169
Brontë, Charlotte, 23, 34, 36, 65, 79, 83, 163, 164, 165
Brontë, Emily, 165
Brooke-Rose, Christine, 8, 168
Brooks, Cleanth, 4, 9, 154, 167, 168, 173
Brooks, Peter, 15, 82, 88
Browder, Laura, 150, 176
Brower, Reuben, 168
Brown, Sterling A., 163
Bunyan, John, 65
Burgess, Anthony, 20, 26, 34, 164, 169
Burke, Kenneth, 9, 153
Burnett, Ivy Compton, 39, 70, 93, 128
Burney, Frances, 21, 172
Burroway, Janet, 168, 171
Butts, Mary, 83
Byatt, A. S., 8, 163, 164, 168

Calvino, Italo, 57, 110, 164, 165
Carey, Peter, 37, 165
Carlyle, Thomas, 132
causation, 3, 7, 52, 73–6, 80, 81, 83, 88, 106, 158, 172
sequence and, 81
see also post hoc ergo propter hoc fallacy
Cawelti, John G., 177
censorship, 131
Chabon, Michael, 165
chapters, 16, 20–1, 26, 155
characterization, 40, 55, 64–6, 157
actions intrinsic to, 55, 64, 66, 119, 128
block, 40, 65–6, 157
description as an aspect of, 40, 64, 65, 157, 167
embodiment of, 56, 66
external, 56, 63, 65–6, 157
generic expectations an aspect of, 56, 65, 144
internal, 65, 157
names as an aspect of, 65, 124, 157

narrator's role in, 40, 65
'personality' as a result of, 56,
  64–5
traits and habits in, 40, 58, 64,
  65, 66, 67, 70, 71, 157
characters, 1–2, 8, 30–3, 44–5,
  55–72, 87, 103, 110, 117–19,
  121, 139, 154, 156, 167, 171–2
animals as, 57
Aristotelian, 71, 139, 158
flat, 8, 59, 67, 68, 72, 157
foil, 67
imaginary persons as a
  conception of, x, 32–3,
  55–9, 64, 69–70, 157, 171
mimetic, 68, 157
narrating, 108, 112; *see also*
  first-person narrative;
  narrators, secondary
names of, 65, 157
plot functions defining, 9, 59,
  67, 70, 84–5, 157
plot inseparable from, 55, 75, 76,
  85
realistic, 139
reflecting, 30–2, 36, 38, 42, 44,
  49, 71, 80, 114, 156
rhetorical roles defining, 68, 157
round, 8, 32, 59, 67, 68, 72,
  157
structural roles defining, 32, 84,
  157
synthetic, 68, 157
taxonomy of, 68–9, 157
thematic, 32, 68, 157
'word masses' a conception of,
  32–3, 56–7, 59, 65, 69, 157
Chatman, Seymour, 9, 33, 42, 44,
  53, 64–5, 66, 70, 74, 76, 79, 88,
  89, 168, 170, 172
Chatterton, Thomas, 133
Chaucer, Geoffrey, 109, 113
chronology, 73–4, 99–102, 104–5,
  109
chronotope, 9, 87, 92, 96–7, 108,
  124, 144, 159, 160, 161
Circle, Prague Linguistic, 9
claims, truth, 118, 119, 120, 123,
  129–32, 135–6, 137, 161
Clayton, Jay, 174
Clemens, Samuel, *see* Mark Twain
closure, 73, 77, 86, 112, 173

Cohn, Dorrit, xiii, 44, 53, 59–64,
  71–2, 105, 122–3, 126, 128,
  140, 161, 170, 171, 172, 174,
  175
Colie, Rosalie, 153
collections, short story, 24–5, 155
Collins, Wilkie, 22, 74, 136
completing analapses, 103, 104,
  112, 160
confession, 135–6, 151
Conrad, Joseph, 42, 163, 165
consciousness
  center of, 8, 31, 38, 45, 60
  representation of fictional, xiii,
    10, 38, 40, 45, 49, 55, 57,
    59–64, 66, 70, 71, 72, 99,
    119, 122, 128, 157, 165:
    narrated monologue, 60–1,
    62, 63, 70, 94, 157, 165, 172;
    psycho-narration, 60, 61, 62,
    63, 70, 157, 165, 172;
    quoted monologue a form of,
    60, 61–2, 63, 70, 71, 157,
    165, 172; self-narrated
    monologue, 172; self
    narration, 34, 36–7, 44, 47,
    109, 111, 122, 126, 156, 172;
    self-quoted monologue, 172
  stream of, 62, 71–2, 158: *see also*
    monologue, quoted
context
  cultural, xii, xiii, 7, 12, 18, 23,
    27, 35, 90–1, 114, 119, 120,
    137, 145, 147, 146
  historical, xii, xiv, 7, 12, 13, 27,
    49, 56, 90–1, 114, 120, 124,
    137, 143, 148, 167
  presentational, 114, 129–31, 161
conventions, x, xii, xvi, 16, 66, 70,
  73, 83, 86, 92, 110, 111, 119,
  120, 121, 122, 129, 135, 137,
  143, 144–6, 149, 152, 162, 176
Cornwell, Patricia, 163
Cortazar, Julio, 80–1
Coste, Didier, 126, 176
Crace, Jim, 164, 165
critics
  Chicago, xii, 11
  feminist, 11–12, 17, 50–2, 56, 73,
    86, 150, 155
  New, 3–4, 9–10, 51, 56, 69, 72,
    107, 154, 167

reader response, xv, 5, 8, 11, 12,
26, 35, 50, 56, 70, 131, 154
Russian Formalist, 8–10, 15, 67,
74, 84, 89, 113, 154, 168
textual, 138, 156
see also feminist, formalist, New
Critical, reader-centered *and*
rhetorical *under* approaches
to narrative
criticism
archetypal, 84, 124–5, 151–2
contextual, xii, 6, 7, 26–7, 91
extrinsic, xii
feminist, 11–12, 17, 50–2, 56, 86,
150, 155
genre, 56, 70, 83
intrinsic, xii, 10, 142
New, xii, 3–4, 9–10, 51, 56, 69,
72, 107, 154, 167,
phenomenological, *see* reception
theorists
practical, xii, xiv, 9
psychoanalytic, xv, 97
psychological, 9, 64, 65, 69,
126
Culler, Jonathan, 171
cyberpunk, 145

Dallas, E. S., 167
Dällenbach, Lucien, 114
Davis, Lennard, 129, 135–6
Deane, Seamus, 20, 164
deconstruction, 11, 64, 174
defamiliarization, 9, 113, 114, 161
Defoe, Daniel, 166
Deleyto, Celestino, 170
DeLillo, Don, 36
Derrida, Jacques, 153
Desai, Anita, 164
description, 4, 93, 154, 157, 167
device(s)
formal, x
laying bare the, 9, 21, 80, 113,
115, 122, 161
plot, 100
dialogue, 87, 92, 95, 97
see also scene
Dickens, Charles, 17, 22, 33, 34,
36, 68, 78–9, 83, 87, 163, 164,
165
diegesis
duration as aspect of, 93, 159

telling in classical rhetoric as, 2,
7, 139, 174
see also story world
digressions, 17, 73, 75, 80, 158,
103, 160
dilation, *see* expansion
Dillard, Annie, 8, 168
discourse, xiv, 4, 11, 17, 51, 64, 65,
74, 82, 87, 154, 155, 171
definition of: in Bakhtin's terms,
51, 87; in Foucault's terms,
51–2; in narratological terms,
17, 51
free indirect, 60, 157, 172: *see
also* monologue, narrated
indirect, 51
level of the, 109
novelistic, 9, 47–8, 51, 64
poetic, 51
discourse time, 4, 85, 90, 92–4,
100, 159
disorder, 17, 73, 75, 80, 81, 83, 85,
90, 99–107, 113, 159, 165, 174
Doerr, Harriet, 164
Dolozel, Lubomír, 122–3, 126, 140
Doody, Margaret Anne, 29, 169
Dostoevsky, Fyodor, 48
Doyle, Arthur Conan, 24, 164
Doyle, Roddy, 164
Drabble, Margaret, 164, 170
dramatis personae, see plot
functions *under* characters
DuBrow, Heather, 146, 153
DuMaurier, Daphne, 65, 164
Duncan, Ian, 149
Dunmore, Helen, 47, 165
Dunn, Kevin, 138
DuPlessis, Rachel Blau, 86, 173
duration, xiii, 90–6, 102, 119, 159
diagram of speeds in, 93

Eakin, Paul John, 126
Earp, Josephine, 133
Earp, Wyatt, 133, 176
Eco, Umberto, 8, 175
editing, textual, 26–7, 28, 138, 156
Edson, Russell, 163
Eggers, Dave, 113, 166
Elam, Diane, 140
Elibron, 27
Eliot, George, 16–17, 22–3, 34, 39,
43, 163, 164

Eliot, T. S., 8
ellipses, 85, 93–6, 97, 106, 159
  see also gaps
emplotment, 125
ends, 3, 18, 75–7, 101, 102, 121,
  158, 173
enigmas, 76, 104, 107, 160
epic, 2, 18–19, 20, 28, 59, 77–8,
  81, 99, 125, 141, 142, 143, 155,
  163, 169
episodes, 20, 27, 73, 79–80, 87,
  105, 110, 114, 155, 158
epitexts, 161
  see also paratexts
Erlebte Rede, 172
  see also monologue, narrated
ethics, narrative, xii, 5, 8, 12, 69,
  155, 168–9, 172
ethos, see Aristotelian character
Evans, Mary Ann, *see* George
  Eliot
Evaristo, Bernardine, 166
events, 1–2, 3, 4, 9, 55, 73–7, 79,
  80, 81–2, 90, 97, 99–104, 121,
  125, 128, 158, 172
  kernel, definition of, 79
  satellite, definition of, 79
existents, 66, 108
expansion, 85, 93, 94, 96, 159
extent, 103, 104, 160

fables, 143
fabliaux, 113
fabula, 4, 9, 10, 74–5, 82, 88, 89,
  154, 158
fabulation, 81
fakes, 129, 132, 133–4, 162
fallacy, *post hoc ergo propter hoc,* 81,
  106, 158
Faulkner, William, 26, 37, 65, 81,
  99, 105–6, 163, 164, 165
feeling, structures of, 91
fiction, 116–27
  adventure, 96, 143
  allegorical, 143
  ancient, 96
  autobiographical, *see*
    autobiographies, fictional
  biographical, 97
  children's, 23–4, 26
  comic, 143
  contemporary, 150–1

deception as a constituent of,
  2–3, 7, 118–19, 122–3, 135:
  see also unreliable narrator
definitions of, x, 1–5, 154
detective, 74, 81, 113, 141, 143
disguised, xiii, 2–3, 128–40, 161,
  165, 175
domestic, 143
early modern prose, 135–6
eighteenth-century, 21, 60, 137
epistolary, 21, 46, 102, 110, 136,
  144, 148, 155, 169
experimental, xi, 41, 47, 80, 92,
  99, 110, 165
fantasy, 108, 123, 141, 143, 145
feminist, 48, 50, 73, 86
formal distinctiveness of, x, 6,
  36, 118, 121–3, 128–9, 132–5,
  161
formula, 70, 141
genre, 24, 66, 70, 155
gothic, 143, 148
historical, 97, 102, 122–3,
  128–30, 133–5, 136, 143, 148
horror, 143
industrial, 143
modern, 24–5, 38, 48, 59, 60, 62,
  63–4, 99, 112, 113, 107, 137
naturalist, 143
nonmimetic, 96, 102, 119, 169
picaresque, 97, 144
postcolonial, 88, 146
postmodern, 3, 41, 47, 60, 64,
  88, 96, 99, 102, 110, 112,
  123, 136, 143
pseudo-factual, 137, 162
pulp, 143
science, 143
Victorian, 17, 19, 21–3, 28, 38,
  48, 60–1, 78, 80, 87, 147, 169
fictional worlds, x, 8, 20, 47, 56,
  58, 66, 91–2, 108, 110, 116–27,
  144–5, 175
fictionality, x, xiii, 112, 116–26,
  128–40, 161, 175
Fictus, Homo, 33, 59
Fielding, Henry, 20, 163
filling in
  analeptic, 103, 107, 160
  proleptic, 104, 160
film, 2, 6, 16, 17, 27, 30, 59, 66,
  80, 91, 137, 142, 145, 147, 170

filters, *see* reflectors
first-person narration, xi, 30, 34–5,
    36–7, 39–40, 42–4, 46–7, 53,
    63, 71, 109, 156, 164
  consonant, 36–7, 44, 53, 109,
    156, 164, 172
  dissonant, 36–7, 43–4, 53, 156,
    164, 172
  plural, 37, 156, 164Fishelov,
    David, 146, 153
Fitzgerald, F. Scott, 65
flashbacks, *see* analepses
flashforward, *see* prolepses
Flaubert, Gustave, 165
Fludernik, Monika, xiii, 72, 167,
    171, 176
focalization, 74, 171:
  hypothetical, 171, 172
  see also situation, narrative
    perspective
focalizers, *see* reflectors
foil, 67
Foley, Barbara, 137, 139
Ford, Ford Madox, 164
forgeries, 129, 132, 134, 162
form
  definition of, x
  dialogic, 48, 51, 79, 87, 157, 158
  dominant, 91, 124, 148, 150, 162
  emergent, 91, 124, 148, 150, 162
  generic, 83, 141–52, 162
  hegemonic, 148
  narrative, x–xvi, 154, 162:
    definition of, x, 1–5; genre
    as, 141
  residual, 91, 124, 148, 150, 162
  spatial, 107, 160
formalism, xi–xii, xiii, 6–7, 48, 154
Formalists, Russian, 8–10, 15, 67,
    74, 84, 89, 113, 154, 168
  see also formalist *under*
    approaches to narrative
Forster, E. M., 3, 8, 26, 33, 59, 67,
    72, 73–4, 88, 154, 172
Foucault, Michel, xiv, 50–2, 157,
    171
Fowler, Alastair, 153
frame-breaking, *see* metalepsis
frame of reference, 114
frames, 108–11, 114, 160
framing, 108–11, 114, 136, 155,
    160, 174

  circumtextual, 114, 115, 136
  extratextual, 114, 115
  intertextual, 115
  intratextual, 115
  see also frame of reference;
    historical context; paratexts
Frank, Joseph, 107
Franklin, Benjamin
Fraser, George MacDonald, 134,
    166
fraud, *see* fakes *and* forgeries
Freeland, Cynthia, 14
frequency, xiii, 81, 85, 93–5, 159
  iterative, 94, 159
  normative, 94, 159
  repetitive, 94–5, 159
Freud, Sigmund, 82
Freytag, Gustav, 173
Freytag's pyramid, 173
Friedman, Susan Stanford, 86, 146,
    173, 177
Frye, Northrop, 84, 88, 125, 151–2,
    153, 162, 177
Fuentes, Carlos, 46
functions, plot, 9, 67, 70, 84–5,
    124, 158
Furedy, Viveca, 114

Gabler, Hans Walter, 169
Gaiman, Neil, 123, 166
Gaines, Ernest, 36, 129, 164, 166
gaps, xv, 17, 35, 44, 49, 56, 81,
    85, 91, 93–6, 97, 98, 104, 106,
    120, 122–3, 159
  see also ellipses
García Márquez, Gabriel, 21
Gardner, John, 8, 168
Garrett, Peter K., 28, 79, 87, 170
Gaskell, Elizabeth, 22
Gass, William, 168
Gelley, Alexander, 175
gender, 12–13, 40, 49, 50, 65,
    169
Genette, Gérard, xiii, 11, 32, 39,
    40, 44, 52, 53, 74, 81, 92, 95,
    96, 97, 98, 100–1, 103, 105,
    114,
124, 129–31, 140, 143, 151, 153,
    154, 157, 159, 170, 172, 174,
    176
genre, xii, 16, 50, 51, 56, 66, 70,
    75, 83, 86–7, 90, 92, 96–7,

108, 113, 114, 124, 125, 130, 136,
141–52, 162, 169, 176, 177
boundaries of, 142–3, 146, 147, 175, 177
historical, 142, 147, 162
metaphors for, 146–7
genres
'super', 148
'the three', 2, 142, 162
Gibbons, Stella, 46–7
Gibson, William, 145
Gide, Andre, 112
globalization, 146–7
Godden, Rumer, 164
Goethe, Johann Wolfgang von, 8
Goldman, Michael, 63–4, 145, 153
Goodman, Nelson, 126, 175
Gordimer, Nadine, 164
Graff, Gerald, 120, 121, 175
Grafton, Anthony, 138
Green, Martin, 177
Greetham, D. C., 138
Greimas, A. J., 15, 68, 70, 84–5, 87, 157
Gross, Sabine, 13
Guillén, Claudio, 141, 153, 177
Guillory, John, 168

Hamburger, Käte, 121, 175
Hardy, Thomas, 22, 27, 68, 163
Harris, Robert, 176
Harryman, Carla, 173
Harvey, W. J., 72
Hawthorn, Jeremy, 74–5, 172
Hawthorne, Nathaniel, 163
Hejinian, Lyn, 81, 173
helper, 68, 84–5, 157, 158
see also actants
Hemingway, Ernest, 93, 164
Herman, David, 11, 13, 14, 15, 35, 47, 53, 171, 172
Hernadi, Paul, 153
heteroglossia, 9, 48, 52, 157
Higdon, David Leon
Hirsch, E. D., 153
Hirsch, Marianne, 174
histoire, 74
history, literary, xiv, 14, 16, 18, 26–7, 34, 35, 38, 86, 90, 114, 128, 135, 137, 142, 148, 150–1, 169

Hitchcock, Alfred, 67
Hitler, Adolf, 132
Hochman, Baruch, 56, 68–9, 70, 72, 157
Hollander, John, 169
Homans, Margaret, 86, 173
Homer, 17, 59, 64, 77–8, 134, 163
Horace, 99
Hornby, Nick, 165
Hulme, Keri, 165
Hutcheon, Linda, 140, 177
Hutchinson, Steven, 173
hybridity, 146
hypertext, 151
hypotaxis, 100, 159
hypotext, 151

ideas, novels of, 143
imitation, *see* mimesis
indeterminacy, 97, 119
Ingarden, Roman, 170
inset, 111, 161
installments, serial, 19–23, 26–7, 78, 130, 149, 155, 163
genre fiction published in, 163
monthly numbers a form of, 19, 21–3, 155
periodicals as a vehicle for, 19, 24–5, 27, 155
sequences a form of, 23–4, 155, 163
interiority, 59, 63–4, 75
interpellation, 114, 161
interpolation, 110–11, 114, 161, 165, 174
interpretation, thematic x, xii, 6, 7, 49, 143
intertextuality, 50, 114, 151, 162
intratext, 151
intrelacement, 103
irony, 43, 50, 113, 125, 137, 151, 152
Iser, Wolfgang, xv, 11, 33, 35, 53, 97, 98, 120, 161, 170
Ishiguro, Kazuo, 35, 43, 94, 164, 165

Jahn, Manfred, 14, 74–5
Jakobson, Roman, 11, 167
James, Henry, 8, 19, 28, 29, 31, 38, 41, 55, 65, 67, 154, 155, 165, 171

James, William, 71
Jameson, Fredric, 139, 140, 174, 177
jargon, xv–xvi, 7, 31, 154
Jewett, Sarah Orne, 25
Johnson, B. S., 80, 106–7
Jones, Diana Wynne, 165
Joyce, James, 25, 36, 39, 40, 62, 65, 68, 152, 164, 165, 176
journalism, 135–6, 137
jurisprudence, narrative, 11

Keen, Suzanne, 80, 147, 151, 173, 176
Kermode, Frank, 173, 176
kernels, 9, 79, 80, 88, 89, 105, 158
keywords, xiv, 28–9, 50–2, 71–2, 87–8, 96–7, 107, 114, 124, 139, 151
Kincaid, Jamaica, 163, 164
kinds, 70, 141, 143, 162
King, Stephen, 23, 163
Kingsley, Charles, 26
Kingsolver, Barbara, 164
Kingston, Maxine Hong, 166
Knights, L. C., 171
Kraus, Nicola, 58
Kristeva, Julia, 50, 151, 157, 162, 177
Kubrick, Stanley, 20
Kurosawa, Akira, 94

Laclos, Pierre Choderlos de, 21, 163
language, ordinary, 11
langue, 8
Lanser, Susan, xiv, 11, 52, 53, 167, 169, 170
Lardner, Ring, 25, 43–4, 163, 165
Laurence, Margaret, 25, 164
Lawrence, D. H., 165
lawsuits, 136–7
Leavis, F. R., 9
Le Carré, John, 164
Lehman, David, 126
Lessing, Doris, 24, 45, 70, 163, 164, 165
letters, 21, 155
level
    discourse, 17, 30, 56, 74–6, 82, 122, 128, 156, 158, 160
    referential, 122–3, 128

story, 17, 30, 56, 74–5, 82, 89, 109, 122, 128, 156, 158, 160
    textual, 30, 56, 74, 82, 160
levels, narrative, xiii, 30, 32–4, 42, 38, 39, 44, 47, 85, 92, 108–15, 119, 122–3, 124, 156, 158, 160, 161, 165, 174
    discourse, 109
    ontological use of, 32, 42, 108, 161
    primary, 85, 110, 112, 114, 161
    secondary, 42, 85, 108, 110, 112, 161
    spatial metaphors in description of, 110, 111
    tertiary, 42, 85, 110, 161
Levi-Strauss, Claude, 11
Lewis, C. S., 24
Lewis, David, 175
libraries
    circulating, 23, 29
    e-texts provided by, 27–8, 9
liminality, 21, 113, 129–31, 134, 146
lines, plot, 77, 79–80, 83, 86, 99, 143
listservs, 149
literariness, 8, 9, 11, 113
literature, African-American, 150
lives, criminal, 135
Lodge, David, 8, 21, 72, 168, 172
Lubbock, Percy, 8, 171
Lyotard, Jean François, 125, 126

Macaulay, Thomas Babington, 134
Manlove, Colin, 177
Mann, Thomas, 165
Martin, Wallace, 15
Mason, Bobbie Ann, 35
masterplots, 88, 158
McCullough, Colleen, 92
McEwan, Ian, xi, 165
McGann, Jerome, 29
McInerney, Jay, 46, 165
McKeon, Michael, 29, 153, 176
McLaughlin, Emma, 58
Mcquillan, Martin, xv, 15
Merivale, Patricia, 177
metafiction, 81, 110, 112, 123, 136, 143, 161
metafictionality, 161

metalepsis, 30, 110–11, 115, 124, 161
metanarratives, 124–6, 161
Michener, James, 92
middles of narratives, 3, 18, 75–8, 81, 121, 158, 173
migrancy, 146
Miller, D. A., 173
Miller, Nancy K., 86, 173
Millhauser, Steven, 37
Milton, John, 163
mimesis, 3, 7, 8, 93, 116–17, 139, 159, 162, 174
   duration as an aspect of, 93, 159
   Frye's modes and, 151
   showing in classical rhetoric as, 3, 7, 139, 174
mise en abyme, 112, 114, 161, 174
Mistry, Rohinston, 39–40, 165
modernity, 59, 63–4
modes
   genres as, 84, 151, 177
   historical, 125–6, 142
   universal, 142, 162, 177
Monaco, James, 170
monologue
   interior, 60, 62
   narrated, 60–1, 62, 63, 70, 157, 165
   quoted, 60, 61–2, 63, 70, 157, 165
monsters, loose baggy, 28, 87, 155
Moore, Lorrie, 47, 165
Moretti, Franco, 124, 148–9, 153, 161, 162
Morris, Edmund, 122
Morris, Errol, 94
Morrison, Toni, 17, 165
Morson, Gary Saul, 145, 153, 177
motifs
   bound, 9, 89
   free, 9, 89
   see also kernels; satellites
Munro, Alice, 19
Murdoch, Iris, 41, 58, 110, 165
Murray, Bill, 94
Myers, Jack, 169
mythoi, 151, 152, 162

Nagel, James, 29
Naipaul, V. S., 92, 165, 166

narratees, 3, 31–5, 42, 46, 50, 52, 53, 119, 154, 156, 164
   dissonance with respect to, 46, 52
narration, 4, 36–50, 74, 90, 154, 159
   anterior, 101, 159
   antinomic, 96, 101, 159
   backward-moving, 101, 159
   discordant, 44, 49, 156, 171
   disorded, 165
   first-person, *see* first-person narration
   forward-moving, 100–1, 159, 165
   intercalated, 102, 159
   intermittent, 46, 102, 159
   multi-personed, 47, 73, 157, 164
   restricted, 38–9, 41, 156
   second-person, 37, 45–8, 157, 165, 171: authorial, 46; external, 46; figural, 46; imperative, 47; intermittent, 46; internal, 46; subjunctive, 47
   self, 34, 36–7, 44, 47, 109, 111, 122, 126, 156, 172: *see also* first-person narration
   simultaneous, 102, 159
   third-person, xi, xv, 30, 34–45, 63, 111, 156: authorial, 39–40, 43–4, 46, 49, 51, 60, 156, 164;
   external, 31, 34, 38–43, 45–6, 63, 70, 111, 156; figural, 39–40, 42, 44, 46, 49, 53, 60, 63, 65, 156, 164; internal, 31, 34, 38–41, 46, 65, 156; limited, 38–9, 41, 156; omniscient, 31, 38–9, 41, 46, 60, 156, 170–1; reflector not the narrator in, 31, 42, 49, 70, 71
   ulterior, 101–2, 159
   unreliable, 32, 34, 35, 37, 42–4, 47, 49–50, 53, 156, 165
narrative
   approaches to, *see* approaches to narrative
   Chinese box, 110, 160
   circular, 96, 159
   conflated, 96, 159
   contradictory, 96, 159
   definitions of, x, 1–5, 16, 32, 154

differential, 96, 159
dual, 96, 159
grammar of, 11, 48, 158
grand, 124–5
historical, 121–3, 124–5, 128–9,
    174
master, 125
minimal, 163, 172
multi-plot, 48, 73, 78–9, 87, 96,
    158, 159, 164, 165, 173
slave, 150
staircase, 112, 161
subdivisions of, x, 16–29, 155
theorists of, *see* theorists of
    narrative
travel, 135, 136
narrative audience, 54, 131–2, 138,
    161
narrative turn, the, 11, 154
narrativity, 48, 121, 125, 128
narratology, xii, xiii, 6–7, 11–12,
    40, 48, 85, 88, 96, 97, 154, 155,
    176
contextual, xiii, xiv, 11–12, 13,
    91, 154
feminist, xiv, 11–12, 86, 155
post-classical, xii, 48
narrators, x, 1–2, 30–50, 79, 103,
    104, 113, 119, 121, 154, 156
authorial, xi, 39–40, 43–4, 49, 51,
    156, 170
characters as, 108, 112
covert, 34, 38, 40–3, 109, 128,
    156
defined, 32, 34
discordant, 156, 171
external, xi, 31, 34, 38–43, 109,
    110, 128, 156
figural, 39–40, 44, 49, 53, 63,
    156
first-person, *see* first-person
    narration
internal, 34, 38–41, 109, 110,
    156
limited, 38–9, 41, 156
multiple, 26, 39–42, 47, 48, 63,
    79, 109, 157
omniscient, xi, xv, 31, 32, 38–9,
    41, 46, 110, 128, 156, 170–1
overt, 32, 34, 36, 38, 40–1, 43,
    49, 60, 109, 156
primary, 111

prophetic, 104
restricted, 38–9, 41, 156
secondary, 108–12, 123, 174
second-person, 37, 45–8, 157,
    165, 171
third-person, xi, xv, 30, 34–45,
    71, 156
unreliable, xi, 32, 34, 35, 37,
    42–4, 47, 49–50, 53, 104,
    156, 165
Naylor, Gloria, 164
Nelles, William, 115
New Literary History, 149
Newman, Karen, 174
Newton, Adam Zachary, 168
New York Times, 134
Nexis, 27
Nolan, Christopher, 100–1
nonfiction, x, xiii, 6, 118, 119,
    120, 121, 122, 126, 128–40,
    142, 161, 165, 169
creative, 134, 136, 176
Norfolk, Lawrence, 26, 128
notices, advance
    proleptic, 104, 160
novel, 2, 6, 9, 10, 16, 17, 48, 59,
    87, 96, 116, 128, 134, 137, 142,
    151, 155, 162, 163, 169
definition of, 18–19
dime, 143
documentary, 137, 162
epic and, 28, 59
great tradition of the, 9
interiority in, 59–64
multi-plot, 143
social problem, 143
theories of the, 116, 135–7
novela, 17
novella, 19, 142, 144, 155, 163
Nünning, Ansgar, 170
Nussbaum, Martha, 12, 69, 168
Oates, Joyce Carol, 37, 164
object, 68, 84–5, 157, 158
    see also actants
O'Brien, Tim, 25
O'Hara, John, 25
Olson, Tillie, 164
Ondaatje, Michael, 165
Onega, Susana, 15, 167
O'Neill, Patrick, 174
opponent, 68, 84–5, 157, 158
    see also actants

order, xiii, 73–5, 82, 85–6, 90,
    99–107, 113, 119, 159, 165,
    174
Ortega, Tony, 133
Ossian, 133

pace, 81, 85, 90, 91, 93, 95, 159,
    165, 167
Palmer, Jerry, 177
Panahi, Jafar, 93
parable, 131, 143
paralipsis, 97
parataxis, 100, 159
paratexts, xiii, 21, 108, 113, 114,
    124, 129–31, 133, 134, 137–8,
    145, 161
  epitexts a variety of, 130, 134,
    146, 161
  peritexts a variety of, 130, 161
parody, 137, 139, 140, 162
parole, 8
Partridge, John, 132
pastiche, 132, 136, 137, 139, 140,
    162
pauses, 93, 159
Pavel, Thomas, 88, 119, 120, 126
people, paper, 33
  see also characters
period, latency, 148
peripety, 9, 80, 87
  see also turns *under* plot
peritexts, 161
see also paratexts
perspective, 30–2, 38–9, 42, 44–5,
    109, 129, 156–7; 167
  preferable to 'point of view',
    44–5
  see also reflectors
Phelan, James, 46, 68, 157, 171
phenomenology, *see* reception
    theory
picaresque, 20
Phillips, Tom, 166
plagiarism, 135, 151
Plato, 3, 118, 139, 154
plot, x, 2, 3, 4, 7, 8, 9, 17, 71,
    73–89, 90, 100, 121, 144, 152,
    154, 155, 165, 172
  character and, 55, 75–6, 85
  conflict a component of, 76, 121,
    167
  defined, 73–5

diagrams of, 76, 173
disruption a component of, 76
equilibrium a condition of, 76
functions, *see* plot functions
generic expectations an aspect
    of, 86–7, 144
reading for the, 82
its relation to story, 73–5
stasis a phase of, 76
turns, 80, 87, 158   typology of,
    9, 17, 75, 83–5, 86, 152
tyranny of, 86
plot functions, 9, 67, 70, 84–5,
    124, 158
plots, multiple, 73, 78–9, 103, 155,
    165
pluralism, xii
Poe, Edgar Allan, 18, 165
poesy, 8, 116–18, 161
poetics, narrative, xi, xii, xiii, 11,
    14, 17, 154, 168, *see also*
    narratological *under* approaches
    to narrative
Poetics, Tel Aviv School of, 14
poets
  the *Gawain*, 34, 163
  the *Pearl*, 34
point of view, 171
  see also perspective
polyglossia, 9
polyphony, 47–8, 52, 64, 87, 157
Porter, Dennis, 177
Posner, Richard, 12, 69, 168–9,
    172
post hoc ergo propter hoc fallacy, 81,
    106, 158
postmodernism, 3, 64, 120, 125,
    139, 173
post-structuralism, xii, xiii, 11, 12,
    50–2, 64, 72, 157, 168
Powell, Anthony, 24, 163
Pratt, Mary Louise, 11, 15, 167
pratton, see Aristotelian character
Preminger, Alex, 169
pre-structure, 129, 136, 161
Price, Leah, 29
Prince, Gerald, xv, 11, 17, 18, 32,
    53, 74, 84, 88, 172
Prize, Booker, 19
prolepses, 101, 103–4, 112, 160
  external, 103, 160
  internal, 103, 160

mixed, 104, 160
objective, 160
repeating, 104
subjective, 160
property, intellectual, 135
Propp, Vladimir, 9, 67–8, 84, 124,
   157, 173
protagonist, and antagonist, 64
Proust, Marcel, 98
psychology, narrative, 11
psycho-narration, 60, 61, 62, 63,
   70, 94, 157, 165
publication, modes of, 16–29
Punter, David, 177
pyramid, Freytag's, 173

Quin, Ann, 165

Rabinowitz, Peter J., 11, 35, 54,
   131–2, 138, 140, 145, 153, 161,
   170, 173
radio, 132
Ramis, Harold, 94
Rand, Ayn, 37
reality effect, 175
recovery, textual, 150
reach, 103, 104, 160
readers, x, xii, xvi, 6, 8, 10–11, 12,
   16, 31–5, 55–7, 64–5, 66, 74,
   76, 81–2, 90–1, 97, 99, 103,
   108, 117–20, 128–31, 136–8,
   145, 154, 156, 169, 170
   implied, 32–5, 50, 70, 119, 156
   real, 4–5, 32–5, 46, 50, 57–8, 70,
      156
reading
   authorial, 35, 54, 131–2, 138,
      145, 162, 170
   close, xii, xiv, 9, 26, 95
   distant, 124, 148–9, 161, 162
realism, 60, 65, 81, 99, 119, 120,
   104, 124, 131, 136, 137, 139,
   143, 151, 169
recall, *see* analepses, repeating
receiver, 33, 68, 84–5, 157, 158
   see also actants
reception theorists, xv, 11, 35, 50
recit, 74
reflectors, 31–2, 36, 38–9, 42, 44–5,
   49, 60, 63, 80, 114, 156–7, 170
   exterior perspectives in, 32, 39,
      42, 45, 157

interior perspectives in, 32, 39,
   42, 60, 63, 157
multiple perspectives in, 26, 32,
   39–42, 45, 48, 63, 157
single (fixed) perspective in, 32,
   38–9, 42, 45, 63, 156
variable perspectives in, 32, 42,
   45, 63, 157
Reid, Ian, 115
repeating analepses, 103, 104,
   160
repetition, 17, 80, 85, 91, 93–5,
   103–4, 167
   proleptic, 103–4, 160
retrospection, 82, 102
return, *see* completing analepses
Richardson, Alan, 14
Richardson, Brian, 48, 88, 96, 98,
   101, 102, 159, 167, 171
Richardson, Samuel, 21, 65, 163
Richter, David, 15
Ricoeur, Paul, 82, 98
Riffaterre, Michael, 119, 126
Rimmon-Kenan, Shlomith, xv, 74,
   88, 98
Robinson, Sally, 169
romance, 8, 19, 20, 78, 103, 117,
   123, 125, 135, 136, 137, 143,
   151, 152, 155, 163, 169
   archival, 133
Roman-fleuve, 24
Ron, Moshe, 115
Ronen, Ruth, 175
Rowling, J. K., 24
Roy, Arundhati, 164
Rushdie, Salman, 164, 165
Ryan, Marie-Laure, 12, 88, 126,
   175

saga, 59, 77
Said, Edward, 173
satellites, 9, 79, 80, 81, 83, 88, 89,
   158
satires, 129, 132, 139, 143, 152,
   162
Saussure, Ferdinand, 8
Scalapino, Leslie, 173
scene, 91–6, 97, 159
science, cognitive, 5, 12–14, 35, 53,
   114
Scott, Paul, 165
Scott, Walter, 134, 136, 165

Searle, John R., 11, 134, 137, 140
semiotics, 7, 167
sender, 33, 68, 84–5, 157, 158
    see also actants
sequences, 155
    genre fiction arranged in, 23–4,
        155
    short stories arranged in, 24–5,
        155, 164
Seth, Vikram, 165
setting, 68, 108, 109, 110, 119,
    124, 143, 144, 160, 167
Shakespeare, William, 78, 112, 135
Shelley, Mary, 110
Shklovsky, Victor, 9, 115, 154
short story collections, 24–5, 155
'showing', 2, 139
    see also scene; mimesis
Sidney, Philip, 65, 116–18, 127,
    154, 175
Simms, Michael, 169
situation, narrative, xiii, 10, 26,
    30–54, 60, 63, 109, 110, 144,
    156, 160, 170
    authorial, 39–40, 43–5, 49, 51,
        60, 170
    defined, 30–1, 44
    figural, 39–40, 44–5, 49, 53, 60,
        63
    preferable to 'voice', 52
sjuzet, 4, 9, 10, 74–5, 82, 88, 89,
    154, 158
Smith, Ali, 49, 164
Smith, Barbara Herrnstein, 167,
    173
snares, 79, 158, 173
Snow, C. P., 163
Society, Narrative, 149, 177
spatiality, 108, 110, 117, 124
speeds, 90–6, 159, 165
    see also duration
Spenser, Edmund, 163
Spiegelman, Art, 166
spoilers, 83
stance, illocutionary, 134–5, 137,
    162
Stanzel, Franz, xiii, 39–40, 129, 170
stasis, 76
Sternberg, Meir, 14
Sterne, Laurence, 34, 80, 102, 113,
    164, 165
Stine, R. L., 24

Stoker, Bram, 165
story, 2, 4, 11, 17, 73–5, 88, 109,
    121, 142, 154, 155, 158, 172
    embedded, 20, 109–10, 111,
        112–13, 114–15, 124, 161,
        165, 169, 174
    grammars, *see* story grammars
    level of the, 109
    narratological definition of, 17,
        18, 74–5
    short, 6, 17, 24–5, 143, 155, 163:
        anthologized, 25, 155; cycles,
        25, 155, 164; defined, in
        generic terms, 18; sequences,
        25, 155, 164; volumes of,
        24–5, 155, 164; *see also* short
        story collections
    short short, 18, 20, 155, 163
    story within, 108, 109–10, 123,
        160
    worlds, *see* story worlds
story grammars, 5, 11, 17, 18, 48,
    73, 87–8, 158
story worlds, 6, 30, 32, 34, 38,
    41–4, 47, 55, 75, 80, 82,
    108–15, 122, 160, 174
Stowe, Harriet Beecher, 164
stretching, *see* expansion
structuralism, xii, xiii, 4–5, 7, 8, 9,
    11, 17, 50–2, 67, 69, 72, 73, 84,
    146, 155, 168
structures, plot, 75, 84, 97, 125
studies, cultural, xii, xiii, 49, 50,
    52, 56, 90–1, 148, 154
    postcolonial, 7, 49, 52
subgenres, 70, 84, 86, 102, 128,
    141, 143, 145, 150, 162, 176,
    177
subject, 68, 84–5, 157, 158
    see also actants
subplots, 78, 158
Sukenick, Ronald, 168
summary
    duration mode of, 91–6, 159
    overt narrator's capacity to offer,
        40
    plot, 77, 79–80, 82–3, 88, 158
Sutherland, John, 29
Sweeney, Susan Elizabeth, 177
Swift, Jonathan, 132
syllepsis, 102, 105, 160
synopsis, *see* plot summary

sympathy, 32, 35, 43, 57, 64, 66, 70

tale
  fairy, 18, 84, 97, 143
  folk, 11, 17, 18, 66, 67, 99
  frame, 42, 109, 111, 113, 160
  interpolated, 80, 109, 111, 161, 165
Tan, Amy, 164
television, 2, 23, 77, 80, 101, 132
telling, 2, 63, 139, 174
temporality, 4–5, 16, 82, 96–7, 121
tenses, 49, 60–2, 101, 102
  future, 101, 102
  past, 34, 47, 61–2, 101, 102, 121
  present, 34, 47, 61, 102
terminology, location of, xiv, 154–62
Thackeray, William, 23,163
theorists
  genre, 141–52
  of narrative 154: Abbott, Porter, 15, 77, 80, 173; Aristotle, 2, 3, 7, 8, 71, 76–8, 79, 154, 158; Babb, Genie, 66, 172; Bakhtin, Mikhail, xiv, 9, 28, 47, 51, 52, 53, 79, 87, 92, 96–7, 124, 152, 154, 155, 157, 174; Bal, Mieke, 74, 88, 172, 174; Banfield, Ann, 172; Barth, John, 8, 110, 111, 114, 154, 168; Barthes, Roland, 11, 33, 50–1, 64–5, 107, 168, 171, 175; Benjamin, Walter, 53; Booth, Wayne, 11, 12, 33, 42, 50, 53, 69, 168, 170; Brooke-Rose, Christine, 8, 168; Brooks, Cleanth, 4, 9, 154, 167, 168; Brooks, Peter, 15, 82, 88, 173; Chatman, Seymour, 9, 33–4, 42, 44, 53, 64–5, 66, 70, 74, 76, 79, 88, 89, 168, 170, 172; Cohn, Dorrit, xiii, 44, 53, 59–64, 71–2, 105–6, 122–3, 126, 128, 140, 161, 170, 171, 172, 174, 175; Coste, Didier, 126, 176; Dällenbach, Lucien, 114; Davis, Lennard, 129, 135–6, 140, 175; Dolozel, Lubomír,

122–3, 126, 140, 175; DuPlessis, Rachel Blau, 86, 173; Eco, Umberto, 8, 175; Fludernik, Monika, xiii, 72, 167, 171, 176; Foley, Barbara, 137, 139, 140; Forster, E. M., 3, 8, 26, 33, 59, 67, 72, 73–4, 88, 154, 172; Frank, Joseph, 107; Friedman, Susan Stanford, 86, 146, 173, 177; Frye, Northrop, 84, 88, 151–2, 153, 162, 177; Furedy, Viveca, 114; Genette, Gérard, xiii, 11, 32, 39, 40, 44, 52, 53, 74, 81, 92, 95, 96, 98, 100–1, 103, 105, 124, 129–31, 114, 140, 143, 154, 151, 153, 157, 159, 170, 172, 174, 176; Greimas, A. J., 15, 68, 70, 84–5, 88, 157; Herman, David, 11, 13, 14, 15, 35, 47, 53, 171, 172; Hochman, Baruch, 56, 68–9, 70, 72, 157; Hutcheon, Linda, 140, 177; Iser, Wolfgang, xv, 11, 33, 35, 53, 97, 98, 120, 161, 170; Jahn, Manfred, 14, 74–5; James, Henry, 8, 19, 28, 29, 31, 55, 154, 155, 165, 171; Lanser, Susan, xiv, 11, 52, 53, 167, 169, 170; Lehman, David, 126; Lodge, David, 8, 72, 168, 172; Miller, D. A., 173; Miller, Nancy K., 86, 173; Moretti, Franco, 124, 153, 161, 162; Nelles, William, 115; Pavel, Thomas, 88, 119, 120, 126; Phelan, James, 46, 68, 157, 171; Plato, 7, 118, 139, 154; Poe, Edgar Allan, 18, 34; Pratt, Mary Louise, 11, 15, 167; Price, Leah, 29; Prince, Gerald, xv, 3, 11, 18, 32, 53, 74, 84, 88, 172; Propp, Vladimir, 9, 67–8, 84, 124, 154, 157; Rabinowitz, Peter J., 11, 35, 54, 131–2, 138, 140, 145, 153, 161, 170, 173; Reid, Ian, 115; Richardson, Brian, 48, 88, 96, 98, 101, 102, 159, 171; Richter, David,

15; Ricoeur, Paul, 82, 98;
Riffaterre, Michael, 119, 126;
Rimmon-Kenan, Shlomith,
xv, 74, 88, 98; Ron, Moshe,
115; Ryan, Marie-Laure, 12,
88, 126, 175; Searle, John R.,
11, 134–5, 137, 140;
Shklovsky, Victor, 9, 115,
154; Sidney, Philip, 8,
116–18, 127, 154, 175;
Smith, Barabara Herrnstein,
167, 173; Stanzel, Franz, xiii,
39–40, 170; Sternberg, Meir,
14; Todorov, Tzvetan, 7, 11,
76, 88, 153, 154, 172, 177;
Tomashevsky, Boris, 9, 74,
89, 115, 154; Tompkins,
Jane, 35, 54; van Dijk, Teun
A., 88; Warhol, Robyn, 11,
12, 46, 169, 170; Warren,
Austin, 10, 142, 154, 177;
Warren, Robert Penn, 4, 9,
154, 167, 168; Watt, Ian, 29,
169; Wellek, René, 10, 142,
154, 177; White, Hayden, 88,
121, 125, 127, 174, 177;
Williams, Raymond, 90–1,
124, 144, 148, 162, 174, 177
reception, xv, 11, 35, 50
speech act, 5, 11, 12, 135
writers as, xi, 8
thrillers, 81, 143
time, 4, 73, 82, 90–2, 99–107, 108,
119, 159, 174
discourse, 4, 85, 90, 92–4, 100,
159
historical, 90–1, 97, 144
spatial arrangement conceived
as, 100, 107
story, 4, 85, 90, 92–4, 100, 159
text, *see* discourse time
timing, 81, 85, 90–8, 159, 174
see also pace
Tinkle, Theresa, 138
Todorov, Tzvetan, 7, 11, 76, 88,
153, 154, 172, 177
Tolkien, J. R. R., 24, 163
Tolstoi, Leo, 165
Tomashevsky, Boris, 9, 74, 89, 115,
154
Tompkins, Jane, 35, 54
Toomer, Jean, 164

topoi, 152, 162
Torgovnick, Marianna, 173
traits, character, 40, 58–9, 64–5,
67, 68–9, 70, 71, 157–8
closure and openness as, 68, 158
coherence and incoherence as,
68, 158
complexity and simplicity as, 68,
158
dynamism and staticism as, 68,
158
flat and round as related to, 8,
59, 67, 68, 72
literalness and symbolism as, 68,
158
stylization and naturalism as, 68,
158
transparency and opacity as, 68,
158
wholeness and fragmentariness
as, 68, 158
Trollope, Anthony, 22, 24, 40, 41,
65, 165, 169
trompe l'oeil, 134
Turco, Lewis
turn, the narrative, 11, 154
Turner, Mark, 175
turns, plot, 80, 87, 158
Twain, Mark, 33
types
character, 59, 64–9, 87, 113, 143,
144, 157
generic, 66, 70, 141, 143, 162
plot, 75, 144, 158

unity, 3–4, 7, 9, 18, 20, 25, 28, 48,
78, 80, 119
unreliable narrator, xi, 32, 34, 35,
37, 42–4, 47, 49–50, 53, 104,
156, 165
Unsworth, Barry, 37
Urban, Greg, 147, 153
Updike, John, 163

van Dijk, Teun A., 88
Vestal, Stanley, 134
Vidal, Gore, 134
visions, dream, 112, 123
visualization, 117
voice, 52, 87
communal, 37, 53, 106, 156, 170
discourse and, 87

double, 52, 61
Genettian sense of, 52, 53
lyric, 52, 157
volumes, 16, 19, 23, 25, 26, 144, 155, 163

Walcott, Derek, 163
Walker, Alice, 163
Walsh, Jill Paton, 58–9, 172
Warhol, Robyn, 11, 12, 46, 169, 170
Warren, Austin, 10, 142, 154, 168, 177
Warren, Robert Penn, 4, 9, 167, 154
Watt, Ian, 29, 169
Waugh, Evelyn, 164
Wellek, René, 10, 142, 154, 177
Welles, Orson, 132
Wells, H. G., 132
Welty, Eudora, 25
White, Hayden, 88, 121, 125, 127, 174, 177

Williams, Raymond, 90–1, 124, 144, 162, 174, 177
Wilson, August, 24
Winterson, Jeanette, 50
Wolfe, Thomas, 27
Woolf, Virginia, 60, 63, 86, 92, 94–5, 165
world-making, xvi, 6, 8, 11, 116–18, 123, 126, 144, 161
historical, 122–3
worlds
'As If', 120, 161
fictional, *see* fictional worlds
historical, 121–3
possible, 116, 119, 122–3, 175
primary, 112
'salient', 119
secondary, 111, 126, 174
story, *see* story worlds
worlds within worlds, 108, 109–10, 161